The Sorrows of Fat City

The Sorrows
of Fat City

A Selection of Literary Essays and Reviews

George P. Garrett

University of South Carolina Press

Some of these pieces have appeared in the following
periodicals: *Chronicles, Georgia Review, The Hollins Critic,
Mill Mountain Review, Modern Fiction Studies, New Literary History,
Princeton University Library Chronicle, South Carolina Review,
Texas Studies in Language and Literature.*

And in the following anthologies: *New Directions in Literary
History; New Essays on "The Great Gatsby"; Just Representations:
A James Gould Cozzens Reader; John Ciardi: Measure of a Man;
Robert Penn Warren; A Collection of Critical Essays; The
Sounder Few: Essays from "The Hollins Critic"; Why the South
Will Survive; William Faulkner: Four Decades of Criticism;
The Road to Glory: A Screenplay; Faulkner and Humor;
Faulkner and Popular Culture.*

Copyright © 1992 University of South Carolina

Published in Columbia, South Carolina, by the
University of South Carolina Press

Manufactured in the United States of America

Library of Congress Cataloging-in-Publication Data

Garrett, George P., 1929–
    The sorrows of fat city : a selection of literary essays and
reviews / George P. Garrett.
      p. cm.
    Includes bibliographical references and index.
    ISBN 0-87249-788-7 (alk. paper). —ISBN 0-87249-789-5 (pbk. :
alk. paper)
      1. American literature—20th century—History and criticism.
2. Books—Reviews. I. Title
PS221.G34   1992   91-30494
814'.54—dc20

Contents

viii

Contents

Author's Note

Here is a representative sampling taken from the literary essays and reviews I have been writing and publishing here and there, over a period of more than thirty years. The pieces which follow were published between 1957 and 1990, and dates of publication are indicated for all of them. I have presented the pieces as they were originally published.

The informal "Prologue," which is also the title piece, presents my own view of the place of literary criticism in one writer's writing life (mine). The "Epilogue," even more informal than the "Prologue," is, in fact, the text of a speech I gave at the Drake Hotel in Chicago in 1989 when I received the T. S. Eliot Award from the Ingersoll Foundation. In a sense, it offers a brief aesthetic overview and a kind of credo. It seemed to me that the first words and the last should be personal ones, spoken by the character-narrator (myself) who bears more formal witness in the other essays in between. In between are essays, then, on various writers and literary subjects, maybe as much as one-fourth of the number of such pieces I have written and published so far. It's a fat book, anyway.

As for the value of all this. That is up to others, finally. It ill-behooves me to make any claims or a case of any kind about this work. I will say this much, however: all the writers I admire, some of them openly admired in these pages, have in common the habitual fact that they always wrote as well as they were able to, holding back nothing, in everything they did, major or minor, heavy or light. I have tried my best to follow their good example.

The Sorrows of Fat City

The Sorrows of Fat City; or, Eclecticism and Other Bad Habits
(1989)

I. Beginning

> *We are using our own skin for wallpaper*
> *and we cannot win.*
>
> —John Berryman

Ralph Cohen, the learned and distinguished editor of *New Literary History*, invited several writers, myself among them, to write something on the place and meaning of literary criticism in their (professional) lives. Who could resist the opportunity to appear in the pages of that heavy-duty magazine? My response took the form that follows.

Oh yes, the title of the piece and of this book. Where does it come from?

Once upon a time, at the University of Michigan, where I was teaching, I attended a lecture by the celebrated Harold Bloom entitled "The Sorrows of Facticity." It was long enough and knotty enough to satisfy all but the most jaded admirer of contemporary criticism at its most abstract and demanding. To my pleasant surprise I found that I could actually follow his argument fairly well, at least until some distraction or other allowed my mind to wander. Once disengaged, however briefly, from Bloom's text and texture, I found that I could never again catch up. But it was an interesting experience, like watching a foreign movie without benefit of subtitles or dubbing. Later at a social reception, I stood in line to shake hands with the critic. And I did so, too, mumbling the usual platitudes of appreciation, when to my dismay, and as will sometimes happen, the line simply stopped moving. And there I was, face to face with Harold Bloom and forced to make conversation, to say something!, until the line moved on, if ever . . . I told him (the truth) that I sometimes suffer from a slight dyslexia and, so, I had misread the title of his talk on the printed posters as "The Sorrows of Fat City." Bloom, a large man, flushed red and scowled with apparent anger. In a wink of time I realized that he was completely unfamiliar with the slang expression "Fat City" and that, in his own kind of wisdom, he had concluded that I was, in a smiling, casual, perfectly offhand manner, making fun of his physical appearance. "Well! Well!" he snorted. "*You* aren't exactly a model of trim and slender fitness yourself!" (All too true!) Just then the line moved on, and I have never until now had an opportunity to explain myself.

(*Good luck to Harold Bloom, if he happens to be reading this essay.*)

II. My History of Trial and Error

This piece must take on the twin forms of confession and autobiography. Neither of which, of course, can or should ever be completely trusted. Not even, perhaps least of all, by the author.

Consider it this way. During a career which seems to me brief only because it has kept me so busy, I have written poems, stories, novels, some skits and plays for stage and TV, screenplays, several odd kinds of words for music, the lyrics for one popular song, as well as long and short book reviews, various kinds and forms of criticism of particular texts in particular contexts, and even (precious little, though, yes indeed, sometimes a little) theory. I have written one anonymous guide book and a little journalism off and on. I have written one literary biography, *James Jones* (1984), and one brief critical study—*Understanding Mary Lee Settle* (1988). And I have worked as an editor, of one kind and another, for half a dozen magazines; also served as an editor or adviser or reader for a number of university presses and, on occasion, commercial publishers. Similarly (it comes with the territory), I have served a variety of foundations—Ford, MacArthur, Whiting, Henfield, the National Endowment—in a variety of ways, and I have judged more contests for prose fiction and poetry than I can ever remember or care to. Few, if any, of these duties even existed for writers when I first began to publish during the late 1940s. Now they are entirely typical exercises for the middle-aged writer who is required to be, in a way his predecessors were not, an active monitor of the contemporary literary scene.

Another odd form of contemporary creative writing, one which surely will not be ignored in any serious history of our literary life and times, is the matter of grant applications. Very few literary artists have been able to ignore the temptation to apply for the available grants and fellowships. The principal rhetorical problem of the grant application, above and beyond and aside from the quality of a given artist's real work, is how to stand out in a huge crowd of competitive applications. And, beyond tactics, what is the best artistic mask to assume? My experience as a judge and juror in these matters has taught me that immense and fascinating creativity, some of it generated by artists of the first rank, has been expended (squandered?) on these things. There is also the equally creative matter of choosing appropriate and excellent allies to write letters of recommendation. I have often found myself astonished to discover significant personal and political alliances where there may be next to no public connection between artists.

None of this counts or considers, as part of my work, a very large number, year by year, of talks and lectures, in varying contexts of formality and informality, mostly literary in focus, but a few political and social, and, on two occasions, sermons from the pulpit of St. George's Episcopal Church in York Harbor, Maine.

And I should not overlook yet another kind of publication—the public reading of poetry or prose. Which has mostly come to consist of reading one's own work, sometimes revised and edited especially for public performance and almost always following the convention of offering introductory and intermediary remarks designed to present necessary background information, to set mood and tone, or to shift mood and tone between two separate items; or, often, simply to interrupt the reading with a little space of time, a breather.

I mention these public readings for a number of reasons. First, that the reading is, in many of the literary arts of our time, especially poetry, for example, a highly significant form of publication, often the most important form. It is difficult not to believe that far more people have heard my verses in public readings, over the past forty years, than have ever read or even seen them printed on a page. More or less by accident, I was giving readings of my poems well before they appeared in any magazines or in book form. And, without being too self-conscious, I would guess that many practices and habits of my writing derive from the fact that they were reasonably intended, first of all, to be heard by an audience unfamiliar with the text in any other form.

For the contemporary poet the largest audience will be composed of auditors at public readings (including, now, tape recordings). Very few poets or critics have troubled much to consider what this may mean. I remember talking with Robert Frost at some length about this subject in the early 1950s. In those days, out of pressing financial necessity, he was giving a great many readings to very large audiences; and while this was satisfying to him in many immediate and obvious ways, it was also troubling him. Because, he pointed out, the steady and regular sales of his published works remained on a uniform level and did not seem to change much despite all of his public appearances. The evidence was clear that the majority of his audience was made up of hearers, not readers.

In any case, the running commentary of the poet/reader becomes a self-reflexive critical act, more than a matter of establishing and maintaining "voice." This is equally true, it seems, whether a poet—like James Dickey, for example—always uses almost exactly the same intertextual materials, including well-timed, "spontaneous" remarks, jokes, asides, and so on; or, at the other extreme, works without much plan, hoping to build a rapport with a specific audience, playing, as it were, in tune and consort with what the poet intuits to be the mood and response of the audience. Either way, the poet's remarks at a public reading become an integral part (sometimes habitual, sometimes unique) of the text even as they profess to present a form of commentary or to presume to offer a kind of explication. In some cases this commentary can significantly alter the auditor's perception of the text. For example, for years the poetry of Ben Bellit was baffling and largely inaccessible to me. Then I heard him read in public. He began each poem by explaining how he came to write it and by presenting the essential situation of the poem. Not many may now remember, but it was the fashion among some poets in the immediate post-World War II years, in America, to imitate certain European moderns by disguising the basic situation of the poem, the poem therefore becoming a commentary on an unknown occasion or situation, simple or complex. Part of the suspense, thus pleasure, of a given poem was to be able to discover "what's going on" and "what it is really all about." Halfway into a poem, one worked outward from inference. "Ah! It's all about a tennis match!" Or: "I see. It's about the death of Socrates." Once Bellit had explained, in public performance, the situation and occasion of his poems, I was better able to understand both the poems and my own earlier failure to connect. Likewise, I allowed for the probability that his other poems may have had some basis in fact and experience and were actually "about" something, whether I was able to guess at it or not. There were others whose public performances modified one's sense of their work: Dylan Thomas, pudgy and slovenly and sometimes drunk and often very funny and self-deprecating, with that wonderfully rich, radio-trained baritone voice which has managed to survive him; Richard Wilbur, whose great elegance also proved to be mostly simple and natural, even gawky, not at all flirting with the high-campy edges of pure self-indulgence like, say, James Merrill; Marianne Moore and Elizabeth Bishop, both of them having distinct and odd (yet oddly similar) little speech impediments which somehow gave their hard-edged, witty texts a palpable spirit of vulnerability; Randall Jarrell, not at all the savage critic and defender of the aesthetic faith, but instead, when reading his poems in public at least, vaguely sweet and sometimes even a little silly, pleading for love and forgiveness more than for respect and admiration; and so many others, maybe the most amazing of all being W. D. Snodgrass, who changed himself completely as a performer by seriously studying the craft of oral interpretation in mid-life.

Probably it can be persuasively argued that the true and complete text of and for an American poet of the last thirty years is to be found in no manuscript, typescript, or printed version, but rather in the collective text of all his public readings. Yet, anyway, it is also indisputable that for the very many who have engaged in public readings, the text is ever after inextricably coupled and confused with the ways and means of the performer.

III. Choosing a Yoke to Wear

I started with the simple assertion that I have tried to engage in as many different kinds of writing as I possibly could. Partly to learn from

---

practical experience. If I were going to teach, if I were teaching to earn my keep, then I would surely need to know as much as I could, from practice and experience, about many different kinds of writing. Partly, too, out of curiosity. Partly, I suppose, out of careerism; perhaps I may have hoped I might stumble upon "success" in one form or another. And partly, in all fairness, because it never occurred to me *not* to try my hand at anything and everything. Sooner or later I would find myself forced to settle down within the limits of this or that. To take on the yoke. "Nobody gets to choose what yoke to wear," as Avianus wrote so long ago.

Yet sometimes one freely chooses to take on a yoke, not realizing, until sad experience becomes a patient schoolmaster, that the apparent free choice was to assume an unsuspected form of bondage. Exercising my hard-earned, high-priced freedom, I failed to consider how forms of genres create institutional demands of their own, the response to which (no matter if made in ignorance or knowledge) involves complex concessions, serious compromises. For example, when I worked briefly for CBS Television, I arrived on the scene with a conventionally perfect contempt for it and was promptly and accurately instructed in the one key fact that I had to know—that television was not, and was never intended to be, an art form or even a form of entertainment. Rather, it was conceived of and managed by its masters as an *advertising* medium. The commercials were what mattered and where the tides of money came and went. What we did was to fill in the space between commercials as cheaply as possible and with the minimum interest and engagement required to keep an imaginary viewer from changing the channel. There was not much room for dancing in those chains.

At the other end of things, for me, was my first introduction to the historical novel with *Death of the Fox*. At the time of writing it, I knew so little about the genre of the historical novel, having read very few of them myself and never really thinking about my own work as belonging to that category, that I suspect it took me much longer to write the book than it should have, certainly than it would have if I had known where I was conforming to tradition and conventions and where I was going off on my own, departing into thin air.

All of which is only to admit to the obvious—that everywhere, in every action, even among the dogs and the dung, one has to contend

---

with more than one's own ideas. One cannot choose but to serve the great tradition. Whether one serves wisely or well is another kind of question, perhaps beyond any reasonable answer.

Another reason for my bad habit of eclecticism is that, although other people do not bore me much, I have a very low threshold for self-boredom. Unnecessary repetition, freely chosen, would bore me to tears and maybe to death.

And, as long as this is a confession, I must admit to harboring a vaguely theoretical basis for my own eclecticism—the belief, largely untested on anyone but myself, that the differences between one literary form and another are largely obvious and superficial and far less important than are all the elements of common ground. It is the notion that if an artist applies himself, with more or less equal interest and commitment, to a variety of forms, then the differences will be less than meets the eye; and, as a corollary, that all of these forms will be equally part of the artist's singular vision, chips off the same sort of Platonic block; which would be the imaginary form where all of the artist's separate investments came together in one account. That is to say, for example, that the poems and play of James Joyce are of value to us not merely because of their complex relationships with his innovative and influential fiction (even though that may very well be the reason that both poems and play survive), but also because *he made them, too*; and, like God, he is somewhat less of an artist in the absence of any part of his creation.

Another self-justification for my history of trial and error in various forms is that I have long believed that the only way I can know myself as artist—in a very different way, of course, than I can come to know and react to the works of others, great or small, living or dead—is by pushing my own gifts and abilities to their outer limits. And finally there is a probably primitive belief that nothing worthy can be made or done without consciously embracing risks, not least the risk of failure. Of course, the definitions of failure change as one ages and changes. We often allow for the arrogance and bravado of youth even as we ignore the evidence of youth's simultaneous depths of humility. Concepts, ideals of justice (and injustice) lead us surely toward humility, even if it is secret, subtle, denied. In youth one humbly believes that it is within the power of others, authorities of all kinds, to award the

---

conditions of failure or success just as they hand out bouquets of reputation or oblivion. Older, yet still performing and producing, the surviving artist believes in justice and injustice only insofar as he may be a fool and, as fool, a faulty artist. It is certainly within the power of others to bless or to wound the artist, but it is beyond the power of anyone to salvage his failures or to shame his successes, although it is, of course, easy enough to ignore the latter.

IV. A School of Piranha Fish

> *Hey, out there!—assistant professors, full,*
> *associates,—instructors—others—any—*
> *I have a sing to shay.*

—John Berryman

The popular perceived dichotomy between the artist and the academy is a distortion of the facts and the truth. Literary artists, both poets and novelists, may have been among the last artists to find place and home in academe, but they have made up for lost time. At the end of World War II, just as the GI Bill helped propel American higher education into one of our major national industries, there were almost no courses being offered anywhere in modern and contemporary literature; and very few writers had any formal or regular affiliation with any college or university. (Robert Frost was a notable exception.) In a few years all that changed. And the change has continued, for better and for worse. There are writers teaching at almost every existing American institution of higher learning. There are hundreds of creative writing programs. It is quite safe to say that, by now, most American writers are associated with colleges and universities; and most of our new writers are coming out of writing programs. The implications of all this have only just begun to be examined and are far from clear. What is clear enough, though, is that the writer of my own generation, and younger, is now likely to be actively involved in academic life, teaching reading and writing for a living.

Years and years ago, my grandfather, the autocratic chief of his tribe of many children and many more grandchildren, once asked me what I wanted to be when I grew up. "A writer," I answered. "Well, that's all right," he observed. "It's as good a way to be poor as any." He was absolutely right about that. During most of the period of my professional career and, indeed, beginning more or less unnoticed a good deal earlier, there has been no real money directly available from writing. At any given time, all the studies and statistics show, there may be as many as a dozen or so different writers in America, few of them regarded as "serious," who are earning an honorable and acceptable living from their writing. The possibility of indirect earning, chiefly from academic association and labor, is new to our times. Was not an option for the first generation of modern masters. This turn of events, allowing writers of all kinds to earn, by writing and good repute, credentials which, in turn, permit them to work as academics, has confirmed and enforced the condition it was intended to alleviate. The writer is encouraged by his institution to publish regularly and, if possible, to gain favorable notice for his work, but need not measure success by earnings. Under this system it is as reasonable to devote time and energy to one form or genre as another. The potential rewards are much the same. An alien and objective observer might try to make an exception of some of the more popular forms of writing—screenwriting, for example, or writing for television. True, these activities tend to be lucrative, in a relative sense; however, based on my own experience and the comparable experience of others, I conclude that these adequate rewards are extremely hard-earned, usually accompanied, at the very least, by such high levels of anxiety and stress, often weighted with such tedium, and at such expense of energy, if not spirit, and with such constant, routine humiliation, as to be hugely self-destructive. They burn out talent and desire. Whereas the conventional image of complaint by the writer in academe is of being nibbled and chewed to death slowly by a school of piranha fish, the world of commercial popular culture is probably best represented as a feeding frenzy of killer sharks.

(In all fairness I should report that the corporate sharks of popular culture often prove to be, perhaps out of sheer corporate necessity as much as anything else, creatures of superior character and ethical behavior to rogue academics. I recall once entertaining a lunch table of

---

hard-nosed and wide-eyed Hollywood agents with tales of the political machinations and chicanery of the English department at the University of Virginia and discovering that they were more deeply shocked than amused. "Do you mean to tell me that people like that are allowed to teach our *children?*" they demanded.)

More by accident than by design, and more as a matter of whimsy than choice, my own training was conventionally academic, more so than most writers of my own age and generation. I used the GI Bill, and such fellowships as I could find and earn, for straightforward graduate study in English at Princeton where, over too many years and with various interruptions, I had also been an undergraduate. It was as good a course of study as money could buy at the time; and partly because I did not take it very seriously, I enjoyed the work and the life a great deal. Years as an enlisted man in the army may not have taught me much worth knowing or remembering, but I had acquired the soldier's habit of going through the motions of whatever was required of me at any given time with a straight-faced anonymity and usually with a perfect, if secret, contempt for whatever we were supposed to be up to and for all but a few of my fellows. I carried the burden of this—rather like the pieces of uniform, the field jackets and olive drab trousers, and so on, that we wore for years after military service was over and done with—into the academic life. It was, as I can see easily enough now, an inapplicable transference of habits; but it nevertheless freed me from any number of commonplace prejudices and also set me free to take delight and instruction wherever I could find them. And I could then allow myself the indulgence of loving and learning from the literature of the past without embarrassment and also without any need to accept, untested and unquestioned, conventional values of then and now. There were good men and true, good scholars to study from and with. Among them (*God bless the reader of these names*, as the ancient formula goes): Gerald Bentley, Laurence Thompson, Carlos Baker, Willard Thorp, Louis Landa, Tom Riggs, Alan Downer, Jesse Reese, D. W. Robertson, Jr., and R. P. Blackmur, among others. And thanks to Blackmur, there were also some poets and writers (covertly) on the faculty already—Randall Jarrell, John Berryman, Delmore Schwartz, and Saul Bellow. These were only a few years older than I and my fellow students, though they seemed to us to be at once much older and,

---

with the exception of Bellow, who managed to preserve his *gravitas*, much sillier than we ever were or would be. They have been much written about and more than a little romanticized in recent years, but then the one small enviable and inexplicable quality they seemed to possess was their modest, local fame. Of course there were also a few well-known and more-envied students around, the likes of Frederick Buechner, Louis Coxe, William Meredith, Galway Kinnell, and W. S. Merwin among them. From the example of our elders we decided (the Salieri lesson) that one need not be especially admirable—or, for that matter, it seemed to many of us then, especially intelligent or sensitive or even talented—to be a writer.

Now when I read the books all about them and those years, I am always aware of something they and now their authors seem to have missed completely—the little cloud of hostile witnesses who watched over their comings and goings. I say, to myself and to them: *We saw you. We were watching all the time. And listening . . . Very little escaped us except the mystery of how you of all people (all except Bellow) somehow managed out of the obvious and shabby chaos of your little lives to produce some work that we honor and admire.*

These people seemed to be the living and breathing examples of the New Critics' new (then) proposition that it was only the closely examined text, in and of itself, not the life and times of any writer, which mattered. That seemed self-evident for all of them, though not so clear for ourselves; for we already knew that at the deepest heart of even our most objective or abstract work lay mysterious revelations and large confessions. These were the springs of self we drank from and bathed in although, true to the fashion, we denied it. Just as, much later, when "confessional" poetry appeared on the scene and so many major and minor poets rushed forward to fabricate their true confessions, often self-serving confessions that any experienced policeman would have found unacceptable and inadmissible evidence, we closed ourselves like clenched fists against that fashion. I think at that moment we took and swallowed whole the prescription of the earlier generation of modern masters that one's proper goal was to disappear into the work of art, to become the work, to have no other life and to be nothing else. Those of us who have managed to live long enough now (*Good luck to the reader of these words*) see clearly enough that this prescription is, as it

---

always was, an impossible ideal and that the old masters (our fathers) were not even briefly true to it.

V. Servants and Agents

All that is needed for admission to the ranks of criticism is a typewriter.

—William Faulkner

Something now has to be said about critics and criticism.

When I was young, I thought I was learning how to read well from the critics I read and listened to and from the few I knew a little as a student "knows" a master. Among these latter were John Aldridge, R. P. Blackmur, Francis Fergusson, Leslie Fiedler, Allen Tate, Edmund Wilson. At Princeton in those long gone days I thought they had much about writing to teach and tell me, much more than all the scholars. Time has precisely reversed that judgment for me. I now remember the critics, sometimes warmly it is true, as characters in a narrative. I remember stories about them and not much else. And I suppose that I must have first heard of the names and books of some of the great moderns and contemporaries from them. No denying that. And, at first, these men, and others known only in books and articles, were powerfully intimidating not only in their intelligence, but also in their assumed authority. Later on, when I was deeply involved in the problems of writing specific texts, the critics were no aid and comfort beyond offering examples of concentration and (sometimes) integrity. At which point I began to lose all but the most casual interest in their discipline and their problems.

My only connections with more contemporary criticism and critics remain anecdotal. The newer people have no more value to my writing life (maybe a good deal less) than the earlier generation. And by now they no longer possess even the secondary ability to point me toward new works and new writers and new directions that I am unaware of. When I was young, it was a matter of fact that the critics had (at some point or other) read more than I had. Now I discover that I am familiar with more writers and more and various texts than they are, even the most, and most justly, celebrated among them. They cannot be much help in refining my appreciation of and for new texts and old verities. And they are no help at all in the endless wrestle with my own words.

Something more. A point of some real friction between the writer in the academy and his academic colleagues. By and large, most of the writers I know of are better read and informed, at least in the outlines of contemporary literature, than the teachers and scholar-teachers of contemporary literature. The result, from the point of view of the writer, is that the academic critics, working within the limits of their knowledge, inevitably become at best servants, agents of and for the contemporary literary establishment. This is exactly what our elders, who resisted the coming of modern and contemporary literature into the formal curriculum, warned us against. "What will be the canon?" they asked. And that is where brutal battles (by at least semi-ignorant armies) are being fought everywhere.

For one reason and another, I have had to write a certain amount of practical and popular criticism, not something I am more than slightly proud of; though I think that the effort to articulate one's reactions to and feelings about the texts of others may have been helpful to me, if only as an exercise in humility.

In fairness, to be just, or, anyway, to give the best appearance thereof, it is necessary to take notice of the criticism of artists. For these days writers produce a great many of the reviews and a not insignificant portion of the criticism of each other's works. Logrolling aside—though it should be said that a lot of the critical work of writers consists of advancing causes and allies and seeking to inhibit, if not punish, rivals and enemies—the present conventions of critical writing by artists seem to call for a stylish obscurity, often an almost impenetrable and thorny (barbwire?) defense of whatever notions may stand at the center of the argument. Artists are not encouraged by anyone, and not much disposed themselves, to aim for clarity and coherence in their critical writings. Their efforts, especially those of the present generation of poets, read like casual translations of the mystical writings of some remote and little known cult or sect. All that can be said for this kind of writing at its best is that it is a knack beyond the abilities and outside of the interests of most educated people. Because this is so, such qualities as integrity, judgment, and influence are not directly involved.

VI. Wrestling a Stranger

Go on, my boy, and strike hard; have a rich and long St. Martin's summer. Try everything, do everything, render everything—be an artist, be distinguished to the last.

—Henry James

When I first decided to go to graduate school—a great many of my classmates had already turned down the fellowship I was offered, one which had, by law, to be awarded to some member of my class—an old lady told me: "I envy you. Academics go through life so gently." At the time, and many times since, I recalled the response of the Duke of Wellington to a lady who told him (once too often) what a privilege it must have been to command the heroic men at Waterloo. Wellington replied: "Madame, the Battle of Waterloo was won by the worst set of blackguards ever assembled in one spot on this earth." Often, at four A.M., tossing and turning in a rage against the latest example of departmental stupidity and injustice, I have remembered her remark and grinned like a dog with a bone at the brutal irony of it. But I think now that she was more accurate than not. Nobody my age in this century has been able to be safely sheltered from the bitter truths of our times. There is no escaping this savage age and its cargo of woe, its hard freight of undeniable sorrow. But, in some important sense, the world of academe is more like the child's game of Monopoly, played with funny money, than the more dangerous games of, say, Trump and Icahn and Boesky and Kluge. Which means that American writers, though now lodged in large numbers in the academy, have not fully escaped experience of and participation in the worst of their times, whether they think so or not. But, by the same token, they, *we* then, for I am among them, are spared some of the consequences of our follies and some of the guilt of our selfish actions.

This piece began, foolishly and selfishly enough, as a kind of defense of my habit of eclecticism in an age of literary specialization. But good intentions are never enough; and even as I put words on the page, the text played protean tricks on me, becoming a pseudoconfession, then finally shifting into the loose shapes and forms of personal history. No matter. I am not sure whether all authorial intentions are, by defini-

The Sorrows of Fat City

---

tion, fallacious or not, in life or in art. What I think we can safely claim is that we often are blessed with the capacity to do and to be more than we ever imagined or intended. And it is the hope of earning that blessing which keeps every artist worthy of his hire hard at work, wrestling an angelic stranger (or strangers) who may yet prove to be no more and no less than a bright version of himself.

I

Living with Elizabethans

1

Dreaming with Adam:
Notes on Imaginary History

(1970)

Two facts, one well known and often recorded, the other less known and seldom, if ever, related to the first: the first that in her old age Queen Elizabeth ordered all the mirrors, in public rooms where she might pass, to be covered with curtains; the second that she ordered great mirrors, enough to surface walls, ceiling, floor, for her inmost bathing chambers. These things took place at approximately the same time. The biographers of the Queen, and they are excellent, have made a good deal of the covering of the mirrors, also dutifully allowing that fully bewigged and made-up and royally dressed, seen at a respectful distance, she seemed beautiful, even youthful, to many observers.

In a work of fiction, where imagination is given more freedom, the two things can properly be joined together. Here is the imagined Walter Ralegh, on the last day before his execution, within the context of an imaginary letter to his young son, Carew.

"In the myth Narcissus is depicted as a man. And rightly so. Only a man (or a brainless beautiful woman) can fall in love with his own appearance. For it is a stranger to him. The woman at her looking glass sees what she sees and knows it. And therefore, I do think, women justly demand the slight subterfuge of flattery from us.

"The old Queen ordered the mirrors in all her palaces removed or covered up in her last years. And this has been taken by some as a sign of vanity and self-deceit. They do not know (or do not remember) that her inmost chambers of bathing where she was alone with herself, as naked as God made her, were made of mirrors—walls, floors and ceiling. To see herself. And not in delusion or vanity or self-love. But naked from all sides, as no one sees himself, so that she would know and never forget the plain truth of herself.

"Meaning she knew her appearance as well as any who make a study of themselves. Yet she took that aging body, that withering face, and painted and daubed and costumed and disguised it until, at a decent distance, she was the picture of a proper Queen. Not out of a vanity or self-delusion. Nor out of the wish to deceive others who might know better. But out of the compelling necessity to be what she must be to rule and never to permit the expectations and the pride of her subjects or this kingdom to be diminished or disappointed.

"She was willing, then, to sacrifice even her own integrity of person in the name of her office and for the good of the Kingdom.

"I think it was too much to ask her to look upon herself in the disguises of public mirrors and to beam approval and signify thereby a total self-delusion."

II

Confession is one kind of beginning, apology another of close kin, and neither is advisable except as the last resort of a well-meaning scoundrel. Better to plead guilty and be silent, or to stand mute, than to present at the outset one's last reserves, the extenuating and mitigating circumstances. Yet that dubious stratagem is now demanded; for nothing is or can be offered here that by any merciful bending and twisting of definitions can be rightly called critical theory of the uses of history in fiction and of the uneasy, continual kinship between the two. Instead of formulation, founded upon authority or growing out of deep experience, all that can be offered is fragmentary, tentative. More of a "mix" than a blending and without benefit of alchemy or magic.

Which may be just as well, if (once again) necessity can be hopefully named virtue. For there is already an ample weight of authority on all sides; theories of the meaning of history and the telling of it abound, and, to a lesser degree, there are plenty of fully formulated, well-presented, documented and demonstrated notions of the uses, limits, and implications of historical fiction. At best I can only share some parts of an experience, leftovers, the chips and blocks and shards from an unpoliced workshop after the conclusion of a piece of work, done but not yet public. Some are particular and some are general. All are

---

random, lacking even the polish of aphorism which can, at least, disguise mutual doubts and, by sleight of hand, divert attention from awkward innocence.

To be particular. I am writing here in terms of an "historical" novel,
my own, recently completed and now scheduled for publication in the
fall of 1970. Its title is *Death of the Fox*, and it is subtitled "An Imaginary Version of the Last Days of Sir Walter Ralegh." It was a long time
in the making, begun first in the early 1950s as an attempt at writing
a full biography.

Begun then, interrupted by all sorts of circumstances, changing with
outward circumstances and with the trial and error of the making and
revising, and changing also over that time as I changed my views and
feelings, and as experience changed me. Begun, interrupted, but never
for long, and constantly changing shape and form, constantly subjected to the process of trial and error, continually and closely questioned. The final writing, myself committed by then by contract and
obligation, began in 1964 and continued until the fall of 1969, interrupted sporadically in this second stage only by mundane conditions,
not by other work.

Thus, for better or worse, it has been a long time finding its form and
coming to be.

My observations and notions are of two kinds: the general, coming
from a gradually increasing awareness of the theory and practice of
other writers, past and present, in working with past time, and including some reaction to present trends and views; and particular events,
technical as it were, created out of the doing and working, the problems, questions, and possibilities which came less out of theoretical or
preconceived concerns (though, of course, those are never wholly absent from any literary work if only manifest in the author's interests,
impulses, and hidden assumptions) than from what might be called engineering or construction details.

At best, then, I can present here, in advance of and in the absence
of the book which must speak for itself and speak differently, some accounting of the gradual formation of an incomplete theory, hand in
glove with the particular elements of practice, neither entirely dependent upon the other and neither free of the continuing interchange and
influence of the other.

The living writer works within, around, against his literary context and consensus. Even twenty years ago the "historical novel," for American writers, was declining in both prestige and popularity. Those handmaidens of the arts (and especially the commerce of the arts in the marketplace) are more often masters than servants. And prestige and popularity, while not identical twins, are very closely related. There are and will be important exceptions, but present evidence is clear enough. For a time, roughly up through World War II, there was some brief flowering of the form, deceptive in that historical fiction, going in time beyond the hauntings and memories of this nation (what the "new" historians call oral history), leaping an ocean of space backward, has never been really a significant territory for American writers except, perhaps, in the form of the satirical demonstration of its insignificance (*A Connecticut Yankee in King Arthur's Court*) or in, for example, the bland and popular pieties which, like the poor, are still here: from *Ben Hur* to *The Robe*. For a time the "sword and bosom" school (*Forever Amber*, etc.) flourished adequately in the mass marketplace. And it might have seemed likely that a corresponding prestigious "serious" fiction would develop to take advantage of this as, for instance, *Portnoy's Complaint* and *Couples* are advantageous responses to the popularity of pornography. But this did not happen, a fact which might be attributed, though only in small part, to the negative or indifferent (in fact the same) critical consensus of opinion. Witness, for example, the wide-ranging and imaginative work of the late David Stacton, who seemed able to write very well about ancient and utterly alien cultures. Most of his books are still unpublished in the United States despite a considerable recognition in Britain and, in translation, on the Continent. The critical distaste for fictional "costume stories" is supported at the highest, most influential level by T. S. Eliot's views of *Murder in the Cathedral*, both in his essays on verse drama and, later, in his introduction to the screen adaptation of that play. Essentially (and over-simplified) his consistent critical burden is that the directly historical avoids what he seems to have conceived of as the chief duty of the contemporary artist, to bring together, insofar as the dissociated sensibility of the modern artist will allow, the elements of poetry here and now, the past ever a part of the present, but never overwhelming it. At a lower level the vulgar success, followed in more recent years by

---

an almost inevitable failure, of the popular arts—in drama the historical plays of Maxwell Anderson, in film the successes and excesses of a long line of filmmakers, from De Mille through George Stevens—did not do much to increase intellectual esteem for the wedding of fiction and history in American letters.

One must stress this national singularity because it is peculiar to our literature and, in fact, goes against the grain of much highly regarded foreign writing. The plays of Camus have enjoyed some interest here, not commensurate with the enthusiasm for his other works, but nevertheless a fact. Par Lagerkvist, in both drama and fiction, is steadily, if modestly admired. And in novel, play, and film the British writers continue the cultivation of the historical muse, and they profit. But the American writer has been steadily more restricted. He remains free to use his own history, provided it is "relevant" to current issues and problems. William Styron's *The Confessions of Nat Turner* was a superb example of the cult of "relevance," of timeliness, if not perfect timing. And the American writer may, in form of a tour de force within the persistent comic tradition, engage himself in satire and celebrative artifice. Example: John Barth's *The Sot-Weed Factor*. But, in general, historical fiction is of minimal importance today. The best evidence is manifest in the bright rows of paperbacks in bookstores, drugstores, etc. Over the past twenty years the paperback has come to dominate both aspects of the commerce of literature—prestige and popularity. It is the most accurate test of both. There are fewer works of historical fiction to be bought in paper than the small but unvanquished rows of westerns and nurse stories.

At the same time, our time, other slight changes have limited the possibilities of historical fiction. The most widely recognized writers, those who began their careers after World War II, still imagined as young but all now firmly middle-aged, have moved more and more into the field of "nonfiction." One of the first was Shelby Foote—also one of the most articulate theoreticians of the relationship of fiction and history—who fifteen years ago deferred his fiction for the sake of his three-volume history, *The Civil War*. More recently the essays and opinions of Norman Mailer have gained him more stature than the sum of his novels; and, with an ad man's bravado and disregard for inconvenient facts, Truman Capote announced the creation of a "new form," the "non-fiction novel," with his hugely successful *In Cold Blood*.

Perhaps some of the apparent decline, if not the "death," of the novel may be attributed to the novelists themselves, abandoning the sinking ship as early as possible. More plausibly, however, one can suggest that the *distinctions*, relatively recent after all, between fiction and nonfiction have blurred beyond much value. This condition is reinforced by the deliberate use of the rhetoric of fiction in contemporary works of nonfiction, the work of Walter Lord, for example, or, more explicitly, Tom Wolfe. And journalism, once the last outpost of "objectivity," has surrendered to the imaginative arrangement of (and suppression of) facts, now dignified as "advocacy journalism."

It could be said that all history, of the moment and of the past, is part of a rhetoric close to that of fiction. Certainly the "revisionist" historians have exposed the imaginative limitations and assumptions of many earlier historians; and they make no great effort to disguise their own. Yet these, too, are limited by their intense concern for the relevant issues. Not all history is irrelevant to the radical activist, but much of it becomes condemned as a game for self-indulgent antiquarians.

Ironically, one result of this stance of shrugging indifference has been a remarkable surge of historical study, and consequently the changing and rearranging of old "ideas," by the historians and by literary scholars. Superb studies have emerged in almost all periods, based more upon a refined definition of the ways and means of modern historical scholarship than upon any desire to "create changes" or to seek relevance to contemporary affairs; resulting, paradoxically, in changes of view more radical than anything yet achieved by the revisionist historians. Paradox within paradox, these historical scholars, bound and perhaps inhibited by a methodology which is insistently inductive, and ravenous for facts, often demanding a weight of evidence far beyond the needs of lawyers or scientists to "prove" a point, have uprooted countless monuments of apparent misconception.

Studies of and in that loose time span we call the Renaissance have increased at an almost inflationary rate, the difference from the economy being that this growth shows no signs of slowing down. In partic-

---

ular all aspects of life and culture, large and small, of the English under the Tudors and the Stuarts have been and are being meticulously re-examined. In specific, there have been, beginning with William Wallace's *Sir Walter Ralegh* and including the 1969 addition *The Shepherd of the Ocean* by J. H. Adamson and H. F. Folland, a whole sequence of biographical studies of Ralegh. These have corrected any number of errors and misapprehensions, brought some fact, previously buried, to light, gathered related information, and, finally, in a speculative way, offered significant reinterpretation of motive and purpose.

Scarcely begun, my biography was out of the question, unnecessary. The impulse to try to come to know the man and the times was undiminished, however. And through his poems, the *History* and the other prose works, I kept close to the original fascination with the man as "subject," not questioning that interest, but accepting it as given. Instead I questioned, sometimes abstractly and sometimes in faulty attempts to begin and finish, what my general guidelines should be. Came back again and again to (among others) lines in the introduction to Agnes M. C. Latham's edition of *The Poems of Sir Walter Ralegh*, especially one—"He might have walked out of an Elizabethan play, a figment of the renaissance-imagination, compact of inordinate vices and virtues and destined to strange ends."

From all these things, then, certain preliminary rules and guidelines took shape.

I would, first of all, ignore the alternative of "relevance" or satire. Others, writers of fiction, were doing things well enough. The search for direct parallels and practical relevance to our times seemed at worst, almost always despite fine writing, high style De Mille, "camp," itself worthy of satire. Even the finest works I knew of seemed distorted by this inhibition. As for satire, Bob Newhart, the comedian, had done that well enough in a five-minute sketch. The firm assurance in either myself or the values of my own time necessary to satirize another time was lacking.

There was yet another possibility, to treat the subject and story in the "poetic" manner, as, for example, Edith Sitwell had handled Queen Elizabeth in *Fanfare for Elizabeth*, a manner less narrative than evocative, composed of condensed, rich, full-toned images carrying the tune and echoing in the mind long after, as her apt title implied. More successful, in my opinion, at once richer and deeper was Marguerite Yourcenar's *Hadrian's Memoirs*, an almost flawless work; and, for that reason, less influential than exemplary. I would keep those works in mind, models of excellence, if not for imitation. Would, by the same rule and for quite different reasons, think of Anthony Burgess's brilliant and exasperating virtuoso piece on the young Shakespeare, *Nothing Like the Sun*, which succeeds beyond all expectation though it violates most of the premises I have so far stated. And I would come to know, not systematically but well enough, a variety of past and present fictions of the times, one very great pleasure being the four Tudor novels of R. H. Benson.

But to be interesting enough to work on over a length of time, and as it happens, to be true to my feelings for the man and the times, my work would have to be different from any I had known and enjoyed. I felt that the strategy of "relevance" was an unnecessary inhibition. Obviously a man writing now could not escape his own time and place. There seemed no virtue or pleasure in asserting the obvious. Biographically there were few things to add to Ralegh's established chronicle. Inevitably a few small factual details and some interesting relationships turned up, things which in an academic work could be footnoted and added to the available evidence. On the other hand there are blank spaces and mysteries in Ralegh's life. Here the writer of fiction could move easily where the biographer and historian must go on tiptoes. The conventional direction of the novelist is to fill in these blank spaces with imagined detail, to stand boldly, attributing one motive or another for the seemingly inexplicable action, siding, then, with one historian or another by turning his careful surmise into a definite stance.

I rejected this possibility for a number of reasons, but in large part because the blank spaces and the dark corners seemed so much a part of the man and his character. Whatever the reasons for them, I would accept them as inherent mysteries, would find another way of using them in fiction.

Perhaps the clearest example is Ralegh's early career as a soldier, several years spent in the brutal religious wars in France when he was a very young man indeed, referred to briskly and memorably in a few instances in his *History of the World* (thus still part of the equipage of his sensibility almost a lifetime later), but otherwise very vague. His military actions in Ireland later are, as they were at the time, well-enough known and have given the biographers considerable material for characterization. Acts of courage, ruthless cunning, and the bloody day's slaughter at Smerwick have been well scrutinized; and these are important. But Ralegh was in his late twenties then and a combat veteran by nearly ten years. Moreover, he had already been to the bright center of things, the Court, and thus far, failed in that more complex and more treacherous battlefield of smiles, frowns, and false promises.

It was not difficult, nor would it be for anyone living in our own time, to imagine a return to combat after ten years and a taste, no more, of a kind of life he could not have well imagined before he had experienced it. Those years in France when a boy became a hardened veteran soldier remain blank of fact and speculation in my portrait, but are instead conjured up in images, in sudden remembered flashes, imitating his own way in the *History*.

And this, then, was a general rule: though allowing myself the freedom of all imaginary work, I would keep to the decorum of fact except in very rare cases where it seemed to me that the evidence was sufficient to be more definite than speculative. Fitting and proper in *this case*, because it seemed that the essential mystery of the man, in his time and ever after, has been essential to his character. And that mystery is larger than the man, is the quality Miss Latham hyphenated as the renaissance-imagination.

The *ideas* of the period have been explored and treated by some great scholars. I know which current explorations of ideas I prefer and admire. But this would not be a book of "ideas," lest it should, like some of the lesser works of scholarship and criticism, become purely and simply a defense of one viewpoint or an attack on another. Ideas, the history of ideas, would be building blocks, not excluded, but not dominating the work.

Critics of contemporary writing often overlook the very large element of choice involved in the writer's language, tone, syntax—all the elements, functional or decorative, we name style. Other writers, especially the poets, do not ignore this in reacting to the work of others; indeed, it is the primary (and often the final) consideration. Auden is directly articulate about this in his essay "Squares and Oblongs," and in several of the prefaces to collections in the Yale Younger Poets series. But our critics, even those dealing almost exclusively with language, do not often allow for the writer's responsibility in choosing the language for the work or, in many cases, *a* language for all his work, which then becomes, in the terms of rock music, his "sound." We hear a good deal of the cliché "finding his own voice." Which implies, together with the sense of discovery, an *accidental process*. But any writer, a man attuned to the texture and sensuous affective qualities of words, has at his disposal (and within the physical limitations of his own ear and the predilections of his psychology) a wide range of possibilities (and thus choices) for style as a whole and in the multiple parts which compose it. American writers, blessed and cursed with a singularly shifting, changing language, at once cumulative and acquisitive, and, unlike many of their contemporaries working in other languages, permitted free and easy use of the flexible spoken language (itself, then, being taken into the catholic written language), have more choices to face in proportion to the freedom they possess. When an American writer "finds his own voice" for his own time and place it is no small accomplishment. No wonder, then, that one of the problems bedeviling the American writer who would deal with history, or for that matter anything foreign to his immediate "experience," is language. What style, what sort of dialogue to use? Eliot has written of this dilemma eloquently enough, posing the questions but offering no answers, in any number of critical pieces. In general there are a number of possibilities. Possible, but probably discarded, is the pop novel and Hollywood tradition, most useful in satire or farce: Janet Leigh in *The Vikings* (written by that impeccable stylist, Calder Willingham)—"that Viking is the man I love"; Anouk Aimée as the queen in *Sodom and Gomorrah*—"Greetings, Hebrews and Sodomites!" A more acceptable and conventional solution is the use of a heightened, slightly old-fashioned, neutral sort of language, hopefully not too stilted, and unobtrusive enough to be "transparent." Beyond this, by a step or two, is the creation of a "new" style, by definition personal, therefore eccentric, one which will serve to conjure up the ghosts and ruins for the writer and, rhetorically, permit the reader to participate in this incantation. No doubt the supreme, and unique, example is *Finnegans Wake*, undertaking the dream of all history; but besides being a once-and-for-all-time work, it also works from the present. The dream is the *now* of the novel. Djuna Barnes's *Ryder* is a superb example, but so eccentric as to be almost unreadable. John Berryman's *Homage to Mistress Bradstreet*, allowing for the differences between verse and prose, seems extremely successful despite some great excesses. Where he succeeds most admirably he kept in mind his own chosen motto for the work, Keats's statement that the delight and surprise of poetry should come from "a fine excess."

My own choice was at least in the direction of these latter, with the private stipulation that the language must be readable, at least within the context of the work, accessible to an imaginary reader. I read and reread a great many Elizabethan and Jacobean writers. Not systematically, which might have been easier and more efficient, but, I felt, would have arbitrarily inhibited the playful process of assimilation. Thumbed through glossaries and compilations of folk wisdom, etc., occasionally jotting down notes, but these notes to be discarded in the writing. The rule developed: to use what remained in consciousness at the time of writing. More lingered there than I might have expected, but for the most part it served a functional purpose in early drafts, a sense of being physically in *touch* with the language, rhythms, the styles of the times. Later on I could (and did) excise most of the eccentricities. They were expendable. The aim was that having been present once in the making, these elements would now be implied, haunting the styles which remained. Since actions of imagination were the chief burden of the story, it was not possible to settle for a neutral tone. The imagination is cloudy, not transparent.

One thing that most aestheticians can agree upon (beyond which they all part company and go separate ways) is that a work of art begins as a sensuous affective experience communicating expressive form. It is one thing to seek to create a sensuous affective experience in words, dealing with known and familiar things. It is quite another to imagine and recreate the surfaces of a world and a time, and a man, that world ever more different the more one "knows" about it, so alien in fact, so removed that it is difficult to believe at all.

Perhaps that's what Keats meant comparing the imagination to Adam's dream. From the one point of view we are able to imagine, Adam's, it is an act of faith.

So it was, though I could not know it until I was done, that a *theme* developed. It grew almost directly out of original choices and predilections. To approach the renaissance-imagination required a commitment of one's own imagination. The proper theme of the work, then, is the human imagination, the possibility, limits, and variety of imaginative experience.

To begin to move toward this I had to unlearn much, even as I sought to learn more; to unlearn, if only for dazed heady moments like holding one's breath a long time, some of our simplest assumptions.

A most rudimentary example is our deeply imagined, therefore almost ingrained, chronology of technology. Whether we rejoice in technological accomplishment or, more often, are dismayed and dumbfounded by the awful dangers of it, we accept with only minor exceptions the progressive theory. What we see and feel, what is *our* sensuous affective experience, is constant refinement and "improvement," development of techniques. We therefore work backwards, stripping away the things we know well, to reach the past where they were neither known nor imagined. The result is, even for some of the ablest minds, acceptance of a sense of development, progress and improvement, in technological matters at least. Even the most nostalgic of us are committed to this view.

Tudor and Stuart England, where suddenly so many new things came to be, would seem a likely place to demonstrate the validity of our own myth. And, indeed, it would take an enormous volume merely to list the *things* newly introduced into England during that time.

There is a kind of ritual observance of all historical novelists I know of, regardless of their differing premises. They feel an urgent need to be exact, as precise as they are able to be, about the things of the time, feeling that by means of these they may manage to summon up the ghosts who used them. It is here, in and among things, that novelists can be more pedantic than the most solemn cartoon image of the scholar. With differences, though, scholars and novelists share the same myth or metaphor of technology. I have read brilliant books by scholars whose dedication and intelligence is dazzling, on all aspects of

---

Elizabethan life—architecture, arts and sciences, housekeeping, horse-manship, crafts, labor and social conditions, sailing and navigation, etc. And sooner or later each and every one of these scholars has demonstrated the modern technological myth, what might be called "the technological fallacy."

Take, for example, an area where much extraordinary scholarship has been done—the voyaging and, in particular, the ships, the sailing and seamanship of the times. Our best scholars have long since recognized the marvelous sailing ability of the Elizabethans. Their achievements border on the miraculous when one, working backwards, considers how little they knew, how "primitive" the things they worked with. But . . . It could be argued persuasively, I think, and with substantial evidence that the Elizabethan galleon was ideally suited to its purposes. Its sailing and handling defects were offset by virtues and strengths not present in later "improved" sailing vessels. Many of the dangers and troubles of sailing ships a hundred years later and after were simply not present to plague the Elizabethan sailor. The whole concept of sailing changed radically in the century after the death of Elizabeth. Judged by the new concept and purposes, the older methods do not measure up. Seen from another time, when there are more sailors than ever but sailing is a recreation, it can be (though it has not been) convincingly argued that Elizabethan ships and sailors were "better" than most of what came after them. The same condition, here vaguely and there clearly, appears to be true in many things. One great difficulty in any argument is that so very little has survived the times. The wars of the seventeenth century, great fires, and the cheerful discarding of old for new have left us with a few great houses and a miscellany of things, random odds and ends, for the cases of museums.

In a larger sense this leads toward an abstraction, the idea or metaphor of change. Americans of all persuasions, it would seem, are agreed that we live in "changing times." The conservatives would slow down the changes; the liberals would embrace them; the radicals would hasten the process by *making* changes. Yet there are two positions which cast shadows of doubt upon the truth of the changing. Some thinkers (Aldous Huxley, for example) have pointed out the undeniable fact that in large part all of the apparent changes we have witnessed in fifty years are simply the working out, the inevitable development coming from the *real* changes, which were more theoretical than practical and took place at the turn of the last century and in the first years of this one. For example, after the Wright brothers flew their powered kite it was only a matter of time and engineering before a man could walk on the moon. It may well be said that we, the living, though well-deceived by appearances, have seen very little change, have, in fact, devoted ourselves to exploitation of changes long since made. And, deceived in a larger, more metaphysical sense, we call ourselves either victims or celebrants of change. By the same token, it can be well argued that the period of the Tudors witnessed radical changes. And it can be demonstrated that, even as they lamented the aging of the world and the abrasions of mutability, the Elizabethans seem to have welcomed and embraced the new, the changing. The reign of Elizabeth can be detailed as a period of marvels, with outward and visible things changing constantly and, often, overnight. (Symbolically, Ralegh once introduced into England a new style of dress and tailoring in one night after entertaining a distinguished Frenchman and his entourage who affected it.) The Queen herself led the way, apparently delighting in all manner of change. Yet no one, except certain of the Puritans, themselves quite new to the scene and soon enough to effect the greatest changes England had ever known, seemed greatly concerned about changes. There was nostalgia, to be sure, conventional longing by a few for the days of the longbow and the simple life; but for all the newness, from the introduction of the fork to the implications of Ramist Logic, the prevailing mood was one which took these changes for granted . . . like the weather. Dig a little deeper and it soon becomes apparent that the reign of Elizabeth was deeply conservative, that one of her great aims was to recover the qualities initiated, then dissipated by her grandfather, Henry VII. It seems that she was lodged in the past, studiously seeking to avoid the folly of seeking to master the future which was the undoing of Henry VIII, likewise turning away from Mary's attempt to *restore* the lost past, learning her negative lessons from the observed disasters of the reigns of Edward and Mary. Freed from concern about the future by circumstance and by choice, schooling herself in the past and aiming to recover rather than to restore, she found herself oddly free to live (dangerously) in a continual present. And so, ironically, possessed a longer future and a longer past than any other monarch before her. Yet while England burned with change, turn and counterturn for half a century, it was, we can see now, a time of relative sameness and stability. And with her death that inner quiet, persistent at the heart of outward clamor, died too. To be followed, as surely, it seems, as the working out of an equation, by England's deluge. Which, if true, means finally that whether she wished it so or not, her refusal to commit herself to the future made that future inevitable.

This can only be dimly imagined and with difficulty. It *could* have been imagined easily enough by any number of Elizabethan historians, Ralegh among them for certain and Shakespearean as well, for they delighted in the working out of intricate mysterious patterns in time and called the pattern Providence. And because the signs of Providence were most accessible not to reason alone, but to the reasonable imagination, neither Ralegh nor Shakespeare nor any other historian of that time seems to have been much troubled by the unimagined distinction between fact and fiction.

III

Which, by devious ways, leads me to an ending not far from where I began. Without benefit of much theory, or, perhaps more accurately, with the benefit of many examples of theory and practice to choose from and among, my working theory of the use of history in fiction came from the work. The end is not to *understand* a piece of history and to make it live again. (Who could presume to follow after Tolstoy?) I should be condemned under the social and Marxist terms of Georg Lukács, in his profound arrangement of the subject in *The Historical Novel*. Others, my betters and in truth my masters as scholars of the time and place, would (and will no doubt when the time comes) prefer that the distinctions should not be ignored, believing that the distinctions between history and fiction can be liberating to both, can lead the novel, or whatever it is to be called, into new, original, and delightful forms and can free the historian to ignore it if he chooses. Writers of fiction and "nonfiction" will wish the same thing for a different reason, seeing the fusion of methods as confusion. Those who seek radical change, new or reactionary, who find so much of history irrelevant, will find this method lacking in relevance too.

I have no answer to any of these. Except this one, that in the working out in fact of a long-imagined fiction, I came to cling to the notion that the proper subject and theme of historical fiction is what it is— the human imagination in action, itself dramatized as it struggles with surfaces, builds structures with facts, deals out and plays a hand of ideas, and most of all, by conceiving of the imagination of others, wrestles with the angel (Wallace Stevens's "necessary angel") of the imagination.

Therefore to write imaginary history is to celebrate the human imagination. Not one's own, for the subject precludes the possibility of doing what R. P. Blackmur called to heroize the sensibility. The subject is not art and the artist. Flaubert did that best in *Salammbô*, and who needs to imitate his triumph? The subject is the larger imagination, the possibility of imagining lives and spirits of other human beings, living or dead, without assaulting their essential and, anyway, ineffable mystery, to dream again in recapitulation the dream of Adam, knowing, as he did not until he awoke, that it is true; for Adam dreamed in innocence. We can only imagine that condition.

And what is the value, if any? Not of a book to be published later and to stand or fall on its own accounting. Not to the writer, who in the writing rather than the publishing, gains all that matters or can be gained. Rather, what use and value from this only vaguely formulated theory of the use of the past in fiction? To which I can answer only this much. We have no poverty of thinkers. If sages are few, honest intellectuals are plentiful, and their voices are heard. And there are plenty, a growing number, of course, equal or superior in intellectual power, who in reaction or revolution would cast aside the mind and follow feeling, sensation, impulse where they may lead. Too often both are abstractionists, peg-legged dancers, one-eyed princes (knaves?) in the kingdom of the blind. The human imagination, an energy in motion and never abstract, permits the wedding and intercourse of thought and feeling, each responsive to, respectful of the other. It may well be that the present (though it is the past by the time two words are on a page or, for that matter, one sequence of images flashes across the movie screen) is the most fitting place to awaken the imagination with some hope of such a felicitous union. To live well in the present demands as much imagination as can be mustered. But to live in the

---

present fully one preserves the possibility of exploring the past. One may choose to deny that one's present world is in any part fictitious. The past, however, is chiefly fiction and must be imagined before it can exist. But the past is forever in the present, even when it is forgotten, and the attempt to imagine it, whether as writer or reader, requires a sacrifice, an expense of vanity (like the old Queen alone in her mirrored room), offering in reward for that a recollection, vague beyond imagining, shared by the living and the dead, of something beautiful, and forever joyously new.

2

Why They Left Home and What They Were Looking For

(1985)

I need to be clear from the beginning that what I am doing here, as my title implies, is personal, speculative, as much a matter of imagination and good guessing as anything else; though I hope it is solidly based on the facts of life and the period of the beginnings of colonization in America, as we know these things. You have heard and will hear from others with much greater and deeper authority and expertise on the period and on the large historical currents which came together to encourage our ancestors to come here to begin a new life in what was for them a new land. My own expertise, insofar as it may exist at all, is limited. Is mostly a matter of experience, the experience of spending a good many years writing two novels (I am now working on a third one) set in Elizabethan and Jacobean times. To do this, of course, required a great deal of time spent on research, or what may be claimed to be an odd kind of research, much of it in books and records; though, I am happy to say, some of it was spent on the ground, in the field as it were, moving among the haunted, if not hallowed, places (all too often in ruins nowadays) in England and Scotland where those who chose to come here, and those who did not, once moved and lived and left some traces and, more strongly, a profound sense of their spirit behind them as if to challenge us to try to imagine and thus remember them. I call it "an odd kind of research" because though it involved much reading and study and arranging and rearranging of patterns of factual information, it was also marked by the undeniable truth that, above and beyond the most rudimentary facts, I did not know at any given time exactly what I was looking for or, indeed, what to expect. In that sense it was always more of an adventure than a chore. But for a writer, fighting and missing contractual deadlines, one eye always cocked at the calendar where first the months, then years leafed past, as they used to in the montage of old-timey movies, it was more than a little scary. The research itself could quite easily have gone along if not forever, then at least for the rest of my allotted days, without ever arriving at any real destination. And that might not have been such a bad thing, after all. I can think of many worse ways to spend a lifetime. For better or worse, however, I couldn't afford not to write my books. The problem was how to know enough (of whatever it was I needed to know) to feel at ease writing about strangers in an imagined and mostly imaginary world, as distant from us in time as the outer reaches of this galaxy are in space. I looked and listened and waited, as patiently as I could, for voices to begin to speak to me.

Much of the work, almost all of the writing, was done in a wooden boathouse set upon an earth and rock pier jutting out into the York River in York, Maine. This earth and rock pier was once the first town pier, replete with its warehouse and the village marketplace directly behind it. I sat and wrote in my boathouse on the place of the first pier in the first village that was settled and colonized in what was then called the Palitinate of Maine and was governed, from a distance, by Sir Ferdinando Gorges. Who was, as it happens, a cousin of Sir Walter Ralegh. We now know what they knew well then that for one reason and another Europeans had been coming to this coast of Maine, most often to the offshore islands but sometimes inland, for a much longer time than anyone has yet accurately reckoned. Most likely—there is a great deal of evidence, some of it quite recently discovered—the Vikings were there. There are plausible hints and clues that there were others even before that. But certainly the English, among others, were coming in the early years of the sixteenth century for the seasonal fishing and to set up their fishing camps, some of which were quite elaborate, solid as settlements; for exploring, also, and for some modest trading with the Indians. Sir Ferdinando decided on what became York as his choice for the first permanent settlement in Maine because it had already been cleared and somewhat tamed. There had been a village there inhabited by agricultural Indians for a long time. Sometime around the end of the sixteenth or the beginning of the seventeenth century, more or less coterminous with the end of the reign of Queen Elizabeth, they simply vanished. It is speculated that they all died by disease or during one of the innumerable tribal wars in that area. At any rate it was a likely place, empty of its original inhabitants, when, in the early years of the seventeenth century, Captain Christopher Levett sailed the *Yorke Bonaventure* through the tricky, rocky mouth and into the calm harbor of the York River (then called the Agamenticus), looking for appropriate places for settlements to be planted. He recommended this one, as follows: "There I think a good plantation may be settled, for there is a good harbor for ships, good ground and much already cleared, fit for the planting of corn and other fruits, having heretofore been planted by the Savages who are all dead. There is good timber and likely to be good fishing. . . . "

And so they came and have been there ever since, including some of the original families—Bragdons and Blaisdells and Moultons and Sewalls and Stovers and so forth; my boathouse is insured by Bob Bragdon, directly descended from one Arthur Bragdon who came to York, in his middle age, from Stratford-on-Avon where it is next to impossible that he did not have some perfectly clear memories of that town's second most famous citizen, an uninterrupted History. Not entirely uneventful, however. For on the day after Candlemas in 1692 a large band of Abenaki warriors, in the service of the French, attacked the village (in fact composed of three separate hamlets) at dawn and killed and carried off more than half of the inhabitants. Two garrison houses withstood the attack, one, Captain Alcocks's, located about 100 yards down river from my boathouse. Captain Alcocks who reported as follows to Captain John Floyd, who brought troops to the rescue from Portsmouth: "All gone. Everything we built and planted, every mark we made on this place is gone. There is nothing left but bloody corpses and cold ashes." For the next decade or so they all slept in the garrison houses, but they planted crops and rebuilt the village. And there it stands still. For symmetry, if nothing else, I should mention two other things. That I am not the first southern writer to live and write there, one time and another; Sidney Lanier and Thomas Nelson Page and Mark Twain owned houses there. And that the first encounter with the war party of Abenaki was when a young boy, checking a line of traps at first light, came upon a great pile of snowshoes set against a rock. He was captured but lived to tell about it. And he was the third Arthur Bragdon of York, Maine.

Why They Left Home and What They Were Looking For

I mention all these things only to show that after all my reading and all my travels and sight-seeing, I was writing my novels in a place as good as any I can think of for summoning up ghosts. It wasn't a haunted place, really; but it was a kind of enchanted ground. And there were moments when I felt the living energy of that enchantment. Moments when, without any warning, I felt the presence of others at my elbow, ghostly presences, to be sure, but as palpable as any shadow, including my own. Moments when, out of the shadows, I seemed to hear their voices speaking.

I cannot speak for them by any means. But I can speak of and about them out of my own experience which, in the end, proved to be as real as the sum of all the years of research.

Let me begin by stressing that these ghosts, these substantial shadows, were and are, appropriately, paradoxical creatures. They are our kin and are much like us; and yet, by the same token, they often seem as alien to us and as indifferent to our concerns as any imaginable visitors from outer space would be. And in and of themselves they heft and hold, in some kind of balance, contradictory forces, motivations, aims. I think that capacity, the ability to maintain quite contradictory and simultaneous impulses, a kind of elegant cultivation of inconsistency, is one of the dominant characteristics of the restless race of our ancestors who came here to create a new life for themselves even as they also intended to recreate, to carry over the best elements and qualities of the old.

Put it another way. They were at once weary to death of the life they had known and perfectly willing to risk life and limb, to risk everything, in the hope that they might escape from a tedious world which seemed to be, among other things, running down, grinding to a halt and good riddance to it; yet, at one and the same time, their thoughts and hopes were all on the future, the shine and possibility of the new, not necessarily the new and different; for much of their hope for the future was for reformation and restoration of the tried and true, preservation of the familiar in a foreign place. It was a simultaneous and contradictory attitude—one that has baffled so many modern historians—combining an apocalyptic nihilism (as weary and sophisticated as that of any modern or postmodern European intellectual) with a simple and hopeful idealism of a kind which might easily have embarrassed even a stereotypical hippie by its incredible naïveté. We have to understand that these people, perhaps more honest than we, their descendants, were capable of loving and hating life deeply even as they lived it. They were less fearful of the turbulence of inner contradictions and, thus, in that sense, more at ease with themselves than we ever can be, even though serenity was far from them and even though living amidst all that expense of energy must have been, at times, like burning alive.

But all that is much too abstract for them. Put it more simply. They left home because they were deeply discontented. Discontented with many things. And yet they were aware of their discontents precisely because they were also the healthiest and happiest generations on the British Isles for many generations before and after. Mixed feelings, then. I can't think of anything about which the Elizabethans and Jacobeans did not respond and react with mixed feelings. It was not necessary for them to trouble themselves to sort these things out. But it is altogether requisite for us to do so if we have any hope of beginning to understand them and what they were up to.

I am not thinking much of matters of policy. True enough that, beginning most seriously with the long reign of Elizabeth, the Queen and her Council for many good reasons made it national policy to inspire and to encourage (albeit as cheaply as possible) all kinds of voyaging and trading, exploration and privateering, even colonizing, though this last was always least successful even as close by as Ireland. Policy, as we know, can sometimes arrive at its stated goals, but not often without joining forces with individual desires. In the Queen's time trade, exploration, privateering and naval warfare helped to create the private wealth and, equally important, the wealth of experience, the consequent skills, which in the end served to make the settlements in the New World possible at the same time they became most desirable. And the failure of many colonial schemes in Ireland taught some hard and useful lessons, too. But none of these things had much meaning until the time arrived when enough of the people, first of England, then, after the accession of James I, of Britain, had had enough. Until much that had seemed new turned old; until what was remarkable became habitual and commonplace; until enough was enough yet somehow, positively and negatively, insufficient to satisfy expectations.

Why They Left Home and What They Were Looking For

The great Queen was a political magician and managed to gratify the expectations of the first full generation of her two-generation reign mostly by myth. After the long Wars of the Roses, the ups and downs and often terrifying times of all the Tudors before her, it seemed likely her time would be as brief as that of her sister Mary and her brother Edward. She promised peace and prosperity and soon enough announced that these desirable goals had been achieved; this in spite of the fact that there was scarcely a day of peace during her entire reign. Her first years were racked by most serious and bloody internal rebellions and overt and covert plots against her government. The plots and conspiracies continued throughout, but by the middle of her years, England was deeply involved in a series of bloody and expensive foreign wars—in France, the Netherlands, Ireland, and against Spain everywhere including the seven seas. Still, peace was the word; and many people, most of them, believed it no matter what the evidence against it. Or put it another way. It was another contrariety—they found themselves able to believe and not believe it at one and the same time. Similarly the truth of prosperity. True, many great fortunes were made. Or so it seemed; though in almost every case it was purely and simply the adroit rearrangement and redistribution of land and existing capital without any significant growth or development. Her father, Great Harry, had at least had the seized lands and wealth of the Church to change the wealth of England once and for all. Elizabeth had a kind of high-class shell game and very quick and clever hands. Many of the outward and visible signs of the new prosperity, particularly in the ostentatious restoration and building of great houses for the great men of her kingdom, served mainly to disguise the decay of the towns and cities, the simultaneous growth and decay of the city of London and the suburbs, and to divert attention away from the undeniable fact that her palaces and public buildings were becoming disreputable, her chief fortifications, excepting Berwick upon Tweed and the Tower of London, were falling into ruin. It is said that not a new church of any importance was built anywhere in England throughout her reign. It is significant, I think, that the great spire of St. Paul's, struck by lightning and burned in 1560, was never rebuilt. It took the Great Fire, half a century after the Queen, to clean up London and allow for the rebuilding of the city. For a long time, nevertheless, the Queen, herself, managed by example and subterfuge to convince her people that they were enjoying peace and prosperity and unity as well, that they were a united people, spared the savage divisions and discords of other peoples all around them. In a relative sense this was true. The Netherlands, France, the states and petty kingdoms of Germany and Italy were gutted and bled white by a century of religious wars. But in England the majority Catholic population and the minority Puritans battled each other and the Queen's Church of England with a passion and a vehemence that belied all the claims of unity. And she herself (and her ministers too) was as savagely repressive as need be to keep control and keep her passionate religious factions in line. In the end she killed more people for the sake of religion than her sister, Bloody Mary; but she managed to do so without claiming or receiving credit for it. Indeed she is remembered now and was honored then for not opening a window on men's consciences.

What I am saying is that for nearly fifty years the Queen (by whom and which I mean the government of England, Court and Council and Parliament) was given full credit for her good intentions even in the face of all evidence which spoke against them. That her good intentions were taken as true and thus became the truth.

As Sir Walter Raleigh says, in the novel *Death of the Fox* and nowhere else that I know of: "We are all false witnesses. And yet the sum of our witnessing may be true." In another place in that novel, in an imaginary letter written by Raleigh to his son, Carew, and later burned for the sake of verisimilitude, he tries to explain the essential Elizabethan paradox to his Jacobean son. It should be remembered that Raleigh is of special interest since, though a child of the Queen's times, he fell between the two generations of her reign. "New the world seemed to us then, all things shining with newness. And that was the magic of the Queen. She dazzled and delighted with seeming changes, as if to deny all our past and to celebrate the future. To those who were young it seemed as though, touched by the wand of her scepter, the world was freshly gilded and beginning again. A false garden it may have been, after all. But God knows it was rich and cunning."

However, in another place in the same letter, Raleigh tells the boy: "All things, even the stones of palaces, fall to age and weariness and ruin."

What, in fact, came to pass? In the second generation, especially in the last decade or so of her reign, the Queen came closest to achieving her intentions. In fact England was as close to peace and prosperity and unity as it had been for a century past and would be for another. But the younger generation, skeptical and ambitious and pestered by the dichotomy of appearance and reality, refused to believe in it any more. They did not exactly hate the old Queen; but, with the best of them hating themselves for the thought, they looked for her demise with some eagerness. It was seriously entertained as well that the end of the world was at hand. Needless to say, a good many people were disappointed when the apocalypse failed to arrive on time. The Queen died quietly, as peacefully as a cut rose a contemporary said, and James of Scotland succeeded her without a civil war. Hopes were high. Briefly. For it was then that the truth, a truth anyway, came out. The kingdom was broke. The old Queen's jewels were paste. Instead of enormous wealth James had to settle for slim pickings. And her old shell game was beyond him. He cultivated other forms of duplicity, but neither he nor all his horses and all of his men could put back together again the great, shared popular duplicity whereby Queen and country had for so long pretended that all things were well. In no time at all the Jacobeans were looking back on the time before as "Merry England" and were ashamed of themselves for having been so discontented in those best of times. Self-esteem may be a much exaggerated source for good behavior and a good life. But, by and large, self-loathing, brief as that state of being can be borne, leads to nothing good. Soon enough would come bloody revolution, bloody Restoration, next the Glorious Revolution, and through it all a flood of emigrants seeking new lives in new worlds.

All that was still to come. But the proximate causes and basic reasons for the beginning of the great modern migrations of the eternally restless Anglo-Saxon and Celtic tribes, migrations which only ended when the British Empire dwindled into the British Commonwealth of Nations and the old country, the old island, was left with only the dregs and less, the *orts* to use the Elizabethan word, of its original population, the basic reasons people left home for good to go in very real danger and discomfort, to risk their lives in gambling for a new life, were all in place. They went, from all classes and at all levels, in the hope of improving their fortunes, to be sure. A calculated risk, made somewhat more sensible, if not any less risky, by the fact that in the old world their chances of improving their fortunes to any extent at all were very small. And more than that they went for simple things. For land, even a little of it to call their own, which they could not have in the old world where all of the land was taken. For such basic things as fuel and shelter. In the old country, as in some weary places in the Third World today, even ordinary firewood had become precious, too expensive for most people. And coal was expensive and dirty—and, believe it or not, the Elizabethans and early Jacobeans were fastidious. People in England and Scotland were tired of being cold. America was trees and timbers for building and burning. They came, too, as is clear in their writings, for food, the game of the wilderness (there was no wilderness in the old country, only *wasteland*) and the chance to plant and harvest crops, new and old things, in unspoiled earth. And, you know, they came for clean air and clean water; for the Elizabethans were much concerned about pollution and could not see any end to it. And, for a time until technology finally rescued them from itself, they were right. Things were getting worse, not better. The Industrial Revolution was coming. Though they couldn't have named it, they felt it well enough. A hundred years after the death of Elizabeth, and for a couple of hundred years after that, the people of Britain were a foot shorter and lived a little more than half of the life span of the average Elizabethan who managed to survive the perils of infancy. By the twentieth century the urban English were about the size of their medieval ancestors. Raleigh was six feet four and, though taller than average (as he would be today), not truly exceptional for his time. By and large, Elizabethans ate well, exercised, and lived healthy lives. But plagues of one kind and another, including the Black Plague, were beginning again to sweep through the country in the last years of Elizabeth and the Jacobean years. And there were famines and shortages of food.

They left home, then, to keep their health and to save their lives, if they could; though the risks were great and a great many lost their lives before they managed even to begin a new life. They came, too, looking for peace. All they had ever known in the old country were wars and the rumors of war. They knew well enough that they might have to die defending life, hearth and home in the new world. Contrary to much of our contemporary received opinion, they had a great respect for the Indian as a worthy antagonist and a brave warrior. Truth is, they ranked the Indian well above the Irish. But, at least they would not have to be shipped out to die badly in Ireland or the Lowlands, ill-equipped and poorly led, against the Spanish infantry.

All these were good, solid reasons, ones which, I am certain, would work quite as well now if a new world were offered to us. . . .

Some of the sense of the accumulated common discontents I have presented in the final chapter of *The Succession,* set during the Queen's last Christmas in 1602/03. Here is a little piece of that passage:

Time Again for Christmas Season

Time again in spite of strange weathers. Spring, summer, and fall too wet or too dry. Winters too cold. Ice and a red sun brooding in gray sky. Lean poor harvests leading to scarcity of grain and meat. Prices never so high. Hard times for the poor and, truly, for all the common folk. Aggravated by rumors of private hoarding. And never mind the truth; for rumor has the same power to create fear that truth does. Already we hear of good country people, rivals now of fatter pigs, going to gather acorns to make bread. And there are some people who foresee the time when not a few in this kingdom will have to go down on their knees. And not chiefly to pray but to graze like and among the immeasurably more valuable sheep. People will feed themselves on leaves and nettles and grass and bark and roots. And soon they will take on themselves the latest fashion of bloated belly and green-stained lips and teeth and tongue. Like the Irish. Poor, benighted savage Irish dying in their sad bogs.

Time for celebration again, also, in spite of wars. War on the high seas and the war of sieges, endless skirmish and ambush in the Lowlands. Of which no wise man can see any ending. Not in victory or defeat. Not until there can be peace with Spain. And war in Ireland, as always; though some see hope of victory there.

Wars taking place elsewhere. Far from Court. From wherever the Court may light in its restless, immemorial progress to no place in particular. If far from court, then far from London, too, with all its swollen rage of busyness and idleness, ebbing and flowing tides of buying and selling, unceasing search for new pleasures.

Wars often forgotten in city and country alike. Except for the late, slow-traveling news of deaths and wounds. A village gained, a castle lost. Ignored or forgotten except for sudden musters. Which can send large numbers of grown and able-bodied men into hiding or disguises (O England now has many sturdy, hairy, poxy milkmaids whenever there's a muster!) until enough poor fish are caught. These being chiefly the slow and the stupid and the purely unlucky. Who will be marched away to the tunes of jeering from safe windows and from behind walls and hedges.

Wars ignored at the Court and in the City until sometimes report arrives to tell of some worthy enemy captured and held for ransom. Or perhaps a prize taken at sea, crew and cargo. Now that is news that can quicken and kindle imagination!

Wars, then, far from the palaces and mansion houses where a healthy man can prove his courage and spend his sweat at the bowling alley or the tennis court. Or at dancing, late into night, in a pair of jeweled, satin dancing slippers. Places where the greatest risks are only wagers. Not wagers of life and limb or even honor, but of money and land. Betting on anything, everything that may or may not happen. Betting on fighting cocks in the cockpit. Or the baiting of bears and bulls by the dogs. . . .

Wars whose straggling marches and forlorn retreats are forever at enormous distance from the long, slow, lazy, solemn summer Progress of the Queen. And likewise from the long, slow, lazy time of autumn when the Queen and her gentlemen and ladies do ride out not to do battle, but for sake of hawking and hunting and horseback riding amid the sweet-wine glories of the season's red and gold. . . .

Time come around again for the festive celebration of Christmastide in spite of crowds of lean, hard faces, blank-eyed, rigid with apathy (when they are not frantic with rage). Hurt faces of vagabonds and other masterless persons. Who can be seen in forests and wastelands, on shoulders of high roads, and sometimes even moving among decent folk in remote villages. Among these you can find enough survivors of war to encourage rogues to counterfeit themselves as discharged soldiers of the Queen. Forgotten by the Queen and their fellow countrymen, crippled by wounds and by the inexorable grip of poverty.

We shall enjoy the revels of this Christmastime and shall never mind, if we can, the decay of hospitality in so many country manor houses, seats of stingy housekeeping in this hard-hearted age of rusty iron.

Pray against danger of the sweating sickness and infection of Plague in the new year to come. Plague has already traveled here from the Lowlands and other places abroad. To work its black spells. To waste and kill man, woman and child. Plague has come close to the City, prowling among the back alleys and muddy lanes of Southwark this summer past.

Some say that worse than plague and sweating sickness are coming. Some are reading the signs and saying the end of the world is near at hand. . . .

End of the world or no—and will anyone care to hazard a wager on that?—so many things are going so badly in this time of the Queen's old age. Consider the subjects, if not the long-winded and rolling rhetoric of lawyers' words, of the Proclamations lately published:

"Enforcing All Former Statutes Against The Forestalling of Grain . . . Ordering Hospitality To Be Kept In The Country . . . Enforcing All Statutes And Orders Against Poaching and Hunting . . . Enforcing Martial Law Against Army Deserters, Mariners, Vagrants And London Vagabonds . . . Enforcing All Statutes Against Rogues and Vagabonds . . . Enforcing Martial Law Against All Unlawful Assemblies . . . Enforcing Statutes Against Handguns . . . Banishing All Jesuits and Secular Priests . . . Ordering Punishment Of All Persons With Forged Credentials . . . Offering Rewards For Information On Libels Against The Queen. . . . "

More dangers than libel against Her Majesty are being feared. The Queen has ordered her guard to be doubled. And, for the first time that anyone can recall, the Queen goes armed. She keeps a sword within reach. Sometimes, struck by flashing rage or a gust of sudden, unappeasable fear, she will thrust her sword through an arras. In case there were spy or assassin hiding there.

True, these are sorry and dangerous days.

Now two questions are sure to arise. Were they not seeking religious liberty? And, in a larger sense, though they may not have imagined it, were they not, like their countrymen left behind, prompted by the stirrings of political and social liberty? To which the answer is yes and no. Some did come to find a place to practice their religion. Almost all who came surely hoped that the new world would be free from the religious controversies which troubled the old. And as for the dream of political and social liberty, well, that would come later. At the time they wanted distance, and the self-government which long distance allowed, from the old world. Mostly they had not yet imagined new and different forms of government. Everywhere but Massachusetts there was considerable alarm when Cromwell seized control in Britain.

Behind all the practical good reasons, as I have tried to indicate, lay one large and complex reason. They had grown weary of the weight of duplicity, the burden required to endure in the old world. Often we see these people, out of our past and vague memory, as part of the beginning of something, anyway far behind us in the steadily progressive accumulation of past time we call history. We see their world as simple and our own as snarled in complexity. In many ways, some of them logically irrefutable, they saw themselves, their world and its various systems, as old, enormously complex, frequently contradictory, the tag end of something beyond repair or restoration. There are many ways in which this view of reality can be supported by the evidence, not only the evidence they chose to ponder, but also our kind of evidence. For example, take technology—that they did, as well as can be done, what they wanted to do. That only later when new and unimagined things had to be done was our kind of technological progress valuable. In any case, they saw themselves as, at best, clever survivors of a system which had asked too much of them. And then there was a new place, a new world where all things would be more simple, where what was good and true and beautiful from the old world might be brought along and preserved, where what was new and valuable might be acquired simply, by labor and courage, patience and dedication. From our vantage point we can see that they were more innocent than they realized, at least to believe in and hope for such things, briefly forgetting what we have come to know so well, that we carry the weight of our inheritance with us wherever we go, that we are wed to our own past in sickness and

---

health, for richer and poorer, and that nothing, not even thousands of miles of raw ocean, can free us from the burden of ourselves and our follies. It is folly, we know, to think otherwise. And yet we must all be grateful to these ghosts for their wistful, childlike, foolish hope. We think we know too much to believe in anything like that any more. Yet even now we envy them the chance they had to wish it might be so and to act upon that wish.

I have tried to put something of this kind of wishing into a moment in a little play about the settling of York, Maine, called "Enchanted Ground." A man and his wife are leaving for the new world, and she expresses her doubts and regrets:

SHE: I shall greatly miss my herb garden.

HE: Tush, woman. Everything grows well there, they say. . . .

SHE: But I shall be sad without the scent of lavender and lemon balm, without my spearmint and black peppermint, the wild thyme and the sweet bay. How can we celebrate a wedding or mourn the dead without rosemary?

HE: You shall have your herbs, I promise you that. You shall have a garden as quick as we can turn the earth.

SHE: Will there be wildflowers in spring and summer? Do you think I shall ever again see the meadow buttercup or the lilac cuckoo flower? Will there be fireweed and harebell and St. John's wort?

HE: God knows, woman, not I. But it must be a land of flowers, for the sailors say you can smell the sweetness in the air a full day or two before we sight land.

SHE: Do you believe that tale?

HE: Well . . . no, but I can hope that it is only a decoration of the plain truth.

SHE: I shall greatly miss the graves of our people in the church and the churchyard. What will we do for ancestors now?

HE: Let them rest easy and quietly here. Someone must be first. We shall be the ancestors of others.

II

Some of the Masters

Fire and Freshness:
A Matter of Style in *The Great Gatsby*
(1985)

I have never yet known, or, indeed known of, a contemporary American writer who did not admire *The Great Gatsby*. This evidence, admittedly and purely anecdotal, is, also in my experience, unique. I know of no other twentieth-century masterpiece in our language, or, for that matter, in our Western tradition, about which this can be said. Let it be said again as simply as possible: I have never known an American writer, of my generation or of the older and younger generations, who has not placed *Gatsby* among the rare unarguable masterpieces of our times. In some cases this admiration is frankly surprising, because *Gatsby* seems to be in form and content so different from what has otherwise engaged the passions and commitment of this writer and the other. It really has not seemed to matter very much which side of the (aesthetic) tracks the writer came from or what side of the street the writer is working. In an era of increasingly specialized special interests it does not seem to be a matter defined or limited by race, creed, color, gender, or country of national origin. And strangely, in an age when we have become so politicized that even the toothpaste one uses becomes, like it or not, a political statement, writers of all political stripes and persuasions seem to admire *Gatsby*, even as, inevitably, they describe the characters and the story in somewhat different terms. Finally, it doesn't even seem to matter very much if the writer in question holds any positive feelings about the life and (other) works of F. Scott Fitzgerald. Many did not admire him in his lifetime—though it is clear he was much envied from time to time. Many do not have feelings one way or the other, nothing beyond a polite shrug, even now. But *Gatsby*, itself, stands by itself—a permanent monument of our literature, a national treasure. And I share the consensual wisdom, though not without a willingness to question it, if only to ask the

question as to where it comes from. In part perversely, because I have
always been automatically contemptuous of trends and fashions, especially *intellectual* trends, which seem to be a contradiction in terms (like
the concept of military justice), I have always preferred *Tender Is The
Night*. It was always my favorite among the Fitzgerald novels, since I
read them, back to back, for the first time, to the best of my recollection, in the green mild summer of 1948 in Princeton. *Gatsby* was assigned reading in a summer school course, the first time Fitzgerald was
ever read at Princeton as part of an official course. It was, in fact, the
first time at Princeton that any American writers beyond the life and
times of Henry James were allowed to be part of the authorized academic curriculum. All that is another story for some other time and
place; but it is not quite irrelevant. The course was new and different,
a departure. It met early, eight-thirty as I recall, in the high-ceilinged,
long-windowed light and shadows of McCosh 10, a lecture hall where
Scott Fitzgerald would have to have found his own place (still num-
bered and assigned seating in his day and mine, though not for long
after) and probably dozed through many lectures as monotonous as the
lazy bee hum from the quadrangle outdoors, taking desultory notes
waiting for moments of light and excitement which came, suddenly
and somehow permanently, at rare times in special courses, and which
made all of it, like the ritual patience of hunter and fisherman, worthwhile. It was an altogether stunning, unforgettable experience to "discover" William Faulkner *(The Sound and the Fury)* and Ernest
Hemingway *(The Sun Also Rises)* in that summer. But it was very
heaven to be in Princeton reading *The Great Gatsby*, as a class assignment (usually while sunbathing through the long, lazy afternoon in the
neat little quad of 1903 Hall), for the first time and then finding, in the
stacks of the brand new Firestone Library, the stories and *This Side of
Paradise* and *Tender Is The Night* and the others. And over at the U-
Store you could buy, and I did, *The Last Tycoon* and *The Crack-Up*,
edited by Edmund Wilson, in the latter of which I underlined with
youth's savage self-indulgence (and self-pity) a couple or three sentences by Glenway Wescott, whom I had met, who was the gray and
eminent and handsome uncle of a boy who lived upstairs in 1903 Hall.
"The rest of us, his writing friends and rivals, thought that he had the
best narrative gift of the century. Did the English Department at

A *Matter of Style in* The Great Gatsby

Princeton try to develop his admiration of that fact about himself, and make him feel the burden and the pleasure of it? Apparently they taught him to appreciate this or that other writer, to his own disfavor."

All of us that summer planned to be the next F. Scott Fitzgerald. One young man, a little older and grander than the rest, seemed well on the way. People pointed out Frederick Buechner, just as handsome as Fitzgerald and a good deal taller, armed with attaché case and portable typewriter, as he boarded the little train, the Dinky, to Princeton Junction and thence to New York. Probably, we grimly and enviously surmised, to have a serious conference with his publisher, to be entertained at lunch in some elegant place (otherwise why the neat necktie on that summer's day?)

Well, we have all come a distance, a far piece, since then, swept by waves of unimaginable change, until, surfacing nearly a half century later, it seems that almost everything has changed beyond memory or repair. One of the things that has not changed, however, that still shines with authentic inner light, is *Gatsby*. That it has this same glowing effect on writers young enough to be my sons and daughters, new enough not to care a serious hoot about Old Nassau (or, probably, Glenway Wescott, Frederick Buechner, or myself), I find an absolutely fascinating phenomenon.

To a certain extent it may be a matter of historical content and the long attractive shadows of nostalgia; but that cannot explain the depth of the novel's lasting appeal. Much of the context and content is lost now in the present. Clearly only a modest handful of American writers and critics alive now, of any age (and forget the foreigners, even the English, who haven't a real clue), possess by birth, education, and experience the assumed knowledge and the imagination to understand the really very subtle social implications and ambiguities which lie at the center, are the very heart of the story of *Gatsby*. Even at the time, the delicacy of Fitzgerald's sensitive recording of a very specific and special world, as envisioned and judged by a very particular and special intelligence, Nick Carraway, must have escaped many of his contemporaries. Significantly, the letters about *Gatsby* he savored from prominent writers he admired, for example the letters from Gertrude Stein, Edith Wharton, and T. S. Eliot, stress and praise aspects of form much more than content. Each differently, they see *Gatsby* as advancing the art of the novel not so much from what it talks about as in the interesting ways and means of its making. As for us, it is very hard now to unlearn all that has happened since 1925; difficult, if not impossible, to imagine ourselves safely on the other side of the Great Depression and World War II and all the wars since then. In one respect, then, contemporary interest in and excitement at the subjects and content of *Gatsby* derives from its odd prescience. Ash heap and eyeglasses, sordid orgy and casual accident, murder and suicide, impotence and unrequited love, these are literary signs we have come to live among as if they had always been there, inherent to any conventional literary picture of modern American life. There is, in fact, a direct line of both influence and authority running from *Gatsby* to a great many of our most prominent contemporary literary artists, both popular and "serious." The signs and portents of Joan Didion, for example, or of Renata Adler are rooted in Fitzgerald's acres of ashes in *Gatsby*, as are the economic minimalism of Raymond Carver, the half-stoned nihilism which pervades the stories of Ann Beattie, the lyrical ambiance of the novels and stories of Richard Yates. Gore Vidal, not deeply sympathetic to Fitzgerald (see "F. Scott Fitzgerald's Case" in *The Second American Revolution and Other Essays*, 1982), is nevertheless clearly admiring of the "small but perfect operation" of *Gatsby*. Of all these, and so many others, by the way, only the quirky Vidal has the depth and subtlety, rooted in old American experience, to understand some of what was eccentric and original about *Gatsby*. At any rate, American writers of all stripes and stamps, from Marxists to reactionaries, seem to be at home with the apparent content of *Gatsby*, to believe in its world, to take it for granted.

It is worth remembering that the downside of "the Jazz Age," namely the Depression, was several years beyond the horizon in 1925 and that the main line of action in the story of *Gatsby*, the summer of 1922, was firmly set in the booming postwar years. Worth keeping in mind that prophets of doom seemed more outrageous and eccentric then than they would a decade later. It is part of Tom Buchanan's foolishness that he sees doom and trouble ahead. Worth recalling that popular fiction in which crimes could be allowed to go without punishment (if only by fate and bad luck) was very rare. After all, in American film and television, as late as the 1960s there was a serious problem of getting Code approval for a story in which vice was not punished one way or another. It was startling in 1925 to let the Buchanans off the hook with a brief judgmental aside by the narrator: "They were careless people, Tom and Daisy—they smashed up things and creatures and then retreated back into their money or their vast carelessness, or whatever it was that kept them together, and let other people clean up the mess they had made. . . . " That they have done what they have done and can walk away from it safely and cheerfully enough, with nobody but the reader and the narrator any the wiser, was as daring as it was remarkable.

There are other things, qualities of which our own ignorance and lack of imagination now deprive us. There is so much drinking in *Gatsby*, and, of course, Fitzgerald was such a heavy drinker at times, and we know all about that now, that it is tricky to keep in mind the fact that both the story and the telling of it are deep in the heart of Prohibition. Which was, as a Constitutional amendment, very much the law of the land. And which was not yet, either by Fitzgerald or others, seen as coming to an easy end either soon or painlessly. Time has turned the underworld and internecine wars, the blood and savagery which accompanied Prohibition, into something close to comedy, perhaps musical comedy. But Fitzgerald knew very well the shock value he gained by having so much drinking in his novel. (As did Hemingway in *The Sun Also Rises*, though that story was conveniently set in Europe.) It is significant that Jay Gatsby and Daisy Buchanan meet again, tentative and a little shy at first, in the proper atmosphere of an intimate and wonderfully awkward little tea party at Carraway's cottage. And, in accuracy and fairness, we have to recognize that, daring as he was, Fitzgerald carefully demonstrates throughout the book the bad results which inevitably follow from excessive drinking. Jay Gatsby is self-disciplined and abstemious; this is a rhetorical plus. The fact that Daisy does not drink is viewed ambiguously, more a matter of "an absolutely perfect reputation" than, perhaps, a sign of virtue. Just so, adulterous affairs and, indeed, even premarital sex, were still to be viewed as essentially criminal vices in polite society; and, to an extent, the views of polite society were confirmed by the Law. Tom's affair with Myrtle (and the fact that she would dare to call him at home!), together with the absence of any apparently serious consequences, to himself at least, coming from it, were conceived as shocking elements in the novel. Tom's promiscuity is rhetorically presented, and so intended to be taken, as wickedness rather than a "problem" or a bad habit. Gatsby's lifetime obsession with the image and reality of Daisy may be more than a little crazy, and more than a little vulgar in its material manifestations—the extraordinary house, the parties, the uncut books, the fancy yellow car and the piles of gorgeous shirts over which Daisy wept; but his dedication to her (including even the folly of asking "too much" of Daisy, asking her to confess that she had never loved anyone else but him) and his love for her were morally solid and appropriate for their time. Knowing better, even knowing why he was doing it, Gatsby had been Daisy's lover. "He took what he could get, ravenously and unscrupulously—eventually he took Daisy one still October night, took her because he had no real right to touch her hand." After which ("He felt married to her, that was all.") he always wanted to do "the right thing." Buchanan, from good family and background, has criminal vices. Gatsby, though a technical criminal of sorts and a man who mingles with strange and exotic types—mysterious Jews, show business types, flotsam and jetsam of society—is possessed by the best American middle-class standards of the time.

Only a few can still believe, still fewer remember, that there was a time not so long ago (O long before *People* magazine!) when celebrity of any kind, even the kind of celebrity Fitzgerald himself had acquired by the time he came to write *Gatsby,* had a chilling effect upon one's social position. "The best people" never appeared in the press except, perhaps, on the occasion of a wedding or funeral. "The best people" did not, beyond the wild-oats days of youth, mingle with celebrities and show business types, famous opera stars sometimes excepted. It is not quite true that American society despised the lively arts, but it is certainly true that most artists of all kinds, even those from good family, were somewhat suspect and a little bit déclassé. The Homeric list of Gatsby's guests from East Egg and West Egg is monumental in its witty snobbery. And as for Jews (the sinister, weak, and shady, two-dimensional Wolfsheim) or ethnics (the pathetic Henry C. Gatz, Gatsby's father, "a solemn old man, very helpless and dismayed, bundled up in a long cheap ulster against the warm September day"), these are not people one might meet except on some most unusual occasion or in the pages of a novel. To understand the prevalent attitude toward the very idea or image of the Jew at that time one can take quite seriously the stance of Eliot in the early poems. Or one can turn to Edith Wharton's letter of congratulations where she asserts "it's enough to make this reader happy to have met your *perfect* Jew, & the limp Wilson, & assisted at that seedy orgy in the Buchanan flat, with the dazed puppy looking on." The truth is, as both Fitzgerald and Edith Wharton knew (both in Europe at the time), the nineteenth century had not yet ended, socially at least, in America. For a moment of almost surreal social topsy-turvy see Nick's celebrated drive with Jay Gatsby into New York, over the Queensboro Bridge:

> A dead man passed us in a hearse heaped with blooms, followed by two carriages with drawn blinds, and by more cheerful carriages for friends. The friends looked out at us with the tragic eyes and short upper lips of southeastern Europe, and I was glad that the sight of Gatsby's splendid car was included in their somber holiday. As we crossed Blackwell's Island a limousine passed us, driven by a white chauffeur, in which sat three modish negroes, two bucks and a girl. I laughed aloud as the yolks of their eyeballs rolled toward us in haughty rivalry.

No comment is necessary. Except, perhaps, to point out that the language, and the reactions of the narrator and the anticipated reader were not only neutral, but decently appropriate for the time. Which was almost the last time they would be so in serious American literature. Popular narrative was (to an extent remains) slow to change and follow. Maybe it should be noted, however, that the *author's* intention in this brief sight gag was clearly to show Carraway's modernity, his openness to and delight in the otherwise shocking (to the reader) confusions of order in America.

All of this is only to make the point that in many ways we are quite far removed, as Americans, as writers and readers, as well, from the content and context of *Gatsby*. The old social guidelines have vanished. Try to imagine how the society of Nick Carraway would have viewed the high life and hard times of, say, John Z. DeLorean.

If it is hard for us to imagine and to reconstruct the world Fitzgerald wrote about and out of, it is only fair to remind ourselves that, some extraordinary prescience aside, our world was beyond his imagining as well. He could not, for example, possibly have conceived of a time when this novel's art might be submitted to the scrutiny and judgment of literary critics and historians, preservers of the totems of the American tribe, who might, themselves, be ethnic or Jewish or even black. That is to say, even as he felt the end of something and sensed many changes, Fitzgerald could not imagine the end of society as he knew it, except by an apocalypse.

In stressing what might be called the societal inaccessibility of *The Great Gatsby* to the contemporary reader, there is another social note worth mentioning. It happens to be something Nick Carraway mentions to us, a point *he* wants to make. Though there are fine-tuned differences and distinctions among all of the principals, there is one common bond. They are one and all outsiders. As Carraway points out in the final chapter: "I see now that this has been a story of the West, after all—Tom and Gatsby, Daisy and Jordan and I, were all Westerners, and perhaps we possessed some deficiency in common which made us subtly unadaptable to Eastern life." That remark, like many others by Carraway, is layered in irony, more than a little ambiguous. But it does carefully call to mind, in case anyone had missed the fact, that nobody at all from the *real* society of the East even appears in this story. Some of the dregs of that society do, indeed, show up at Gatsby's parties; but in truth the whole story is a playing out, on foreign territory as it were, as alien and exotic as the France and Spain of *The Sun Also Rises*, of a story of love and death among expatriates.

I think it can be convincingly argued that we are by now far removed, imaginatively and in fact, from at least the *rhetorical social world of Gatsby*. And a case can be made, persuasively I believe, that precisely because Fitzgerald was so sensitively attuned to that world and because that world was created and dramatized through the words and consciousness of a single character, Nick Carraway, that we are no more likely to find out what Fitzgerald "really felt" about that world, from the text, than it is likely that we shall ever know the views of our language's preeminent anonymous artist. That is, we know much about Elizabethan attitudes and prejudices; and we know much of this from the plays of Shakespeare. But we know precious little about what Shakespeare felt or thought, if anything, *except as an Elizabethan*. In some ways the world of *Gatsby*, though deceptively tricked out with things we know of and can believe in, is as foreign to us as Elizabethan and Jacobean England. And yet there stands this particular novel, by acclamation taken as nearly perfect in all detail, by example taken by writers, and thus readers, as admirable and enormously influential. If it is not really a matter of content or context, then it is, I believe, a matter of form that makes it so. Finally it is, then, a matter of style, an imperishable style, which has made *Gatsby* a permanent experience.

Briefer than it seems to be—for there are any number of adroitly used literary devices in *Gatsby* which are associated with a much more leisurely, old-fashioned kind of story-telling, giving a serious impression of much more abundance than is, in truth, the case, *Gatsby* is also much more complex in its method of presentation than the luminous clarity of its language implies. Most of the critics have taken due note of the influence of Conrad on the novel's strategy, particularly insofar as the story is filtered through the consciousness of an alert and sensitive first-person narrator who stands as a witness to the main thrust of the central action even as he works out a knotty story, with its particular and pressing problems, of his own. Carraway's story of that summer is important to himself. He loses in the game of love, turns thirty, loses, too, in his choice of work and place to be, and by the end (which is in fact the beginning of the telling of this story) has turned his back on all that and gone home for good. Yet the main thing which happens to him, from the reader's point of view, is his fascination and involvement with his neighbor—Gatsby. The character of Carraway, as he presents himself, is complex and not entirely relevant to the subject of style. But it needs to be noted that he is an ambiguous character, one about whom the reader is intended to have mixed feelings; that these mixed, sometimes distinctly contradictory feelings give him more weight and solidity as a character than most witness-narrators; that these mixed feelings add more suspense and mystery to the elements of the story he relates and the ways he chooses to relate them. However, to deal, in partial abstraction, with the matter of form and style, it is necessary to simplify, perhaps to oversimplify what is naturally complex. All first-person narratives are presumed, by inference at the very least, to be either directly told to us, that is *spoken*, or written; in the latter case shaped into the form of a manuscript. *The Heart of Darkness* is a story presumed to be told aloud to a small group of witnesses (including the original narrator) on a becalmed boat waiting for the tide to turn. *The Turn of the Screw,* on the other hand, presents a speaking narrator who kindly allows us to read a written manuscript (written by somebody else) over his shoulder. Both of these effects, though equally strong in original authenticity, as is the case of any good first-person story, at least at its beginning, are also oddly and deliberately distanced from the events which make up the story. That is to say, by definition, from the beginning and for as long as the narrator is both engaging and not apparently untrustworthy, the principal action (event) of any given first-person story is the telling of the story, itself. That is all that is really presumed to be happening—a story is being told. Sometimes it is written; sometimes it is spoken; sometimes, for the sake of celebrating the spoken vernacular, it is, as in *Huckleberry Finn,* assumed to be dictated, as it were, by a narrator and corrected by the author. Third-person stories, by their very different stances, pretend to emphasize events directly rather than the ways and means of telling a tale. It becomes very important, then, for writer and reader of a first-person story to negotiate early on and to determine two related conditions: (a) is the story considered to be mainly written or spoken? and (b) where is the narrator now, and how much time has passed since the events, which are here recounted, have transpired? *Gatsby* is barely underway before we learn (in the fourth paragraph) that this is intended as a written, rather than a spoken, version of the tale, and, indeed, that it is a *book,* presumably the same book that we are here and now reading. "Gatsby, the man who gives his name to this book. . . . " This assumption raises another question, one whose resolution is held in abeyance (suspense) for quite some time. As far as the narrator is concerned, as stated clearly in the opening paragraphs of the story, the events of the story are all over and done with. Things have happened. The teller has experienced them, reacted to them, and in some ways been changed by them. It is all after the fact. But there are various elements of the telling of the story which are clearly in the present tense. Some are merely aphoristic, reactions which have become generalizations and link the time of telling directly with the time of happening: "Again a sort of apology arose to my lips. Almost any exhibition of complete self-sufficiency draws a stunned tribute from me." Or (for instance): "There is no confusion like the confusion of a single mind, and as we drove away Tom was feeling the hot whips of panic." There are many of these present judgments of past actions. And there are other occasions, at regular intervals throughout, where the narrator interrupts past action to assert an act of present memory: "Among the broken fragments of the last five minutes at table I remember the candles being lit again, pointlessly, and I was conscious of wanting to look squarely at every one, and yet to avoid all eyes." Or: "I think [*now,* evidently and distinctly from *then*] he'd tanked up a good deal at luncheon, and his determination to have my company bordered on violence." And: "But I am slow-thinking and full of interior rules that act as brakes on my desires, and I knew that first I had to get myself definitely out of that tangle back home." At the risk of being crudely obvious, I call attention to two elements above and beyond the functional value that these recurring time shifts, between the time of the events described and the time of the composition of the description, serve, by keeping the reader conscious of the two separate, but simultaneous, time schemes. The first of these is to focus our attention on aftermath, to emphasize reaction more than action. The second characteristic is to set in some sense of tension, if not conflict, often within the same sentence, the qualities of the spoken versus the written American language. *Gatsby* is a marvelous experiment, a triumph of the *written* American vernacular, the range, suppleness and eloquence of it. But for the written vernacular language of the times to be fully explored, it was necessary to set it in direct contrast to the spoken language, not only in the contrast between credible dialogue in the dramatic scenes, but, occasionally and within limits, in the narration itself. Thus "out of that tangle back home" and "I think he'd tanked up a good deal at luncheon. . . . " In other words, the written narration, this *book* by Nick Carraway, has to touch, however briefly, on the level of spoken narration in order to define itself clearly. Moreover this capability is necessary if full use of the spoken vernacular is to be accomplished in dramatic and satirical scenes. The overall effect, the created language of this book, Nick Carraway's language, offers up a full range between lyrical evocation and depths of feeling at one end and casual, if hard-knuckled, matters of fact. It allows for the poetry of intense perception to live simultaneously and at ease with a hard-edged, implacable vulgarity. Each draws strength from the conflict with the other. This same tension of time and language is at the center of Carraway's point of view and is expressed early on in chapter two as Carraway, drunk, imagines himself as a stranger capable of including even Carraway as an object in his speculative vision: "Yet high over the city our line of yellow windows must have contributed their share of human secrecy to the casual watcher in the darkening streets, and I was him too, looking up and wondering. I was within and without, simultaneously enchanted and repelled by the inexhaustible variety of life." *I was within and without. . . .* *Gatsby* becomes an intricate demonstration of that kind of complex double vision, of the *process* of it. We are not far into the story (chapter three) before we discover that the "book" Nick Carraway mentioned at the outset, the book which, completed, will turn out to be *The Great Gatsby,* is not yet finished, is in the process of being written. "Reading over what I have written so far, I see I have given the impression that the events of three nights several weeks apart were all that absorbed me." This additional sense of time (narrator pauses to reread what he has written so far) almost, not quite, allows for another kind of time level—the time of revision. At least it asserts that what is being reported has been carefully thought about and can be corrected if need be. And at the least it makes the time of the composition of the story closely parallel to the reader's left-to-right, chronological adventure.

A bit later, in a number of ways, we are encouraged to *participate* actively in the narrative process as, for example in chapter six, where Carraway explains and defends a narrative choice:

> He told me all this very much later, but I've put it down here with the idea of exploding those first wild rumors about his antecedents, which weren't even faintly true. Moreover he told it to me at a time of confusion, when I had reached the point of believing everything and nothing about him. So I take advantage of this short halt while Gatsby, so to speak, caught his breath, to clear this set of misconceptions away.

Here focus is so clearly on the process of making and of the free, if pragmatic, choices involved, that the reader is strongly reminded of the story as artifact, though, ironically, it is Carraway's selective virtuosity that at once supercedes and disguises Fitzgerald's.

Meantime narrative virtuosity becomes increasingly various and complex as we move deeper into the story. In chapter four we are given a first-person narration, in her own words, spoken by Jordan Baker, "sitting up very straight on a straight chair in the tea-garden at the Plaza Hotel," concerning Daisy and Gatsby in 1917. This is told in a credible and appropriate vernacular for Jordan Baker—as recalled, of course, by Carraway. More romantic and lyrical by far is Gatsby's own story which is told (out of sequence) in indirect discourse. Carraway finds a third-person, high style appropriate to the inner mystery and turmoil of the young (and mostly nonverbal) Gatsby. By this time Carraway has so dominated the material of the story (even his speculation and tentativeness can be taken as the authority of integrity) that he is capable of creating a language which can dramatize in rhythmical images the inward and spiritual condition of Gatsby as a young man:

> But his heart was in a constant, turbulent riot. The most grotesque and fantastic conceits haunted him in his bed at night. A universe of ineffable gaudiness spun itself out in his brain while the clock ticked on the washstand and the moon soaked with wet light his tangled clothes upon the floor. Each night he added to the pattern of his fancies until drowsiness closed down upon some vivid scene with an oblivious embrace. For a while these reveries provided an outlet for his imagination; they were a satisfactory hint of the unreality of reality, a promise that the rock of the world was founded securely on a fairy's wing.

In chapter seven another form of indirect discourse, this time a third-person account of the death of Myrtle Wilson, matter-of-fact and vaguely journalistic (as if, as is later implied, its source were indeed the newspapers), is employed. "The young Greek, Michaelis, who ran the coffee joint beside the ashheaps was the principal witness at the inquest. He had slept through the heat until after five, when he strolled over to the garage, and found George Wilson sick in his office—really sick, pale as his own pale hair and shaking all over." Carraway returns to this place—"Now I want to go back a little and tell what happened at the garage after we left there the night before"—out of chronological sequence, in chapter eight, with an almost purely dramatic third-person omniscient scene, which, in any literal sense, has to be wholly *imagined* by Carraway, but which offers brief moments of sensory perception and thought by both Michaelis and George Wilson. Stylistically this unit is quite distinct, as is Carraway's imagined version of

Gatsby's last moments, here quite candidly blending overt speculation with an implausible certainty to form a single poetic vision:

> He must have looked up at an unfamiliar sky through frightening leaves and shivered as he found what a grotesque thing a rose is and how raw the sunlight was upon the scarcely created grass. A new world, material without being real, where poor ghosts, breathing dreams like air, drifted fortuitously about . . . like that ashen, fantastic figure gliding toward him through the amorphous trees.

This high moment is a direct reversal of the more usual pattern of perception in the book where the sight of the ashen figure (Wilson) might have led him next to react with a generalized vision of "poor ghosts, breathing dreams like air." Here, at the last moment of his life, Gatsby, as conceived and imagined by Carraway, reverses reality and unreality just as Carraway himself had done earlier, imagining himself as a stranger in the street staring up at lit windows and wondering. The result of the reversal is something close to prescience, certainly something stronger than premonition.

Finally, this extension of style to the extreme almost absurd edge of narrative credibility allows Carraway the indulgence of imagining direct, and quite vernacular, dialogue from the dead Gatsby. "But, as they drew back the sheet and looked at Gatsby with unmoved eyes, his protest continued in my brain: 'Look here, old sport, you've got to get somebody for me. You've got to try hard. I can't go through this alone.' "

In point of fact, stylistically *Gatsby* is a complicated composite of several distinct kinds of prose, set within the boundaries of a written narration, a composite style whose chief demonstrable point appears to be the inadequacy of any single style (or single means of perception, point of view), by itself to do justice to the story. Which is a story of a world not so much in transition as falling apart without realizing it. New and old clash continually, violently. It is shown to be impossible to escape the one by embracing the other. Carraway, as is his habit, finds an aphorism for precisely this paradox, seeking to explain "the collosal vitality" of Gatsby's illusion: "No amount of fire and freshness can challenge what a man will store up in his ghostly heart."

Nick Carraway's authority, and his insistence on telling his own story together with Gatsby's—and it should be remembered that it is

Carraway who gets the last aphoristic and poetic word, who presents the haunting image of "the green light, the orgiastic future that year by year recedes before us" even as we are swept backward like "boats against the current, borne back ceaselessly into the past"—is to establish a powerful, if illusory, sense of unity which tends to camouflage the variety and complexity of the narration. French critic André Le Vot, in the chapters of his biography of Fitzgerald which deal with *Gatsby*, creates an elegant and impressive paradigm of the use of color symbolism and the constant use of light and dark in the story, contrived to hold the discrete parts of the story, in the subtext at least, in a conventional unified coherence. These things seem to work well for that purpose; and there are other elements and patterns which tend to serve roughly the same purpose, all adding up to an impression of unified style. Beneath the surface, however, *Gatsby* is boiling with conflict and chiefly the conflict of new and old, the inadequacy of the old ways and means to deal with the new world of the twentieth century. Thus behind its seemingly bland and polite surface, *Gatsby* is, in many ways, a wildly experimental novel, a trying out of what would become familiar, if more various, strategies of our serious literature and, especially, of the range of our literary language. With all its apparent acknowledgment of the power of the past, *Gatsby* is a leap toward the future, the invention of new styles, therefore the dead end of something else. Those wonderful letters the young Fitzgerald received from literary dignitaries at the time are explicit in announcing this. "You are creating the contemporary world much as Thackeray did his in *Pendennis* and *Vanity Fair*," Gertrude Stein wrote, "and this isn't a bad compliment." T. S. Eliot called the novel, accurately, "the first step that American fiction has taken since Henry James." And Edith Wharton, wisely, felt threatened. She had a minor criticism, based on the traditional practices: "My present quarrel with you is only this: that to make Gatsby really Great, you ought to have given us his early career . . . instead of a short résumé of it. That would have situated him, & made his final tragedy a tragedy instead of a 'fait divers' for the morning papers.

"But you'll tell me that's the old way, & consequently not *your* way. . . . "

In terms of form, then, more than anything else, in terms of *style*, *Gatsby* is a pioneering novel. Other masters of the first half of this

---

century may have done more radical and extraordinary things with the novel's shape and substance, but, by and large, these other great books were (are), at the least, inimitable. With *Gatsby* Fitzgerald advanced the form of the American novel for the benefit of all American novelists who have followed after him, whether they know it or not. They seem to sense this, to bear witness to it, in their continuing admiration for *Gatsby*. For youthful romance it is hard to beat *This Side of Paradise*. For the purity of nostalgia and the evocation of a period, an era, there is always my old favorite *Tender Is The Night*. But in *Gatsby*, which pretends to be a little of both, youthful romance and nostalgic period piece, it is a matter of style; and that style is for all our bitter seasons.

4

The Major Poetry of
Joyce Cary
(1963)

It is not surprising that the poetry of Joyce Cary is little known. Not much poetry in our time could be called "well known" by any standard of measurement, and the poetry of an artist who devoted most of his creative energy and effort to fiction has all the odds against it. One of the convenient critical clichés we have learned to live with is that serious critics can and, indeed, by a kind of benevolent fraternal collusion, are *supposed* to ignore the poetry of a writer who has made his reputation in another form. Some distinguished novelists support this state of affairs, and not without good reason. Few of them would like to be reminded of their fledgling efforts at writing verses. Joyce Cary's first published book, *Verse* (1908), has almost disappeared off the face of the earth.[1] But what are we to do if the poetic efforts are not juvenilia? What happens when a major novelist writes poetry and sees it published at the peak of his career? We have, for example, the poems of William Faulkner. Most of his poetry was written early, but he collected his poems in *A Green Bough* (1933) *after* he had written and seen in print seven novels, including some of the universally accepted great ones. And we know, or we ought to, from the introduction he wrote for the Modern Library Edition of *Sanctuary*, that he cared deeply enough about his work and his duty to it to revise the galleys of that book extensively, at considerable expense and at a time when he had very little money to spare. It would seem reasonable enough to suppose, then, that Faulkner also cared enough about the poems in relation to his other work, his total work, not to allow them the luxury of publication for publication's sake. The point is that the poems are intended to be judged as minor works by a major artist, done with pride and to the best of his ability.

The example of Faulkner is relevant to Joyce Cary, quite aside from any other things these two lonely artists may have in common. Cary's poems were not well received either, beginning right in the editorial offices of his publisher. Enid Starkie has said that when Cary "had composed his two long poems, 'Marching Soldiers' *[sic]* and 'The Drunken Sailor,' his publishers had not considered them worthy of him, and had tried to dissuade him from publication. He was surprised and puzzled, though not distressed or disturbed, but he persisted in publishing them. He was, I think, calmly confident of his worth and achievement, but without a trace of pomposity, or vestige of self-importance."[2] This was the same Joyce Cary who accepted realistically the necessities of critical fashion: "The original artist who *counts* on understanding and reward is a fool."[3] Safety for the critic lies in the brute fact that neither the poems of Faulkner or Cary have enjoyed much reputation among or received attention from the poets and the critics of poetry. It is possible in both cases to avoid the problem entirely, by taking refuge behind the shopworn assumption that an important literary artist can be blind to his own inadequacies. But this assumption, however comforting, is a dangerous one, based upon the idle hope that because the writer was not a part of the accepted poetic heirarchy of his time, he is therefore a bad poet. A cursory glance at literary history will shatter that notion to smithereens. God alone (and *not* Donald Hall or John Ciardi or whoever the very latest Arbiter may be) knows who will appear to be the significant poets of our time to future generations. Meanwhile we cannot afford to be so arrogant or impudent as to ignore any of the work of the leading artists of our language, not if we really care about either art or language. It is our obligation to know and to examine these works, the work of highly skilled craftsmen, on their own terms and, insofar as possible, to try to shed some of the simple prejudices of literary fashion, even to deprive ourselves of the creaking armor of invincible ignorance and the habitual, Pavlovian gesture.

Cary's two important books of poetry, *Marching Soldier* (1945) and *The Drunken Sailor* (1947), appeared after he had seen much of his life's work published. There were ten novels, including the whole of the first trilogy, prior to the appearance of *Marching Soldier*. *The Moonlight* and *Britain and West Africa* separate the two books. The second trilogy was soon to follow. It ought to be clear, then, that his poetry was not intended to be dismissed or taken lightly.

Marching Soldier is that rare creature of this era, a narrative poem of more than six hundred lines. Published just as the war was ending and victory was in sight, it is concerned with *the* marching soldier, that nameless, faceless, weary combat veteran who endured. There is nothing quite like it in our literature. It bears comparison with some of Randall Jarrell's wartime poems and with Louis Simpson's more recently published narrative poem, "The Runner."[4] But Jarrell's poems are basically lyrics, fragments and parts of a larger context which is implied; and Simpson's narrative is singularly American, really a kind of short story in verse, dealing with the themes of initiation, cowardice, and bravery in the life of a single soldier. Cary's soldier is long past the stages of innocence and initiation. He is a hardened veteran, knowledgeable and sophisticated in war, and serves as a type for all soldiers of all time. The whole poem is seen strictly from the point of view of this soldier, outwardly in the things he notices and reacts to, inwardly in all the accepted values and assumptions of an old-timer. The poem gains concreteness and particularity from an easy, matter-of-fact familiarity with all the gear, the weapons and equipment of modern warfare, and, as well, from the repetitive use of dialogue in an idiom closely approximating that of the common British soldier. I do not know of any recent work in prose or poetry which displays so thorough an assimilation of the strict, complex, and utterly unsentimental code of the combat soldier. Except for a few vivid memoirs and the brutally intense lyrics of poets like Owen and Sassoon and, in our own time, Jarrell, Ciardi, and Shapiro, most of our writers have not tried to handle the subject and the precise point of view that Cary does. Of course, Cary had long personal experience to call on, beginning with *his* initiation in the First Balkan War of 1912–1913.[5] And in *Marching Soldier* he makes it quite clear that the experience of his generation became living history for the next, so that the generation of World War II was already sophisticated. The past had been digested and modified in the guts of the living.

Marching Soldier makes demands on the reader, not the more usual demands of surface obscurity, but the far more rigorous requirements of a deep imaginative commitment, of bringing to the poem an experience of life. The poem is rewarding in proportion to the reader's liberation of his imagination and experience of life. Thus it is a more profoundly difficult poem, in a visceral sense, than if built upon the habitual conventions of the modern lyric mode. The reader must shed some of his conditioned responses to contemporary poetry at the beginning. Yet *Marching Soldier* is distinctly modern, taking advantage of the inherent condensation of verse forms, using the full possibilities of abrupt, almost cinematic transitions, exploiting the full range of the spoken language from the eloquently rhetorical to the flat, monosyllabic ring of dialogue. Structurally it is a clean-lined, simple poem. It begins with a parade, the soldiers, already veterans, marching in steady cadence toward waiting troopships. There is a brief, flashing scene of the women and children watching with wonder and ignorance which may remind the reader of John Manifold's celebrated "Fife Tune." There is a voyage—painfully evocative and accurate to anyone who has had that experience—which ends with an assault landing on a beach. A village is fought for and occupied. Then in a momentary lull comes a quick flashback to childhood, to thoughts and memories of a home front as remote as the stars to these men and adding to the weight of their packs the invisible and overwhelming burden of history. This is followed by defensive action and counterattack. An enemy city is taken by house-to-house fighting. Then following this shorthand history of the war, there is another parade, this time a "victory" parade, though to the soldiers (and the reader by this time) it seems little more than a repetition of the original march.

Cary never withdraws from the point of view of the common soldier. The terrifying texture, the felt experience of war is presented without comment or explanation. This is, of course, perfectly in keeping with Cary's practice as storyteller. It is also part of his stated aesthetic for poetry. Writing for the jacket of *The Drunken Sailor*, he said: "A poem is not an argument but an experience, in the most concentrated form." Both in its conception and in details *Marching Soldier* is fully demonstrative of that view. Technically the poem is deceptively simple. The poet does not call attention to himself or his method. He alternates between two lines: a long line based on stresses, the stresses of the spoken language sometimes heightened by echoes of biblical and classical translations; and a short, spare, choppy line set to the rhythm of hob-nailed marching soldiers. The latter is a virtuoso use of stress and pause within the confines of a short line. And, finally, there is the staccato of the spoken dialogue. The overall effect is one of great lucidity. The method is particularly apt and successful in making possible easy shifts from concrete to abstract, from action to idea and back again. Most important for a narrative poem, there is a deft and credible handling of physical action, the point where most modern narrative poems fail. Here, for example, is a piece of a beautifully realized picture of an infantry assault:

> Troops move in front. "Are we off? I don't know,
>   but we're moving."
> We go off slowly through evening shadows. The shells
>   fall faster,
> Far off, sleepy rifles sound like a toy clock, cheers
>   like a grasshopper.
> We see men run towards a village. They disappear
>   among bushes. Some are left lying.
> "They've held." "I suppose the place was stronger
>   than someone thought."
> "Those church towers are giving the range." "Where
>   are our tanks?"
> "Tanks can't shoot there—that's a famous place."
> Machine guns spray upon us. The church towers watch.

Another brief moment in a similar assault rivals the terrifying poems of Wilfred Owen in its matter-of-fact exposition of simple horror.

> The batteries open up from some valley unseen,
> Their lazy shells have found the road. A man falls
>   against the bank.
> His arm and side are gone. He is dying this moment.
> He watches the blood spurt glittering in the new sun,
> Without surprise, without anger, he says "I'm
>   finished."

Why should he be surprised, a soldier, to die
suddenly,
Why should he be angry, a soldier, at soldiers who
never saw him,
Who do not even know his name,
Who fired from three miles off their pet gun, into
the morning's work,
And hit the mark, a good shot, a job well done? They
fire again, and again men are hit.

This same long, flexible, steady line permits the handling of the
more abstract and speculative, but always dissolving smoothly back
into the specific scene. Here, in lines which echo the killing above, the
common soldier thinks of home:

Should I be angry, should I be surprised, that
thieves wrap themselves in cunning.
That liars shoot off lies, and spread their wings on
malice.
The liar says truth is a fool, and truth becomes his
servant,
The hypocrite breathes upon honesty and makes it ice
for his fortress.
See him sit within shining with the light of
righteousness,
He condescends with our sweat, our blood is the dung
of his garden.
The dodger laughs at us, and his laughter is a wall,
proof against steel.
The coward's eyes despise us, his smile asks for our
contempt
To make it a war medal.
For the coward has a story, he tells himself a tale,
He has made himself a hero, and the hero fears not
even himself.

> I wait here, while the shells fall, and I am afraid
> I ask, will this body obey me?

Cary's soldier is not a hero. Neither is he any of the others who thrive and prosper while he dies: the liar, the hypocrite, the dodger. If they have the last laugh, he has at least the movement when, in spite of all, his body *does* obey him.

Essentially the subject of *Marching Soldier* is a multiple series of questions without answers. It predicates the inevitable fact of peace, but offers no solutions, no promises or programs, no faint hope for a change in the human condition. It is an uncompromising poem, written with victory in view, at a time when above all its possible audience wanted to forget the facts of war and to lose themselves in jubilant celebration. It is, of course, typical of Cary to go against the easy, popular grain. Back in 1943, when the issue of the war was still very much in doubt, he had written with confidence of the victory to come and with deep concern for the peace to follow. Victory was not to be doubted, but peace in the world was to Cary a dubious possibility. In *Process of Real Freedom* he wrote: "I am led to think that the only hope for a permanent world peace is a universal unwillingness and unfitness to make war, that is, a world of real democracies."[6] The terms of this hope are fragile. He acknowledged, with uncanny accuracy for that time, the potential of terror in the future: "Already people talk of racial wars, wars of extermination, to which our present wars, more cruel than any in Europe since the wars of religion in the 17th century, will seem like a skirmish."[7] He could still affirm the possibility of peace and a future for mankind. "If recent history, source of so much pessimism, seems to contradict such a hope, we have to remember that history never repeats itself."[8] But the form of *Marching Soldier* is cyclical. It is clear that by 1945 Cary had lost that slender hope and believed that history *does* repeat itself. The marching soldier will march again, and again, until he is finally killed:

> "We do not ask for miracles, we know that all men
>   must suffer,
> Only tell us why it has been laid upon us,
> Tell us the name, the name of our pain, that we may

make it a friend,
Tell us the name of our grave,
That it may be our bed."

II

"He makes a joke of life because he dare not take it seriously."

—Cary's preface to the Carfax edition of *The Horse's Mouth*

The Drunken Sailor is radically different in form from *Marching Soldier*. Subtitled by Cary "a ballad-epic," it is a very long poem by present standards, more than 1,700 lines elaborately designed to emphasize all aspects of artifact. It is a kind of total book. It is illustrated by Cary; the book-jacket blurb is largely a long quotation from Cary; and, in addition to the text of the poem itself, there are extensive marginal notes by the author in the manner of *The Rime of the Ancient Mariner*. It is a highly grotesque poem, rich in allusion and parody, a prime example of what we now call the Absurd. The central episode (insofar as the poem *has* episodes) is a running battle between a rotting privateer from sailing days and a modern battleship. It is an encounter which the privateer ultimately survives, but through blind accident and by no special virtue of the drunken sailor and his ghostly shipmates. It is as absurd as anything our recent dramatists have conceived. Yet it is still a serious and even terrifying poem. It is this wedding of grotesque humor and high seriousness which has evidently baffled the few critics who have looked at the poem. Andrew Wright, for instance, is aware of the relationship between form and content in Cary's other works and even aware of the relations between the ideas of the poem and the novels; but he is simply bewildered by the form of the poem. He writes: "*The Drunken Sailor* is not, I think a successful poem. It is too long, too freighted with devices, too insistently explicit; and though some of the description is wonderful and characteristically just, fresh and affecting, the poetry as a whole—but particularly the rhyme—is forced."[9] Wright's judgment and evaluation turn out to be in fact simply description. The poem *is* "freighted with devices." It *is* "insistently explicit." And throughout the rhymes are wildly, wonderfully and deliberately "forced." All of this is part of Cary's intention.

We are thoroughly familiar with this particular kind of wry, cosmic humor in modern verse. We have seen it in Ogden Nash, in the poetry of John Betjeman, and sometimes in the poems of Frost and Ransom. It is present, in various forms, in the early Eliot. But it is true that no other skilled poet of our times has carried the method Cary uses to such length, to the breaking point, in order to make a profoundly serious statement. In addition to lengthy passages written in loose and ragged satirical couplets, Cary employs nine basic stanza patterns, ranging from three to sixteen lines. Within these basic stanzas he varies the rhyme scheme with cheerful and reckless abandon. There are parodies of hymns and prayers, of sea chanteys, ballads and songs. There are rudely satirical caricatures of great men of thought and letters from classical times on down to the recent past. There are leaden echoes of many celebrated lines of English poetry, ranging from subtle allusion to the pure horseplay of lines like "The path of glory leads into the clink." There are shopworn inversions and old-fashioned poeticisms standing back to back with modern slang. There are brief moments of the conventionally "poetic," juxtaposed against large patches of doggerel. It is, in short, a mad, drunken kind of poem, a kind of antipoem, perfectly suited to its title and subject. In the face of all this, the lengthy and elaborate allegorical explication of the poem on several levels of meaning, which the author wrote for the jacket, and all the careful marginalia, sometimes couched in the conceptual language of philosophy and sometimes in the jargon of pure pedantry, seem to be part of an enormous joke. They are. And they are not. Though the poem is clearly allegorical, with little attention paid to even the least suggestions of surface reality or probability. Cary is on record as having taken allegory as an inferior form for the artist. In *Art and Reality* he wrote: "Allegory gives a clear, a definite meaning; not to the soul, but to the conceptual judgment, and in a form of dry precept whose falsity is at once detected by the soul."[10] But he also recognized the real appeal of allegory to the artist who feels an overwhelming compulsion to communicate conceptually. "Allegory is an immense temptation to the writer," he wrote, "especially to the great, obsessed writer."[11] Readers familiar with the second trilogy, written under great duress, with time running out for Cary and, in his view, time running out as well for our civilization, a time of madness, murder and self-deception (the weakness and self-deception of Chester Nimmo, the mad passion of Jim Latter), will have noted an impatience with the guise of *fiction* in these books and perhaps, a streak, a shadow of ineradicable pessimism as well. It shows clearly in the crude and powerful self-portrait, Cary's final etching, he made for a limited edition of *The Horse's Mouth*, created in dark, heavy strokes as if with charcoal, though in point of fact it was etched directly on a plate. The eyes are wounded and sad. The face, unsmiling, no longer has the fine jutting jaw or the delicate lines of humor at the edges of the lips so familiar from photographs. It is a deeply lined, taut, pinched face, almost a skull, reminiscent of the faces of the victims of the concentration camps. It is shaded, bathed in darkness. It seems to look from darkness into darkness. It is the face of a man who has seen into the heart of darkness and knows that it is vast, immeasurable, and eternal.

The illustrations Cary created for *The Drunken Sailor*, two of them used for the jacket as well as within the text, offer an excellent clue to his intentions in the poem. The first, the frontispiece, is an etching of a bound angel being rudely, slowly hoisted into place atop a high pinnacle above London. (Curiously he opens with a device like that Fellini later employed to open *La Dolce Vita*.) The workers, all but one who on inspection turns out to be Cary himself, are hideous gargoyles come to life. Their faces are contorted with hate and fury. In contrast the stone angel seems strangely human and tranquil. The motif is threat, impending torture. Torture in all forms is one of the recurring patterns of the poem. The drawing is immediately reminiscent of and is technically based on the famous prison etchings of Piranesi. The second drawing, which is related to a brief account in the accompanying text of Molière as cuckold, shows an old, bald, toothless man (his fine curly wig and elegant coat hang in the background) embracing a nude, amply endowed, and empty-eyed blonde woman. With deliberate anachronism she is shown with a conventional modern permanent wave. The bed on which they are resting turns out to be a two-headed monster, one face a weeping cuckold with horns, the other a wildly grinning, laureled satyr, set together like Siamese twins in parody of the conventional masks of comedy and tragedy. This cartoon is more evidently related to the modern surrealistic tradition and the earlier tradition of Bosch. It has some stylistic kinship with the turn-of-the-century German cartoonists, men like Heinrich Kley. It also reminds us of modern painters like Ensor, Munch, and the German expressionists of the late 1920s and early 1930s. The third illustration is a metropolitan street scene, modern, urban London. Dense crowds of blank, anxious, skull-like faces are packed together in hideous similarity, swept along as by a foul tide or on a conveyor belt to nowhere. Buses crisscross, jammed with sad-faced riders. And over all this looms a huge billboard face, advertising a film. It is recognizably the woman from the Molière cartoon, now evidently a modern movie star, smiling the smile of the monster satyr. "NEW LAUGHS" cuts diagonally across her face like a huge bandage. When we compare the first illustration with the last, we see that it is really the same London, seen in the first from a high, remote, bird's-eye view. Thus we have come full circle in the poem. These illustrations, then, express visually and seriously the basic historical theme of the poem. There is, indeed, a chronological progression in style, manner, and subject, yet *nothing really changes.* Change is inevitable and, in fact, the one constant in human history; but the human condition does not change.

It has been noted by others that the poem in substance relates directly to Cary's views of human history, politics, power, art and life, as found in the novels and nonfiction.[12] And Sidney Monas in an essay-review of the first trilogy has made note of certain verbal and imagistic connections between the poem and the novels of that trilogy.[13] These connections are there and are worth close study. But what are we to make of the poem and all its parts and paraphenalia as a thing in itself? It seems to me a kind of *Waste Land,* written in Cary's very special terms and in an almost unique form. The whole poem can be seen as a bitter, comic-strip nightmare, the rantings, ravings, and terrible visions of a drunken sailor. Using the early Christian symbol of the sea voyage (itself borrowed from the classical tradition by Augustine, upon the "Egyptian gold" precedent from his gloss of Exodus) to represent the life of man, and thus history and the State as the creations of man, alluding to it directly at the outset by naming the chaplain of the privateer Saul (not yet Paul), Cary proceeds to create an anthology in parody of great English sea poems, from the Anglo-Saxon "Seafarer" up through *The Rime of the Ancient Mariner* and Byron's *Don Juan.* It is very literary, and most of the crew aboard his ship of fools turn out to be literary men. Among those named and discussed are Homer, Dante, Villon, Molière, Ronsard, Shakespeare, Christopher Smart, Clare, Cowper, Shelley, Byron, Hugo, Dickens, Dostoyevsky, Baudelaire, Tolstoy, Scott, Wordsworth, Carlyle, Browning, Tennyson, Arnold. These great men, rigidly confined within the bounds of jingling rhymes and mocking verse, are treated as caricatures, held up for ridicule and criticism as they appear in distorted images, much like the grotesque figures seen in a fun house of mirrors. They represent our intellectual baggage. These and other characters—the Sailor, the Crew, a Narrator, the Fugitives, and the Liberty Men—do all the speaking. In this dramatic form the poet himself never appears. The only positive element in the poem appears in the form of the Liberty Men. This will not surprise the reader who is familiar with Cary's *Power in Men* (1939). There he seeks to define liberty, or "real freedom," and apply it to political and social history: "Liberty is creation in the act. It is therefore eternal and indestructible."[14] Of the relation between man's search for liberty and history he continues: "So we have seen many theories of liberty, many attempts to form an ideal state in which man can be both bound by law and free in his own right. History is strewn with the wrecks of these fabrics. But the creative power that made them, the impulse that prompted their making can never weaken or die. Freedom was born without a name. It began its work before man was known, and it continues upon it, in silence and secrecy, even when no one dares to speak of it."[15] This, of course, is the Joyce Cary of 1939 speaking. But it is significant that the one hope offered for man (and the crew of Cary's battered privateer) is voiced by the Liberty Men. They recognize that the voyage is endless, that all safe harbors are illusions; and the truth of this acceptance of the naked facts saves the motley crew and the drunken sailor. They sail on at the end, not sure of anything, always in deadly peril, but at least certain of the constancy of imagination and its labor "that achieves, by continual accomplishment, its own ransom from bitterness, knowing that there is nothing sure, nothing dependable but the spirit of life itself and its invincible desperation which, among the cruelty of circumstance that is the form and effect of its real being, begets for ever in newness and innocence eternal delight."[16] Life is "creation in the act." So is Liberty and man's desire for it. At least in that desire and in the labor to realize it man shares briefly in the life process. And the end and reward of all that labor is, in the final lines of the poem: "To hear from ravaged valleys start / Childish songs, forgot by art."

The Drunken Sailor is a highly sophisticated poem, a mocking one, one which mocks almost everything including itself. All the apparatus for this pseudoprimitive exercise in rhyming—the serious jacket blurb, the elaborate marginal notes—seem to intensify the monstrous joke. It will remind the reader of Nabokov's *Pale Fire*, with its wrapping of devices and artificial gimmicks, its mocking, self-deprecating tone. Still, Cary means urgently what he says in the poem and through the characters. This is the final bitter joke of a bitter poem. But there is still the question of why he chose this form, the one he calls the most limited in that it speaks only to the intellect. One must conclude that it was the urgency of his feelings and the necessity to shock the reader into awareness. It is a mad call to reason, a power Cary recognized as an absolute necessity to the condition of liberty: "For man, therefore, progress depends on the use of his reason. He realizes for himself his instinctive desires, what we call his nature, by the use of independent judgment. That is his means and his only means of self-development. Whether the reason is God's seeking to realize his love, wisdom, and delight in concrete existence or whether it is the product of blind luck, it must have liberty or it cannot do its work."[17]

III

Cary's two major poems have not placed him among the fashionable or celebrated poets of our time. It may be that the future will change this. Maybe not. Cary would be the last to worry. He knew all too well, from experience, the little whims and quirks of the fashions in art. For Cary evaluation was, finally, irrelevant, since it was impossible. What mattered, what constituted greatness was to be *original*, that is, in tune with the creation in action that is life. He comforted himself with no easy illusions. Words he wrote about Gulley Jimson apply to himself: "He is himself a creator, and has lived in creation all his life, and so he understands and continually reminds himself that in a world of everlasting creation there is no justice."[18] For those who admire the creations of Joyce Cary there is no problem. His poems are part of the whole work and the whole man. The very least that we can do is to accept his vision and his purpose and to include them in any consideration of his art.

Notes

1. James B. Meriwether, "The Books of Joyce Cary: A Preliminary Bibliography of English and American Editions," *Texas Studies in Literature and Language*, 1 (Summer 1959), 300–10; "A Note on *Verse*: Joyce Cary's First Book," *Library Chronicle of the University of Texas*, 6 (Winter 1960), 13–16. Some of these early poems are treated briefly in Andrew Wright, *Joyce Cary: A Preface to His Novels* (London: Chatto & Windus, 1958), 41–42.
2. Enid Starkie, "Joyce Cary: A Personal Portrait," *Virginia Quarterly Review*, 37 (Winter 1961), 116–17.
3. Preface to the Carfax edition of *The Horse's Mouth* (London: Joseph, 1951).
4. Louis Simpson, *A Dream of Governors* (Middletown: Wesleyan University Press, 1959).
5. Joyce Cary, *Memoir of the Bobotes* (Austin: University of Texas Press, 1960).
6. Joyce Cary, *Process of Real Freedom* (London: Joseph, 1943), 14.
7. Ibid., 3.
8. Ibid., 15.
9. Wright, *Joyce Cary*, 45.
10. Joyce Cary, *Art and Reality* (New York: Harper, 1958), 163. See also Cary's article "What Does Art Create?," *Literature and Life*, 2 (1951), 32–45.
11. *Art and Reality*, 162–63.
12. Wright, *Joyce Cary*, 44–45.
13. Sidney Monas, "What To Do With A Drunken Sailor," *Hudson Review*, 3 (Autumn 1950), 466–74. Further study is needed of the connections between *The Drunken Sailor* and Cary's verse in *To Be a Pilgrim*. Echoes and fragments of many of the sea poems alluded to in *The Drunken Sailor* appear in *To Be a Pilgrim*, with its dominant image of England as the sea-wanderer. And it is important for a full understanding of Cary as a novelist to see how he used his poetic gift both in the epigrammatic couplets he gives to Edward Wilcher in *To Be a Pilgrim*, and in the remarkable lyrics he gives the native clerk in *Mister Johnson*.
14. Joyce Cary, *Power in Men* (London: Nicholson & Watson, 1939), 9.
15. Ibid., 9.
16. Joyce Cary, *The Drunken Sailor* (London: Joseph, 1947), 62–63.
17. *Power in Men*, 266.
18. Cary, Carfax edition of *The Horse's Mouth*, (London: Joseph, 1951), 319.

5

Whatever Wishful Thinking
May Wish: The Example of
James Gould Cozzens
(1978)

Like many, maybe most, of the American writers of my generation, I earn a large part of my keep by teaching reading and writing to college students who have a limited experience of both. One of the most crippling things they suffer from, as readers and writers, is a diminishing number and variety of exemplary normative models. There are times when you might well imagine that all the known possibilities of and for prose fiction are to be found somewhere between the graceful fidgets of Donald Barthelme and the salad-talk of Thomas Pynchon. Too bad, they (and I include Pynchon and Barthelme among them) could all learn a great deal from the example of James Gould Cozzens, looking at what he has done (his art) and what has become of it (his career).

Rereading Cozzens's work this time, I am struck most by the variety of it, the wide range of what he can do, therefore the choices he is able to make and has made. (A writer who writes only one kind of book is either obsessive and can't help himself or a hypocrite and the hustler of a single brand name.) Choice is the burden and the privilege of freedom. Freedom, as I understand it and within the limits of heredity, environment, and necessity, is something the artist celebrates, aspires to, hopes for. To dance, as graceful as can be, in chains. Absence of models for the student and apprentice means a corresponding absence of choices. Meaning, then, that in art as in life, we are learning to live and work within dwindling and ever more strictly limited freedom.

Of course I can understand why Cozzens is not taught much, if at all, these days in the colleges. In academic circles, especially in the last twenty-five or thirty years during which the study and the teaching of contemporary literature has become eminently respectable, he has never been likely to have or to gain much support. There are lots of reasons. One: the briefly captive "youth audience" is not really capable of dealing, not ready to deal with the materials, both form and content, of the major Cozzens novels. These works—like, for example, those of Joyce Cary or Wright Morris—are far from easy to teach or talk about in the classroom. The best literary works, for teaching purposes, are those with obvious and interesting or entertaining secondary or decorative characteristics. It is much more satisfactory for everyone to discuss style and imagery and structure, for example, than to test the tense and subtle relationship between the characters in the world of a fiction and the people, as we perceive them, in Real Life. Teachers are not interested in embracing difficulty. The teacher is primarily interested in developing himself as a performer. He, or she, looks for the literary work which can offer the greatest occasion for recognizable pedagogical virtuosity. Sometimes it is a work of quality and character. Sometimes it is not.

It is exactly for this reason that a great many highly regarded contemporary American writers (themselves products of the self-same academic system and destined to serve it in flesh and fact) have adopted the reasonable strategy of ignoring those elements of fiction that were once considered primary and have instead cultivated a fiction almost entirely composed of secondary and decorative effects. It could be argued that many of our most highly regarded serious writers have, perhaps wisely, chosen to exploit the superficial characteristics of fiction and to assume a retrogressive stance and pose of deliberate immaturity. Aiming to speak to a special group of the young, who are in this era as innocent and inexperienced in reading as they are of the lives of grown men and women, some of our best and brightest writers have come to depend upon tricks and pyrotechnical effects to capture and hold limited attention spans. And they have come to affect a rhetorical sensibility which lies somewhere between the infantile and the retarded. This combination of a sophisticated technique with a simplistic authorial sensibility has generated some of the most breathtakingly trivial literature since the great rash of sonnet sequences in the final years of the sixteenth century.

In any event, none of Cozzens's books was written for the academy or to make critics and teachers feel and look good. Since the New Academics (direct descendants of the New Critics) depend for their very survival on the celebration of the trivial, there is bound not to be much place for the work of Cozzens in their scheme. And there are other causes of and opportunities for conflict. Professors are more or less professionals and might be expected to have some sympathy and understanding at least for the main line of Cozzens's "professional" novels. But professors are not nearly so well paid as doctors, lawyers, and even the military. (I exclude the clergy.) Most professors hate the professionals. Moreover, for a very long time and dominantly so since World War II, in politics the Academy has been a sort of sacred grove, strongly dedicated to the Left. For many reasons—not the least of them being his techniques of story-telling which are, at least superficially, highly objective and dramatic—I cannot honestly gauge or infer the politics of James Gould Cozzens. I can tell more or less where the characters stand. His central characters, whether liberal or conservative, among the American professionals are not revolutionaries or even Marxists. For some time in America (unless you happened to be lucky enough to be a Southerner and thus mostly outside of conventional labels and indices, beyond the pale, as it were) it has been dangerous for the career and reputation of any writer not to be a clearly identified member-in-good-standing of the Left. Even though he was southern, William Faulkner's career suffered more than once because of this. So, for a time, did Hemingway's and Fitzgerald's and O'Hara's and Dos Passos's. Cozzens has suffered too. Using the thoughts and feelings of some of his characters as evidence, together with some vaguely recalled scraps from the celebrated distortions of the *Time* magazine cover story of many years ago concerning *By Love Possessed*, critics have conveniently labeled Cozzens a rigid reactionary. Therefore, in the thinking of at least some academics, since the Constitution appears to prohibit the outright suppression of annoying literature, truth and social justice require that his work should be ignored.

II

Although on rereading I found Cozzens's fiction much more various than I had remembered, still I can justify the memory because the main line of his mature work seems to be centered in the "professional" novels: *The Last Adam* (1933), *Men and Brethren* (1936), *The Just and the Unjust* (1942), *Guard of Honor* (1948), *By Love Possessed* (1957), and *Morning Noon and Night* (1968). There is always some overlapping in these novels, if only because the professionals inevitably deal with and relate to each other. But essentially we have a fiction built upon and around the lives of characters who are twentieth-century American professionals in the areas of law, medicine, the church, and the military. The central characters are (mostly) mature men of various ages who believe in their disciplines and who are, in fact, the men whose work has the power to shape and direct the quality of life in this country. No other serious American writer, except John O'Hara, with whom Cozzens shares some concerns but whose purpose was always somewhat different, has succeeded in dealing so effectively and seriously with this class and group of people. Which seems to me important for a number of reasons. First of all, because it is these people, the professionals, who have in fact and for better and worse most profoundly influenced American life in this century. Judging by most of our fiction, you might assume that the United States is chiefly populated by criminals, antiheroes, wise children, schizophrenics, clowns, and, of course, plenty of professors and artists. It would be easy enough, on the strength of most serious and recent American fiction, to assume that nobody much puts in a day's work in the U.S.A., and certainly nobody does anything that might be called honorable or interesting. You might infer that the few among us who are sane are to be found trout fishing in Idaho or running from the bulls in Pamplona or white-water canoeing in north Georgia. The so-called middle-class American in the workaday setting has often engaged the attention of popular writers, but the more prestigious, literary writers have simply avoided the problem, its challenges, and risks.

Which is strange. Because if we are even to try to understand what has been happening in America in this century, we have to understand the professionals. Witness both the heroes and the villains of Watergate. It is also a simple fact that almost all of the actual and potential "reading public" in America, throughout this century and no less now than earlier, is composed of mature men and women of the professional class. They are the only ones who have either time or interest or money for reading. There is no real "youth audience" for books of any kind (including paperbacks) outside of the briefly bookish and limited context of American higher education. In fiction and in poetry the heroes of college students are, almost exclusively, *assigned* heroes. It is no wonder that these heroes have brief lives in the light. Remember *Lord of the Flies? The Catcher in the Rye?* Renown and repute are gifts coming from an extremely self-centered group with a very short memory. Otherwise, aside from the captive audience of students, none of the other groups, which have been cultivated for purposes of exploitation by American publishers, has existed as a reading public except in the wishful thinking of the aforesaid publishers. The simple and statistical truth is that, so far in this century, Blacks don't read books, Chicanos don't read books, Native Americans don't read books. Ethnics don't read books. (The one great exception is the Jewish minority. Jews read lots of books and are a real audience.) Even Liberated Women, it seems, don't read books outside of the academic context. If there is going to be any audience at all for books by or about Blacks, Chicanos, Native Americans, Orientals, Ethnics (pure or impure), Liberated or Total Women, or even students, it is to be found in the standard "reading public" of America. Which is to say it will be middle-aged, upper-middle-class, professional in orientation, and predominantly female. The plain fact is that for all of this century in America the people who buy and read the books have been and still are mostly the wives of professional men. It is a small audience and appears to be dwindling.

The relationship of Cozzens to this audience should be interesting and instructive. His first novel was published in 1924, so he has had an active professional career of more than fifty years. Of course, we have to admit first and then keep in mind something that is not generally accepted by the critics and historians of modern American literature— that whatever else may be said about the state of letters in this country, the workshop and the marketplace, it is radically different from that of the earlier generation of American masters. For the first generation of twentieth-century American writers, which has to include Cozzens as a younger member, it may or may not have been respectable to be a novelist, but it evidently seemed a reasonable thing for a grown-up to do, even though the odds were bad and the required sacrifices were considerable. At this stage it is no longer a rational ambition to wish to be a serious novelist. I have said elsewhere, and still maintain, that it makes about as much sense today to write a novel as to set out to be a professional kite flyer. So when we look to the writers of the earlier generation for instruction and example, it's best to remember that, at least in the beginning, they were clearly saner than we are.

Having lived and worked long and well into our own era, Cozzens seems to have kept up with the times. And, as it happens, he has something recent and direct and explicit to say on the subject of success. It is something which he wrote to go along with his biographical sketch in the 1976–77 Bicentennial Edition of *Who's Who in America*. As an innovation for this special edition, the editors solicited statements from biographees, "statements of those principles, ideals, goals and standards of conduct that have helped them achieve success and high regard." Cozzens complied with the editorial request, though not, I'd guess, in precisely the terms they had in mind. His statement sounds more than a little bit like the words and thoughts of his own Henry Worthington in *Morning Noon and Night*. Cozzens wrote: "The longer I watch men and life, the surer I get that success whenever more than minor comes of luck alone. By comparison, no principles, ideas, goals, and standards of conduct matter much in an achieving of it." Notice that he ignores the other most ambiguous part of the query—"high regard."

Coming from a certifiably successful American, that statement reads like what the theologians call a hard saying. Certainly if success (and consequently failure as well) come "of luck alone," then neither praise nor blame can attach to either condition. It follows, then, that only a fool would hope for the justice of more than minor reward or greatly fear the risk of failure. It follows that success and failure, in the terms of *Who's Who*, are meaningless.

Cozzens should know something about both success and failure. In his time he has had more than one best seller, and he has won important prizes. At one time and another he has been praised by many of the best-known critics and reviewers. By the same token he has also been subjected to the most outrageous (bordering on the purely malicious) kind of personal and artistic attacks. He has made the complete circuit with Fortune's wheel, seen both sides of the rainbow. It follows that his views on good luck and bad are to be taken seriously.

Luck (in the separate senses of both Fortune and Providence) plays an important part in all of Cozzens's fiction. In *Morning Noon and*

Night, Henry Worthington thinks and talks a good deal about luck, and in one place he has some comments on the part it plays in the literary situation in America. Here is what Worthington has to say on the subject:

> The publisher who has unprofitably published a book, like the writer who wrote it, is taught nothing. The lesson they learn is only that they are out of luck. I used the word advisedly, for adducible figures from our publishing studies seem to show beyond doubt that neither merit as a piece of writing nor excellence, by literary standards of the moment, as a creative work is the determining factor in making a book a best seller. Indeed, as far as merit goes, so many books of no merit (that is, subsequently conceded to be without any) have had very large sales that, considering these alone, the hypothesis that badness does the trick—you find it proposed by almost every failed-writer-turned-critic in the literary-circle jungle—may seem tenable. It is not tenable because, whatever wishful thinking may wish, there are other figures to show that books of much and evident merit (that is, by subsequent critical consensus held so to be) often sell equally well.

Anybody lost in "the literary-circle jungle" today would be well advised to read Cozzens and to listen to Worthington. Perhaps with some regularity. Also with the understanding that in one small respect the advice and counsel are out of date. With few enough exceptions to make the rule seem ironclad, no serious fiction sells well in this final quarter of our century. That is (and I like to think both Cozzens and Worthington might appreciate the irony of this), the difference between "success" and "failure" is so small that these very terms are virtually without meaning. Just so, the most "successful" novels published today would, in a relative sense (and I am as sure as Worthington that figures would bear me out), have to be called "failures" when compared with the most successful fiction of the previous generation. Yet even that fact, as Cozzens has shown us, is irrelevant.

III

Take this, if you will, as it intends to be, informal and personal, one working writer's brief attempt to express gratitude to and admiration for an influential writer of another generation. In that sense it has to be about "influence." Which is, I suppose, a word for teaching outside the classroom. In addition to the pleasure and instruction available for all readers of the fiction of James Gould Cozzens, there are special lessons for the writer. At a bad time for the art of writing, one of our most productive craftsmen has much to teach the rest of us. He offers a superior example of the integrity of the craft, of the daring refinement of language, of the creation of fully realized characters who matter, of structures and patterns of experience which seem, in the major novels, to shadow the complex patterns of Fortune and Providence in our lives. Technically he can do it all and without seeming effort or wasted motion. It may not be possible, or even particularly useful, to use Cozzens as a specific model or to deal in the same way with the same kinds of subjects and materials; but every writer, certainly every apprentice and journeyman, can learn almost all that is worth knowing about technique from studying his work.

More important than that, however, is the example of the man and artist. Not the private man, who is, in spite of attention, unknown; but rather the man in the public light, bearing with equal grace his good luck and his bad. A cliché among the writers of my own generation, offered up when exchanging complaints, is: "Oh well, no matter what happens it can't be as bad as it was for Herman Melville." True enough. . . . It also can't be any better or any worse than it has been for Cozzens. That the best and the worst can be gracefully borne is as much a challenge as a consolation. That neither success nor failure need be a crippling condition, that it remains always possible freely to choose to do honestly and to do well without regard to what Cozzens calls luck, seems to me one of the most important lessons I can hope to pass on to my students whether they learn to read and write or not. Of course, it would help if they did learn to read. Because then they could find it for themselves in the novels of James Gould Cozzens.

6

The Good
Influence of John Ciardi
(1987)

*Not everything that happens is a learning
experience. Maybe nothing is.*

—John Ciardi, "For Instance"

I am thinking here of influence not in the complex, gnarled and often crabbed senses of it as adopted and advanced by the gospel according to Harold Bloom; not, then, as some kind of intellectual haunting, not as a matter of any great and shadowy anxiety nor in the least as any kind of competition between the past and the present. Nothing of the sort. What I am thinking about is at once more simple, and, I would like to think, deeper, though it can be described in a language without the cover and concealment of adroit obfuscation. All of us who try to write poems do so under various influences. In our age, an age (to claim the very least) of the widest kind of literary diversity, of the wildest plurality of forms and voices and tones of voice (and, alas, standards) we are all constantly on the lookout for worthwhile and imitable examples. We seek to learn by and from both good and bad examples. In the absence of widely accepted standards of excellence we are forced not so much to define our own as to find our own from among the apparent practice of our peers and, especially, from the strategies and tactics of the elders, our immediate predecessors who have lived and worked in roughly the same literary world as ourselves. Here John Ciardi's example is particularly important; for he stood as one of the very few among that generation of elders who remained fully active and productive as poets. From many, maybe a majority of the others, the lesson to be learned by their example might well be to quit early, if

---

possible, while ahead, to be dealt out of the game soon enough to rest on laurels, to cut your losses or to take your winnings, adequate or meager, and run.

So that is the first lesson. John Ciardi taught by example: that with a little luck or a lot of hard labor, it may just be possible to continue being a poet, to keep on writing poetry, with, of course, all the risks inherent to that life and calling, a vocation proudly demonstrated by his last book of *new* poems, *The Birds of Pompeii* (1985).

But I am running ahead of myself already. At this stage the only point I wanted to make, a very general one, was that, for the kinds of influence I am thinking of, we of roughly my own generation turn to the elders just behind us, John's generation; for it is from them, their good and bad examples, that we have the most useful things to learn. It is the useful things, what can be begged or borrowed or stolen, even (yes) what can be copied, that we are concerned with. Poets even as near to us in time as Eliot and Pound and Yeats, as Wallace Stevens and William Carlos Williams and Robert Frost, for example, have much less of this to teach us; partly, of course, because they were, each in his own way, so successful in their conventional rebellion from *their* elders that we have already forgotten who most of their prominent predecessors were and what on earth the whole fuss was all about; but partly, also, because the world they lived in and wrote about, though it partakes of a good-size chunk of this selfsame century, is radically different from our own and might as well be (it often seems to me) separated from our times by the dark gulf of many centuries. There are times when it honestly seems to me that we are closer to the lives and times of Wyatt and Chaucer, or Villon, perhaps, and certainly of Virgil, at least the Virgil of the *Eclogues*, than we are to the early Eliot or the later Pound. I am naturally assuming the spontaneous and coterminous equality of all the honored dead, at least in their continual haunting of the present and of the living. And I am not considering the usual contemporary critical distinctions between modernism and postmodernism, distinctions which seem to me about as important, or unimportant as the case may be, as the length of skirts, the height of collars, the width of necklines. Our grandparents witnessed the end of something, itself perhaps an illusion and a brief one, but nonetheless something which might as well be called Civilization. And which may well have been Civilization for all we know. We come along later and deeper in the dark ages of the brutalized twentieth century. We have only the faintest recollection of the almost unimaginable times before. Even our nostalgia is lavished on barbarous times. In John's times and wars, and in mine, which overlap, we have been witness to the murder of hundreds of millions of people. Rivers, maybe oceans of blood have been flowing. Imagine what it would be like for all of us if it were not characteristic of blood to clot and dry quickly. By now half the world would be drowned in human blood, just as the world would be tipped over by the weight of our injustices to each other. Never mind the gothic horror of that image. Instead, consider more simply that John's generation and mine have been witness to many terrible things. As a matter of course. We share that with each other and have to look to each other for comfort and solace, for some understanding.

Nobody but one among us, a creature of these times, could have written these lines of John's, ripped out of context from "Useless Knowledge," the penultimate poem in *The Birds of Pompeii*:

> . . . These are notes
> for a sermon on the sanctity of survival
> to teach that life is not worth dying for.
>
> But have we a choice? I have flown my hot missions
> in a flammable bottle when I could have been grounded
> on permanent garbage detail. What's wrong with
> garbage?

Nobody living fully in the second half of this century needs much of a gloss or an explication of those lines.

But maybe equally important, when you cast aside the big cosmic forces and issues, which casting aside is the first gesture of the veteran soldier, throwing away every piece of inessential equipment as he goes into combat; casting aside huge and vague facts for homely truths, we have to admit that the life of the poet, the profession of letters in our time is quite distinctly different for us than it was for that luckier, earlier generation. The social and economic details of this era of ours are at once obvious and tedious to talk about. And I won't trouble you with them except to say that where, with precious few exceptions, they, our literary grandparents, were adequately, if not always well-heeled, there are now precious few ladies and gentlemen of letters left among us. There are, it is true, a few writers, among them poets, who are the fortunate children of considerable inherited wealth, for whom the vocation of literature is, therefore, a matter of free and easy choice, but of next to no risk (except the risk of failing as a writer, and there is at least some possible insurance against that if you can afford the extraordinary premiums). But most American poets these days come out of the hard-pressed, overtaxed, American middle class, some quite recently arrived there. Some have arrived there, in a literary paradigm of "the American dream," on their own, from hard and meager beginnings. John Ciardi is one of these latter. Read *Lives of X* (available again, thanks be, in *Selected Poems* [1984]), for the unsentimental story of it. Then maybe read the newer "Audit at Key West" for the other end of the story, the acute awareness of the killing weight of inflation on old and young American dreamers.

> . . . The world is divided
> into those who managed to buy in time, and their
>   children
> who can no longer afford to and must wait
> for their parents to die.

Enough of belaboring the obvious. I hope I have made the point that we share a world which is much the same to each other and is distinctly different from the one just before and maybe the one to come after . . .

Well, then, maybe a word about that—the youngsters. I am not sure that our younger poets, some of them our very own students, have very much to teach us except, by merely being there and being young, the immutable veracity, not a cynical syllable in it, of the statement that youth is wasted on the young. It is also possible to learn from them to accept the fact, without undue embarrassment, that we were mostly foolish when we were young. But one does not look to or among them for models on how to live and how to do anything except to be decoratively young. We can, of course, be injured in various ways by the young, but we cannot be seriously influenced by them.

One final, perhaps quirky observation. Though the very young, our children already now young adults, have no choice but to share our world, its same ever-expanding record and inheritance of unbroken and bloody barbarism, the large majority of them, in America at least—finally, it's America I am thinking of and talking about—most of them have only witnessed the bitter truths of these bitter times indirectly and thus vicariously. The overwhelming majority—for the first time in our whole national history—managed adroitly to avoid the national experience of a major war, the war in Vietnam. Except as an abstraction or as something on television. Which, abstraction and/or reduction to cleverly edited two-dimensional representation, begins by being so severely distorted as to be untrue to those of our generations. You will see that I do not consider fleeing to Canada or Sweden or graduate school, no matter how perilous, to be an equivalent experience to military service. Not the same thing, nor even part of it. Those who did not serve were sheltered from it by those who did. All of which means (or *may* mean) that they, the children of the 1960s, have yet to learn what others, including ourselves, have by heart; that maybe the influence, like the buck, stops here; that, by and large, they may as yet lack the sad experience to be able fully to understand the work of John Ciardi and, thus, to be influenced by it and by him. Maybe. But though we wish them well, I can't imagine a single manjack among us who believes it is even remotely possible that they will ever manage to get through their lifetimes in this century, and the first of the next one, entirely unscathed, unbruised, and unbloodied.

On the other hand the old masters—if we may so designate the earlier, Eliot-Pound-Yeats generation—were mature and gifted poets of great sensitivity and keen imagination. And yet, tested against the weight of actual experience in World War I, by which I mean the living work of the brilliant combat poets like Owen and Sassoon, Isaac Rosenberg and Robert Graves, and so many others, their work seems somewhat pale. Literary judgments for the moment aside, one has to look to the work of people like John Masefield and Kipling, both honor graduates of the school-of-hard-knocks, to find the gritty impact of experience which can approximate that of the younger poets of that era. And it is interesting to note that those last parts of Eliot's *Four Quartets*, written during and after his direct experience as an air-raid warden during the Blitz, arrive at a kind of poetry more directly experimental than intellectually derivative, something he had not demonstrated before.

To return to the proper subject, then. We, the writers of various kinds of my generation, look especially to the writers of John Ciardi's generation for pertinent and relevant examples; and we are much influenced by them. A good many of us gladly consider ourselves influenced by John Ciardi. And I would like to say a few things about the nature of that influence, first in general, then in particular, and, finally, personally.

In a general sense John Ciardi has been hugely influential because he placed or found himself in peculiar positions to be so. Nobody sets out to be an influence on others, to be influential, except maybe our natural parents who have a bounden duty to be so, or the varieties of demagogue which the tides of this century have thrown up, demagogues of all kinds and persuasions who seem, in all their guises, to share some common and irresistible itch to be able to manipulate their fellows and to prevail over them, if possible, one and all. But, almost incidentally, there have been various ways, in these our times, by which an individual writer can exercise a considerable influence on others, writers and readers alike. And John Ciardi has been influential in most of the available ways that I know of. I am not speaking here, not yet, of the most important influence of all, the example of his poetry. Which is, of course, the way and means most poets are deeply influential upon each other. I will be speaking to and about that, but as a personal matter (if also, I hope, an exemplary one). Most powerful, that influence is usually most private. Not always. But I think, at least in these times, that the more public the direct influence of a poet, the more likely deleterious it will be. A few years ago half the beginning poets in America were writing, as best they could, in the manner of Mark Strand and Charles Simic. There were times when it seemed that most of the younger poets wanted not to be like Strand and Simic, but (by some weird incantation) to *turn into* either one or the other or both indistinguishably. There was a brief period when it seemed possible that every poem being published in America was being written by the same poet. But just when it all seemed too depressing for words, that whole thing vanished like ground fog succumbing to first sunlight. Even Strand and Simic, separately and equally, slowed down and changed a little and the poetry of young Americans began to assume its appropriate plurality again.

The Good Influence of John Ciardi

Ciardi has plenty of admirers and disciples, but his public influence has been of a different kind. As poetry editor, over years, at *The Saturday Review*, he chose the poems to publish or reject for that magazine. Likewise he determined which books to review or not to review, to praise or to blame. Similarly in his regular columns for the *Review* he had an important opportunity to advance or to challenge ideas. Not merely literary and critical ideas, but others as well. Surely there are readers who still remember well how courageously Ciardi challenged some of the political and social bad habits in postwar America. Editorial positions are, by definition, influential; though it must be said, in honesty, that much of their potential for influence resides in the office and not in the holder. Thus today poets like Howard Moss (*The New Yorker*) or Peter Davison (*Atlantic Monthly*) or even, for example, Reginald Gibbons (*Tri-Quarterly*) or Daniel Halpern (*Antaeus*) have, for a time at least, a kind of automatic power to influence the lives and work of other poets, an influence more weighty and significant than their own achievements might ever allow. And, indeed, the whole matter of editorial integrity and influence, the uses and abuses thereof, merits serious examination as a central part of the literary history of the age. And certainly John Ciardi's time at *The Saturday Review* is an important example of contemporary editorial influence. My recollection of all this is that Ciardi was an exciting, and sometimes controversial, editor and at the same time a highly responsible one. He was an honest editor—a quality more rarely found than the uninitiated might surmise. For a good many years, then, his influence, honest and moderate, was a powerful one and, I think, a healthy one. Which is more than most editors can ever claim.

I say this as one whose every submission to that magazine at that time was summarily rejected and whose books of poems, when reviewed there at all, were (in my opinion then) roughly handled. I can assure you I wasn't happy about it at the time. But there were positive and useful things to learn from the experience, and I like to think that I learned some of them and that they came to serve me well to help me through darker and rougher times (at the hands of villainous amateurs) later on. I have lived to tell the tale. Which may have been a test the tough-minded editor intended; for anyone who couldn't take the heat, who couldn't pass through the modest obstacle course of regular rejection and critical chastisement and still carry on about his proper business, should no doubt look for another kind of life and art. All of us have had to do some judging and editing along the way. Most of those we pause to praise are unimpressed, being convinced they fully deserve a full measure of praise and devotion. And most of those we criticize hate our guts for it. But it is important to learn what do to with and about negative responses to our work. One learns to question one's own habits and assumptions. Sometimes one learns to change habits, to modify assumptions, upon the strength of just and lively criticism. Sometimes one recovers from self-interrogation with a confirmed and strengthened sense of the worth of something which has been criticized by others. And that, too, is a valuable lesson, Ciardi wasn't always right, not by a long shot. But his criticism raised good questions. It was enormously useful.

Without ever discussing or, for that matter, ever even mentioning the editorial experience to John Ciardi, what it did to and for him and how he may have influenced others, I have an idea that it was an experience from which he learned many things. And once it was over, he discovered that he had given up, with that position, some of the amenities of the literary life which went with it. The truth is that some of John Ciardi's finest poems were written in the years since he served at *The Saturday Review*. It is important to note, however, that while all of Ciardi's books published before he left *The Saturday Review* were widely reviewed, and regularly reviewed in *The New York Times Book Review*, those published since then were sparsely reviewed, and none was reviewed in the *Times*. We have all been witness to, recently, the ugly spectacle of a fundamentally boneheaded (and, at least in that sense, dishonorable) review of Ciardi's *Selected Poems* and Karl Shapiro's *Love & War, Art & God* in *Poetry* magazine (a magazine Shapiro once edited and where Ciardi had often published first-rate poems), in which the young reviewer criticized both distinguished poets for their failure to keep up with the latest trends and fashions. As if to be fashionable, and by choice, were the beginning of wisdom.

Ciardi is, and has proved himself to be, too tough and too honorable for any of this kind of thing, at high and low levels, to have made any real difference to him. It certainly has not injured his poetry, either, or stifled his Muse. One of the things he learned, I imagine, from exercising a certain literary authority as an editor and then losing it when he gave up that position was what he already knew well enough—that, by and large, this world is populated by knaves and fools, some of whom can be dangerous to the health and welfare of others. He has, in fact, written about that truth well and often, and never better, in my opinion, than in the poem "Faces." Look it up and read it in *Selected Poems*, the story it tells of an act of gratuitous and stupid cruelty, almost fatal in its consequences, done to the speaker by a perfect stranger whose face he never clearly saw in the dark and for which (that face) he has been looking and finding models ever since:

> . . . But why tell you?
> It's anybody's world for the living in it:
> You know as much about that face as I do.

It may not be redundant here to note that Ciardi, the critic has indicated an alert awareness of what is going on in poetry, an eager desire to know what the poets are up to. But (see his piece "The Arts in 1975" in *Contemporary Literary Scene II*) he has also pointed out—and I believe he is the first poet and critic to do so—the wild variety of the present scene in poetry, questioning the capacity of anyone to keep up with it. Allowing that contemporary "American poetry lacks a dominant mode," he writes:

> If anything, it is given over to partisan groupings that ignore what is not of the in-group. Imagine that our publishers, in a spasm of madness, commissioned twenty poets, each to assemble a "representative" anthology to be titled *American Poetry Today*. (The fact is, of course, that the cost of permission fees has seriously inhibited the making of anthologies, but imagination is free.) Now list at random twenty poets to edit these anthologies. How many American poets, do you suppose, would appear in all of these anthologies?—I mean poets alive today. How many who are prominently featured in one anthology would not appear in *any* of the others? Would any one of these anthologies offer a reasonable survey of American poetry now? Would it be possible by reading them all to discover some significant common ground on which American poets meet?
>
> Speculation is for its own sake. I suspect that every answer would find factionalism as our only common ground. But division is not necessarily

an evil. It tends at least (or does it?) to heed variety. In art, variety is always the soil of hope.

This description of reality seems to me as accurate as it is profound. The fact that our anthologies of the 1980s gather together the same poets *as if* there were a genuine consensus, as if there were some common ground, just as our professional reviewers tend to review the same poets and the same books, does not contradict Ciardi's view. Rather, it is strong evidence of a certain kind of collusion, precisely the "factionalism" he pointed out, and, to the extent that it pretends to be definitive or even representative, to precisely that extent it is dishonest criticism. It is easy to disagree with Ciardi the critic, but his integrity is demonstrably beyond all questioning.

Well then. Ciardi exercised much practical (and often useful) influence as an editor and critic, as a creator of anthologies and textbooks. Also as, for years, a teacher and as director of the celebrated summer workshop at Bread Loaf. As teachers we are (perhaps fortunately) seldom aware of how influential we may have been. Some of our students succeed in the very same subjects we professed to be teaching them. And John had his string of successes of this kind at Rutgers and elsewhere. I am impressed by the variety of the work of the poets he has taught. What do Miller Williams and the late Frank O'Hara have in common? Ciardi was their teacher. Though he gave up full-time teaching, Ciardi was clearly a born teacher and an experienced one. He taught writers beyond numbering. He taught good things and he set a good example for them. But he has taught even more readers that there are good things to read, even in this rusty age, things which are worth a grown-up's time and energy. And who knows how many children have been taught to relish the delight and instruction of poetry from the experience of his many delightful and instructive books of children's poetry? Certainly there are good lessons, good things to learn there for poets in general as well as for those other poets who wish to learn to write poems for children.

Because I have never set foot on the grounds of Bread Loaf and have always been the kid at the knothole at the ballpark, I think I can speak (briefly enough) with some objective authority about it. At Bread Loaf, which Ciardi directed and managed for such a long time, he exerted a major influence on the future (thus the present) of American letters. Consider that, at the outset, it was a bridge, too, between several generations; for in a real sense it was Robert Frost's show. And Frost was the presiding spirit of the place. If Frost was the Old Man, Ciardi was the executive officer, the troop commander. Years of American poets and fiction writers passed through the basic training, the flash and fire of Ciardi's Bread Loaf. It is a debatable point, one that is argued with some vehemence on both sides, but my best judgment is (still viewed from the knothole) that Bread Loaf ain't what it used to be. Not like it was when it was Ciardi's enterprise. There are new names and a new crew, some of them highly celebrated writers. But some essential link with the spirit of Frost, some basic sense of the energy and the original purpose of the place was lost when Ciardi's resignation was accepted. The reports that I receive, the vibrations I also am attuned to, tell me that Gene Lyons's famous article about Bread Loaf in *Harper's* (or was it *Atlantic?* No matter . . .) was a devastatingly accurate account of the new and not-improved regime there.

There were some other gatherings and conferences headed by Ciardi after that—like the Ohio Valley Writers Conference at the University of Northern Kentucky in 1985—where something of the old energy and excitement was regained and restored, enough so that it is easy to believe in the validity of the original model, to have an example of what it must have been like.

All these things, then. Editor and teacher and director, and not to overlook Ciardi's influence as the translator of *The Divine Comedy,* taken together with his innumerable lectures, public appearances, readings (that is, John Ciardi as *performer*), his old days on TV, his appearances on National Public Radio, gave Ciardi a visibility and served the art of poetry in America. Much credit has gone to Frost first, and later to Dylan Thomas, for helping the cause of poetry by popularizing the form by which it reaches its largest numerical audience—the poetry reading. Probably Ciardi gave more readings, over a longer period of time, than Frost and Thomas taken together. Certainly he deserves as much credit as they have earned for establishing this kind of marketplace for the works of poets. And he deserves credit from a multitude of poets for creating this additional possibility for poets to earn a living, sometimes an adequate one, for their work.

I have only touched on the surface of things, but I hope it is clear that we all owe a large debt to the public John Ciardi and his good influence. Finally, however, it is the private influence of the poet and his work to which other poets, often separately (though there are friends who shared most of all their friendship with and admiration of John Ciardi, those for whom he has known as "The Godfather" and "Big John," among other nicknames), are most beholden. Finally, it is the poetry that matters most, both for the pleasure of reading and for learning from it, to other poets. I am sure that we have learned different things from it, each according to our own needs and hopes. All that I can say and celebrate is what I have learned and most admired.

One of these things has been John's concept, both theoretical and practical, of "the unimportant poem." He spelled out this idea in a number of places, no place more clearly and simply than on the jacket of his own book *For Instance* (1979): "I write only unimportant poems," says Ciardi. "The smaller the better. Perhaps small enough to be life-size. That is never much, but all there is, and therefore everything." Simple, but profound. *"Perhaps small enough to be life-size."* We have lived in and through terrible times full of Big Events, what the Chinese used to mean ironically by the "interesting times" it is a curse to live through. Against the enormity of the times and all the noisy clamor of them some poets have linked arms with the hucksters and hype merchants, seeking some kind of marching-band authority, if only by size and scope and apparent originality seeking to say large things. Others have turned away and inward, seeking the inversely important by the cultivation of the deep and shadowy regions of the subconscious. And, as Ciardi was among the first to admit, some good things have come from both directions. But both, using the chaos of the age as a rationale ("How can you write little poems while people are starving in Ethiopia?"), have turned away from the quotidian wonders which are the beginning of wisdom for poets, especially (it seems to me) American poets who have learned to rejoice in the ordinary experience, even as they explore it. Moreover, it is our special strength and characteristic to treat readers as honorable equals not by "talking down" to them nor by, to use the southernism, "big-mouthing," but rather by speaking well about persons, places, and things which both poet and reader can be assumed to know and care about. There is a poem in *For*

Instance which shows and tells this thing, what "the unimportant poem" is all about exactly:

Saturday, March 6

One morning you step out, still in pajamas
to get your *Times* from the lawn where it lies folded
to the British pound, which has dropped below $2.00
for the first time since the sun stopped never
setting on it, and you pick it up—
the paper, that is—because it might mean
  something,
in which case someone ought to know about it
(a free and enlightened citizenry, for instance)
and there, just under it—white, purple, yellow—
are the first three crocuses half open, one
sheared off where the day hit it, and you pick it up,
and put it in water, and when your wife comes down
it's on the table. And that's what day it is.

Lifting up the terrible abstract weight of all the world's news in the actual *Times*, the poet-speaker uncovers the first three crocuses, "one sheared off where the day hit it." An injured, useless, unimportant thing which becomes art (just as an "unimportant poem" can be) when he saves it, puts it in water for another's delight and thus gives the day its true name, meaning, significance. It is a paradigm of the poet about his proper business.

The paradox of the "unimportant poem" as advocated and practiced by Ciardi is that it does, in fact, allow the poet to deal with all kinds of worldly matters, including events large and small, in ways that few other poets have been able to. The Big Band boys are up there on the tower conducting the half-time show. The Deep Image poets are down at the bottom of the well and can only see a little dark circle of starry sky. It is a strange and exciting thing to see stars in the daytime, but wells deep enough are few and far between and you can't stay down there very long. The concept of the "unimportant poem" liberates us to write out of what we imagine happens to us in the real world, to make something out of our own experience. But poetry really isn't about *experience*, it is all about language. And so the "unimportant poem" is wildly liberating to us, inviting us to use a whole range of language—tones, voices, dialects, high and low modes. Ciardi, a master of the American language and its long history, was ideally suited for this kind of freedom. His precision allowed him to make easy leaps and jumps back and forth between the stages of the spoken and the written, between high and low voices within the context of a single poem, often of a single stanza. There can be, therefore, abrupt shifts, "cuts," in the language of film, as radical and graceful as any created by the seventeenth-century metaphysical poets. Riffle through the pages of *Selected Poems* and you'll find a multitude of good examples. If you want to know one of my special favorites, for the sake of many kinds of living language (including the deliberate use of jargon and cliché, thus, in this context renewing both), take a good look at "Trying to Feel Something." The paradox of "the unimportant poem" is that because it is so liberating, it cries out for forms. To contain the energy. A net and some lines to make some rules for the game. Ciardi was, as it happens, a great and subtle master of verse forms. If you idle through *Selected Poems* you will find yourself in a gallery of forms. If you are a poet, you will be challenged to try your own hand at them, to see if you, too, can put living words and living things within the cage of some strict form and then see if you can hide the cage from all but the most alert and curious observers.

We are moving back into a time of forms—everybody knows it. The good poets will be looking to John Ciardi for examples. So will the bad poets if and when forms are truly fashionable again.

All that I have said about the good influence of John Ciardi, public and private, adds up to the truth that he gives hope to the rest of us. Maybe, just maybe, we, too, can keep writing, growing, changing, becoming long after so many others have settled for rigidities (certainties?) and reputation. Maybe, with his example, we can teach ourselves to be tough enough to continue, hitting and missing, suffering and rejoicing, maybe even arriving gratefully and honestly at the earned place of the last line of "For Myra out of the Album"—"I have been here, and some of it was love."

Afterword:
Three New Books by John Ciardi (1990)

The late John Ciardi had a story he used to tell when, as often happens, writers talking together began to swap bitter tales of woe concerning rough treatment suffered at the hands of their publishers and the disappointments which fall on just and unjust heads equally like the rain. He liked to summon up a week which began like any other and then took a sudden turn for the worst he could imagine when a new director, arriving at the Rutgers University Press, announced that Rutgers, which has published and kept in print a half dozen of Ciardi's books of poems, not only was discontinuing the publication of poetry, but also was remaindering all copies in stock, getting rid of it all as soon as possible. Two days later Lippincott, which had half a dozen of Ciardi's children's books in print, made precisely the same announcement. In less than a week Ciardi was, for the time being, completely out of print. For the past few years, beginning well before his death (on Easter Sunday, 1986) and continuing posthumously, the active and energetic University of Arkansas Press has almost made up for that grievous loss—to readers as much or more than to the poet—by handsomely publishing various gatherings of work by Ciardi, old and new, known and unknown. These latest three are significant additions to the list. *Echoes* presents forty-five previously unpublished poems, of various forms and lengths, which were found among his papers after his death. Taken together they are vintage Ciardi—lyrical or narrative, funny or angry or both at once, spun out gracefully in a virtuoso's mixture of formal patterns. Richard Wilbur was on the money when in a jacket blurb, he called this book "not a batch of leavings but a warm and delightful leave-taking." Ciardi, himself, remains celebrative to the end, even in a hard-nosed poem like "A Traffic Victim Sends a Sonnet of Confused Thanks to God as the Sovereign Host" which concludes with a couplet of the prisoner-poet's essential freedom: "But I'm still free to scratch a thanks on the wall / To say you host a sweet world, all in all." *Poems of Love and Marriage*, twenty-four poems around the stated theme, brings together some of Ciardi's most popular poems ("Men Marry What They Need") with new ones. Taken together this way,

---

they prove him to be one of the finest poets of modern love. Ciardi spent a lot of his lifetime teaching and lecturing. *Fifteen Essays* is a selection of the best of his good talk. He said some wonderful and memorable things. Here's one: "I have learned not to send a poem on a prose errand." And another, more specific to our times: "I would rather be confused by Shakespeare than clarified by my broker."

7

The Recent Poetry
of Robert Penn Warren
(1965)

So you didn't know? Well, it's time you did—
though one shuns to acknowledge the root from which one's
own virtue mounts.

—Robert Penn Warren, "Clearly About You"

If you choose to begin with 1935, the year of publication of Warren's *Thirty-six Poems*, then it is simple enough to state that for thirty years he has been writing poetry of distinction and importance. Including his book length narrative in verse, *Brother to Dragons* (1953), there have been six books of poetry, and during that time Warren's poems have received a good deal of critical attention. He has won many awards and honors—the Pulitzer Prize, the National Book Award, the Shelley Memorial Award, and others. He has served as Consultant in Poetry at the Library of Congress. All of which adds up to a simple fact. Even if the poetry of Robert Penn Warren were to be considered in abstraction from his closely related achievements as novelist and short-story writer, as critic, editor, and teacher, still he would obviously have to be counted among the very small number of outstanding and genuinely productive poets of our time.

Judged by that second and much less frequently invoked standard of judgment, productivity, the continuing creation of poems of high quality over a considerable period of time, Warren's achievement is more rare. He stands almost alone in the sense of continued growth and change in his poetry. Most of our poets have chosen to reflect the specialization of industry and the age, no matter how much they howl against it. Each finds his particular way, what the peer group prefers to call "his own voice," and then proceeds to cultivate and exploit it with the single-minded devotion of the mythical manufacturer of Brand X. Perhaps closer to the mark, each imitates the insistence of the latest popular crooner whose sighs, groans, bumps, and grinds are immediately identifiable to the most careless listener and which, through the bounties of success, may eventually be called a "style." Take yet another image for the American poetic scene. The young poet begins as a sharecropper, hoeing his hard row, living in relative squalor at the fringes of a large plantation at the center of which stands a sort of Selznick-style mansion house, a kind of national monument, museum, and tourist attraction where only a few, widely recognized, very important poets live. These are chiefly those who have long since laid down the shovel and the hoe of hard labor and, while waiting for a first-class chariot ride, are willing to settle for clean fingernails, uncalloused palms, the sweatless and riskless roles of lecturer, reviewer, critic, and sometime judge for one of the prizes and grants which are available, able to be tossed with benevolent noblesse oblige to the most obedient and best-behaved youngsters and the faithful middle-aged who know their place. For that young poet out there in the hot sun the ideal, the dream of glory is, of course, to get out of it, to escape the weather, the work, the danger, and to move into the comfortable shade and dignity of the old manse. And, like ambitious young men since time began, they are willing to polish any number of boots, to kiss any number of famous and ample posteriors, because that beats staggering along behind a mule and a plough.

Our present poetic situation is not conducive to growth or change. In the past twenty years, years some have called affluent, it has become a kind of dancing court, a splendid hall of mirrors ("Mirror, mirror, on the wall / Who is Donald Andrew Hall?"), a genteel society of mutual admiration and profound self-esteem. It should be added that there is always at least one chamber reserved for those distorted and disturbing mirrors which are intended to make us all appreciate, even more than we naturally do already, the essential symmetry of our natural selves. Here the well-paid, well-fed jesters, wearing traditional cap and bells, play in happy mockery, the kind of mockery whose sole purpose is to emphasize the altogether enviable status of the status quo.

The American poetic status quo is conservative (a little to the right of Ivan the Terrible) in literary matters and takes a dim view of productivity. The prolific, the versatile, the *changing* are more feared by the establishment than the world, the flesh, and the devil combined.

Paradoxically, Warren began his poetic career with the assurance of a decent place within a respectable group in the hierarchy. He was an acceptable young "fugitive." The influence of this small group, small in number and even smaller in gross product, can hardly be overestimated. It is not only critically, as has been widely allowed, but also by the example of their work and success, that this little group has been so influential. This is a little surprising, for the essentials of good, sound fugitive verse, exemplified at its best by the best of Ransom and Tate, are traditional and traditionally southern. Their verse is formal and, for the most part, shuns innovation in language, form, and subject matter as if it were a social disease. Their work is deeply rooted in the old, historical southern assumption that there is a clear-cut boundary, formidable as any curtain of iron or bamboo, between the proper precincts of prose and poetry. Viewed against the backdrop of southern literary history, the very slight changes effected by the fugitives in poetry or prose are as negligible as the works of man considered in the context of geologic time. In poetry there was a mild increase in the intellectual surface and content, which has sometimes been advertised as "obscurity," and there was the admission into the realm of the acceptably poetic a gentle irony which might be called a kind of academic gag-writing. Taking a signal from T. S. Eliot's brief, though famous bow in the general direction of John Donne, they quickly codified a set of laws and bylaws of poetry and fiction; then, with almost missionary zeal, they became fugitive indeed, all but a few of them fleeing the benighted South, for the security and culture of the suburban North.

In some of his earliest poems Warren demonstrated his ability to turn this kind of poem almost to perfection. And, ironically, it is by these poems that he is usually represented in the anthologies today. The familiar final quatrain of "Bearded Oaks" is a really marvelous example of Marvell translated into twentieth-century English:

> We live in time so little time
> And we learn all so painfully,
> That we may spare this hour's term
> To practice for eternity.[1]

"Love's Parable" (*Thirty-six Poems*) is pure Donne and shows its origin proudly in its syntax, deliberate inversions and archaisms, and here, for example, in the dominant image of the opening stanza:

> As kingdoms after civil broil,
> Long faction-bit and sore unmanned,
> Unlaced, unthewed by lawless toil,
> Will welcome to the cheering strand
> A prince whose tongue, not understood,
> Yet frames a new felicity,
> And alien, seals domestic good:
> Once each to each, such aliens, we.

Warren might easily have stopped right there, and not without some honor; but he is gifted as a superb storyteller, and he is also more deeply related to the living heart and guts of the southern tradition than any of his mentors. Even among his early poems there are ones which break the rules and have a very different kind of validity and excitement. The variety is clearly evident in *Selected Poems 1923–1943*. There is "The Ballad of Billie Potts," a sustained narrative poem which is particular and concrete, exactly local, and riddled with homely imagery, some of it part of the folk tradition, some designed and contrived as a close approximation of it.

> Little Billie was full of piss and vinegar,
> And full of sap as a maple tree.
> And full of tricks as a lop-eared pup.[2]

In a group of poems with a Mexican setting he had begun to show an ability to handle the concrete scene and real action in verse that could rival his abilities in prose. For example, this flashing, cinematic moment from "The World Comes Galloping" (*Selected Poems*):

> Then at the foot of that long street
> Between the pastel of stucco and the feathery pepper
>   trees,
> Horse and horseman, sudden as light, and loud,
> Appeared,

And up the rise, banging the cobbles like castanets,
Lashed in their fury and fever,
Plunged:
Wall-eyed and wheezing, the lurching hammer-head,
The swaying youth, and flapping from bare heels
The great wheel spurs of the Conquistador.
Plunged past us, and were gone:
The crow-bait mount, the fly-bit man.

Not many of our poets could write down a gallop like that one. *Selected Poems* shows a mature and gifted poet, able to use various voices and ways, some apparently inconsistent with each other if one accepts the dictum of the Establishment and looks for one voice only.

Then came *Brother to Dragons: A Tale in Verse and Voices* (1953). The critical debate about this poem goes on, and no doubt it will continue. It ought to, for in *Brother to Dragons* Warren did what everyone had declared impossible. He wrote a book-length narrative poem, highly original in many aspects of both form and content; and he sustained it with power and grace, *as a poem*, from beginning to end. More than anything else, this work managed to bring together the concerns and themes which had separately haunted his poetry and his prose. For any study of his whole work it is crucial. For a consideration of Warren as poet, it marks a turning point, proof positive that the stuff of prose and the stuff of poetry could, in fact, be wedded and live happily together. In a sense, then, after *Brother to Dragons*, Warren was liberated, free to turn to something new if he chose to, equally free to carry along with him whatever he wished from his own poetic experience.

Promises: Poems 1954–1956 lets us see what the direction would be. It is technically different, with new, rolling, long lines based often on stresses and speech rhythm, and new and interesting variations on traditional stanzaic forms. The *language* is different, able now in simultaneity to encompass the prosaic and the "poetic" to create out of disparate parts a total effect of poetry. The earlier virtuosity is here replaced by the much harder trick of surface simplicity and an easy and familiar mystery of the whole range of the living language, from commonplace to "highfalutin" rhetoric. Nothing, no subject, no word, no notion, is to be cast aside as "unpoetic." It is an explosive book and a bold one. A declaration of independence. To those who had counseled reticence and rigor it must have seemed that he was speaking to and of them in the little poem "Work":

> The hand that aches for the pitchfork heft
> Heaves sheaf from the shock's rich disrepair.
> The wagoner snags it in mid-air,
> Says, "Boy, save your strength, 'fore you got none
> left,"
> And grins and wipes the sweat from his hair.[3]

Promises has poems set in Italy, in history, in the South, and in the country of the imagination, but it is a deeply southern book and more inclusively southern than any of the work of the celebrated fugitives. It belongs to what might be called the grand tradition of southern writing, the one which includes so much more than our schoolmarms and schoolmasters (our own Ichabod Cranes), the one which includes our novelists, our backwoods humorists, our lawyers, politicians, and preachers. There are many things which come together in that tradition. Briefly, some of them are: a love of the land which was, and is still in many places, a *beautiful* land, a sense of its history, a strong bond of family, a sense of humor which bubbles out of the ground like fresh springwater in surprising places, and a way with language.

In literature it is this last quality which most clearly distinguishes the southern writer from any other. It is a legitimate child of the tradition of southern rhetoric in life—religious rhetoric, and more specifically political and legal speech. From the beginning of this nation until now, the New England writers have *preached* at people. The more recently arrived, the sophisticated urban writers, learned to talk English from James Cagney movies—out of the sides of their mouths, lively, nervous, and never quite at home with the idiom. The southern writer comes from a race of talkers of another kind. He loves rhetoric for its own sake and without embarrassment. He has a fine, given tradition of it: pulpit rhetoric, grave or comic, calm or evangelical; political oratory, the sounds, not always empty for being stentorian, of a rip-roaring, stumping, and stomping political campaign, a firing-off of rockets, roman candles, catherine wheels, and sparklers in a dazzling display of truth and falsehood; and the long, honored tradition of courthouse rhetoric, great speakers and great men who first voiced this nation's aspirations and follies, our ideals and vices, who once for the pure joy and hell of it would battle as fiercely over the ownership of a hog as the rights of man, seeing no incongruity there, stump or pulpit; bench and bar, they loved the English language, and they taught it to perform, to turn somersaults and to jump through hoops of fire. This love of language long since found its place in southern prose, including the prose of Warren. But until *Promises* it was strictly segregated, separate and utterly unequal, from the world of poetry. In *Promises* Warren achieved a graceful integration.

Now place the book in a scene. The literary scene in which the literary stockbrokers and entrepreneurs were asking themselves: "What will Lowell do next?" "What will become of Richard Wilbur?" "Do you suppose the Beats really *have* anything?" "What will Ciardi think about all this?" "What will James Dickey say?" "Who will get Archie's High Chair at Harvard?" and, above all, "Do we dare to eat a peach?" Into this piddling and unimportant scene came *Promises*, perhaps inimitable, yet offering the example of a poet going his own way at a time when conformity was (and still is) not only expected but also demanded, an experienced poet making a bold sight change and hitting the target again and again while the others were (and still are) trying to learn the basic manual of arms. The poems of *Promises* were different from the earlier poems, yet withal a natural development, spun out of personal need and experience, clearly impossible without much mileage and all the earlier work behind them, clearly the work of a finished poet who was not a victim of the General Motors mentality—a new model every year—nor even, a self-made success through the success of his fiction, evidently much concerned about his place at the establishment feeding trough.

For himself *Promises* must have marked a new sense of freedom and expansion. One which, for a literary parallel, can only be compared to that last astounding harvest of W. B. Yeats. For the young writer it should stand as a living example of the real dream of every real artist, that vision of a late-blooming garden which grows not by hothouse care and protection, not by a florist's dutiful, commercial urging, but richly from the sparse, sandy soil of patience, courage, and fortitude. The baffled Establishment, busily preparing its annual hoop-rolling contest and daisy chain, threw up its hands and awarded Warren the prizes for the year. Then promptly forgot the whole affair. Rushed off with a sigh of relief to the nearest newsstand to pick up the latest *New Yorker* and see what their friends (each other) were up to. There is a fine madness to the poems of *Promises*. None of its poems ever appeared in *The New Yorker*.

There are many interesting and original qualities evident in the poems of *Promises*. Some of these call for special emphasis because they point toward a new direction, one which has, in fact, been followed by Warren in his most recent collection, *You, Emperors, and Others: Poems 1957–1960*. In form and language Warren shows himself more truly a child of the metaphysical poets in these new poems than in the earlier, more obviously and strictly imitative examples. Here, without trying to imitate the language, style, or imagery, he demonstrates a kinship with the whole manner and substance of the metaphysical poem. The metaphysicals, as we all know too well, have been celebrated for the power and originality of their controlled incongruity, for seemingly unrelated ideas and images judiciously yoked by violence together. It is, then, the absence of a strict decorum which marks their poems; or, when a surface decorum is observed, there is, as in Marvell, an ironic, sometimes mocking attitude toward the observance and, thus, the form itself. The former quality shows itself in the ready mixture of high, low, and middle voices, in a range of speech which may, within the same verse unit, jump from high oratory to slang and right back again. And speech is a key word, the viability and excitement of the spoken language as well as the literary tongue. Along with this, inevitably, goes a certain deliberate roughness of form. And all this, whether a literary fashion or an articulate aesthetic (let scholars fight *that* one out), becomes important in its result or effect. Which is the *dramatization* of the mind, body, and spirit, the sensibility of the poet (or speaker in the case of a dramatic monologue) in action. It is the dramatic presentation of the action in progress, rather than the after-the-fact, lyric evocation of a real or imagined experience. This method, then, is daring, has great risks. For the action of the poet's sensibility, exposed in the very act of groping to create the poem, itself becoming the poem which the reader is experiencing and, thus, remaining unfinished until the experience of the poem is finished, this action must be interesting in and of itself.

One gains small insight and less pleasure from watching a sensibility of limited interest groping toward an obvious conclusion.

This, in turn, means a number of things. The poet who would try to write metaphysical verse, then as now, must be a man of the world, experienced both as a man and as a poet-rhetorician. In the best sense he must be sophisticated. It is not, then, a method for the young. Moreover, the method implies that parts and pieces of the well-wrought poem, whether single images, lines, or stanzas, are in themselves meaningless and without interest, however striking, when abstracted from the whole poem. The poem is the unit, not its parts. It shouldn't be necessary to add here that this method goes directly against the grain of much modern critical theory. All those poets and critics who judge by looking for the validity of the line as unit or the realized stanza are, right or wrong, barking up a very different tree.

So it follows, quite naturally (*organically*, one of the fugitives might say), that Warren would experiment with new verse forms as well as play around with old and honored ones. And it follows that, as he found his way, the units would become larger and larger, looking beyond the individual poem to the entire sequence or the book, which, however various, would itself be yoked together. This can be clearly seen in the fact that in these two most recent books Warren has grouped more and more poems together as subunits under one title.

This new method is begun in *Promises* and superbly realized in *You, Emperors, and Others* whose book jacket (*mirabilis!*) for once honestly and simply states that it is "an extension of the lyric voice which made *Promises* such an important literary event." The voice is not a *new* voice. It is a development, a unified version of all the separate, earlier voices into one strain. Image and symbol detectives will easily find the evidence, many of the same images and symbols revised and recurring, to relate the later and earlier poems. Many of the themes and subjects are, of course, the same. The most obvious difference is in the form, in the toughness and verbal activeness of the lines, in the full use of strong, hard-textured, often "unpoetic" words and sounds. For example, the opening stanza of "Gull's Cry" from *Promises*:

> White goose by palm tree, palm ragged, among stones
>   the white oleander,
> And the she-goat, brown, under pink oleander, waits.

I do not think anything in the world will move, not
   goat, not gander.
Goat droppings are fresh in the hot dust; not yet the beetle;
   the sun beats.

It is not just the clear-cut scene nor the *things* which evoke it, but it is also the words themselves, as things with sound and texture, which work here for the hard, clear, clean effect. The intrusion of the speaker in the third line, which might be deplored in a lesser poet as distracting from the scene, works. And the sensitive reader will notice that the end rhymes in this quatrain are not intended to ring like little bells. On the page they are decorative. In the listening experience of the inner ear they serve almost as internal rhyme. For a superb example of the ability of Warren to cram extraordinary variety into small space, to keep both the inner and outer life fully dramatized, look at the concluding couplet of "The Child Next Door," which deals with a retarded peasant child:

I think of your goldness, of joy, how empires grind,
   stars are hurled.
I smile still, saying *ciao*, saying *ciao*, and think:
   this is the world.

One should not ignore the importance of Warren's new direction and achievement within the current literary scene. For more years than it's worth worrying about, modern poets have been trying to find some way to do exactly what Warren has done—to find form, manner, and voice able to contain at once a whole sensibility, a whole spectrum of thought and feeling, faithful to the multiplicity of both the outer and the inner life. Theodore Roethke came as close as anyone in some of his finest poems. But what was presented was an irrational sensibility, one which could communicate, but only by means of shards and fragments painfully dug from the dark strata of the unconscious. Where Roethke might have gone is a moot point, now that he is dead. In some of his recent poems Robert Lowell has shown an inclination to move in this direction; but, for all his energy and power and for all the seeming candor of his confessions, there is one essential quality missing—

coarseness, a healthy vulgarity which might relate his experience to that of another human being. This base and simple element is essential to the alloy which is a whole sensibility. Lowell is painfully conscious of and articulates the vulgarities of the world he lives in, but some inhibition, perhaps the inevitable result of the urban-intellectual milieu, the *literary* world, prevents him doing more than naming the parts. Which, after all, any *New Yorker* writer could do, always implying in the very act of naming that "all this has nothing to do with the real *me*."

Younger poets, too, have been conscious of and chafed against the limitations of the modern lyric mode. But not having lived long enough or learned enough to be interesting, they seem to be left with the alternative of joining either the nose-thumbing, clever crowd, the so-called Beats, or returning to basics, to what might be called "candid-camera poetry," as exemplified by the recent verses of Robert Bly, James Wright, and Louis Simpson.

I mention these things, relating Warren's work to the literary scene, the current fashion show, to point out that whether or not the establishment knows it or likes it, Warren's recent poetry is a very important part of that scene. The poems are important and successful because the poet has all the qualities needed to make them work. He has intellect, sensitivity, and critical acumen; he has extra literary experience as a storyteller and dramatist; he belongs to a strong, vital literary tradition; and he has deep roots, has kept alive a healthy memory of the dirt farm. In short, unlike many of his contemporaries, he can tell the difference between horse manure and shinola without running a lab test.

Using a wide variety of verse forms, ancient, modern, and original, and treating a variety of subjects, Warren has one central theme in *You, Emperors, and Others* which gives the book the unity and coherence of a single poem. The voice is that of an older man, looking back with some nostalgia, viewing the present with intelligent skepticism and sometimes satirical distaste, glimpsing the future, which includes the brute, simple fact of death, with anxiety. The subject or theme of all the poems is classical—the tears of things. Yet this ancient and honorable theme is raised to a higher power by a strongly Christian sense of joy. Along with *history*, the word *joy* occurs over and over again in the resolution of these poems and serves to link the poems together. Whether the poem is an elegy for a boy who fell off a freight train or a ruminative treatment of a Roman emperor, the method is much the same: a long, hard, unblinking look at the naked truth as he sees it, by which exercise is earned a brief vision of the ineffable truth. This is nowhere more explicitly evident than in the final unit in the book, "Nursery Rhymes," tough and sardonic songs of experience, clad in the pleasant rhythms of familiar children's poems. There is something in these poems of the feeling of that masterpiece of modern film art, Fellini's 8 ½ (Warren's book like Fellini's film is at once deeply autobiographical and wildly imaginative), where, at the lowest point, all illusions of Marcello having been stripped away, all losses named and known now to be irrecoverable, with blank despair apparently the only logical conclusion, there is the sudden, earned moment of pure vision. Here, for example, are the last stanzas of "Mother Makes the Biscuits," a peripateia immediately following a catalog of worldly afflictions:

> Clap hands, children,
> Clap hands and sing!
> Hold hands together, children,
> And dance in a ring.
>
> For the green worm sings on the leaf,
> The black beetle folds hands to pray,
> And the stones in the field wash their faces clean
> To meet the break of day.
>
> But we may see this only
> Because all night we have stared
> At the black miles past where stars are
> Till the stars disappeared.

With a very few exceptions (I think, for example, of the poems of John Hall Wheelock and Babette Deutsch), we have not had the good fortune to witness the continued development of an American poet from youth to old age and, with age a certain wisdom. Most of our poets finished, *as poets*, young, left us the undeniable virtuosity of their youthful, lyric voices; a condition so emphatic that many have come to believe that only the young lyric voice is the truly poetic. One might call up Yeats as a poet in English who had a sudden surplus of energy and wrote magnificent poems out of the bone-vexing times of decay and long shadows. I have no hesitation in suggesting that Warren's later poems, in the full power and energy of his hard-earned liberation, in the full freedom of language and form, which exploded in *Promises* and has been consolidated in *You, Emperors, and Others*, are more important to us than the late poems of Yeats. One need not accept wholly and whole cloth his vision. Indeed, that would be impossible without first having lived and worked as long. But for anyone interested in the art of poetry these late poems are important. We have a modern poet whose career and history show a steady growth and blooming which can be compared to those of Picasso and Stravinsky. Quite suddenly the whole history of the establishment seems unimportant, trivial. For poetry is not written by schools or establishments, but by single, lonely poets. If Warren were to conclude now with his final book it would be enough. But in another of the final nursery rhymes, "Cricket, On Kitchen Floor, Enters History," Warren offers us at least the promise of more poems, Lord willing and himself alive and able:

> History, shaped like white hen,
> Walked in the kitchen door.
> Beak clicked once on stone floor.
> Out door walked hen then;
> But will, no doubt, come again.

Though the texture is dry, the texture of old bones pared down fine from the last fat, those who care about American poetry are grateful that one man has come this far. Will be more grateful if he will come again.

Notes

1. Robert Penn Warren, *Thirty-six Poems* (New York: Alcestis Press, 1935). All quotations from *Thirty-six Poems* are from this edition.
2. Robert Penn Warren, *Selected Poems 1923–1943* (New York: Harcourt, Brace, 1944). All quotations from *Selected Poems 1923–1943* are from this edition.
3. Robert Penn Warren, *Promises: Poems 1954–1956* (New York: Random House, 1957). All quotations from *Promises* are from this edition.

8

Warren's Poetry: Some Things We Ought To Be Thinking About

(1990)

That boy's a wonder—has more sheer genius than any of us; watch him: his work from now on will have what none of us can achieve—power.

—Allen Tate to Donald Davidson (1924)

Aside from the fact that Warren is the complete man of letters, one of the last of the vanishing breed, we should always remember that he is first and foremost a poet.

—George Core, "Robert Penn Warren"

So much has already been written for so many years about Robert Penn Warren's poetry—some of it by very public and distinguished critics and some of it also criticism of an exemplary and surpassing excellence—that it seems to be almost redundant, if not irrelevant, to come forward to add yet another reiterative voice to the chorus. And yet there are in Warren's case, as in the case of any major and influential literary artist, some old things to be said again, things to be reminded of and reconsidered, and some newer things, modifications of the critical consensus, or at least some slightly different angles and points of view to be presented. I have at hand no statistics, no charts and graphs, but it seems altogether likely to me, no false claim, that Warren's poetry has received more attention, certainly more *continuous* critical attention for almost half a century, than the work of any other poet in our language and of our time. Other major figures have lived to see their work, if not themselves, initiated and established in the pantheon which, if no certain admission to literary immortality, is nonetheless a sort of promissory note, a passport against future obscurity and oblivion. But these others (one thinks, for instance, of Robert Frost and T. S. Eliot) were, as working poets, past their prime, no longer seriously performing. Warren, on the other hand, was something unusual in our literary history, a poet early recognized, early and often criticized—and usually with appreciation—who went on busily and vigorously writing poetry and, perhaps as important, growing and developing, changing and, indeed, blooming as an artist deep into late old age, into the last months of a long life. Warren is not the first of our elderly poets, not the first voice to speak to us out of shadows that had been mostly silent until modern times. For example, John Hall Wheelock, whose earliest work appeared at the time of World War I, created significant new work in his late eighties and early nineties; and, it should be noted, that as an editor at Scribner's Wheelock introduced us to new poets, to the first books by James Dickey and Louis Simpson and Mary Swenson and David Slavitt, among others. And, as the American population ages and advances in medical science allow for the possibility of a more active and vigorous old age for more and more people, it is unlikely that Warren will stand as quite such a surprising example of the potential for a lifetime of creativity. But an example for the future, a model of excellence and achievement, he is bound to be.

Too much can be made of this essentially minor point, but it is worth remembering that, as a poet, first to last, Warren earned most serious attention, and often the serious praise, of three generations of America's most influential critics. Excluding his own powerfully influential friends and mentors, Tate and Ransom and the others, he found himself receiving encouraging notice from the publication of his first collection, *Thirty-six Poems* (1935). Morton Zabel's review in *Poetry* (April 1936) not only celebrated Warren's "exacting craftsmanship," but also pointed to and encouraged him toward the future: "But the most compelling sign of his worth as a poet appears in the independence he has shown in growing beyond his studious youthful efforts at style and the formidable influences that supervised them." This same kind of encouraging appreciation, usually pointing forward to new directions, led and followed him, as poet, for more than fifty years. Calvin Bedient's very important, if somewhat overwrought and overwritten study, *In the Heart's Last Kingdom: Robert Penn Warren's Major Poetry*, came along in 1984; and *Robert Penn Warren*, from the Modern

Critical Views series, edited by Harold Bloom, was published in 1986. (I have in hand Warren's own personal copy of that volume with its flyleaf inscription in Bloom's hand: "For Red/Homage/to a great poet./ Harold.") From Zabel to Bloom and Bedient is a long haul. Pretty powerful company. And this is not even to consider the generations of poets who wrote about his work and, overwhelmingly, honored it and the man. After his own generation, you have such worthy celebrants as Delmore Schwartz and Randall Jarrell and Robert Lowell. Soon after that come people such as James Dickey, James Wright, and Richard Howard; with inevitable negative cases being argued by, for example, Donald Hall and Sterling A. Brown. The ranks of a slightly younger generation of poets are impressive also; though it should always be remembered that by the time these ambitious young poets appeared on the literary scene Warren was well-established in the venerable position to do them some powerful good or ill, the latter if only by ignoring their efforts and palpable ambitions. Nevertheless, together with the caveat that in general all these younger poets are, for whatever reasons good or bad, too uniformly judgmental of other poets (which Warren never was), these newer poets deserve mention if only as examples of Warren's continuing and powerful influence in recent times: J. D. McClatchy and Laurence Liberman, Dave Smith and T. R. Hummer; even Stanley Plumly.

Honors and awards came early to Warren, beginning with the Caroline Sinkler Award (1936) and persisted without slacking off, including two Pulitzer Prizes for poetry, a National Book Award, the Bollingen Prize. Warren's space in *Who's Who* came close to matching Earl Mountbatten's. He was in due time awarded so many honors, honorary degrees, medals, etc., that some anonymous wag called him the General Pinochet of American Literature in honor not of his politics at all, but rather the top-heavy tinkling appearance of over-decorated Latin American leaders.

Finally, in what amounts to a crucial critical recognition and accolade for any working poet, Warren has been included in most of the worthy anthologies of American poetry since even before the appearance of *Thirty-six Poems*. There are some odd exceptions. Helen Vendler, for instance, in *The Harvard Book of Contemporary American Poetry* (1985), gave space to James Dickey and Dave Smith, both separately much influenced by Warren, but found no place for the original. But others, ranging from Conrad Aiken's wonderfully eclectic and idiosyncratic *Twentieth Century American Poetry* (1944 and 1963), and John Malcolm Brinnin's elegantly exclusive poetic Social Register, *The Modern Poets* (1963), feature Warren's work prominently. So does Richard Ellman and Robert O'Clair's *The Norton Anthology of Modern Poetry*. In their headnotes both these latter books have the highest kind of praise. Says Brinnin, simply enough: "The wide public success of his novels, among them *All the King's Men* and *World Enough and Time*, has at times obscured the fact that he is one of the most accomplished of American poets."

There was a time, and not so long ago, when status in American poetry was earned and conferred by appearance in one or another version of Louis Untermeyer's *Modern American Poetry*. Warren came aboard, and remained so ever afterward, in the fifth revised edition of 1936. And Untermeyer's brisk headnote of the time offers some valid early appraisal: "Intellectual in its origins, Warren's verse remains closer to the earth than the work of his confreres; fertile in strong images, its strength no less than its fecundity rises from Kentucky soil. The critical mind is always at work here, but not so insistently as to inhibit the creative imagination."

Amid all the wealth of criticism and critical materials, one must pick and choose the most useful and beneficial. I find substantial contribution to the appreciation of Warren's poems in various works, early and late, by Cleanth Brooks, Louis D. Rubin, Jr., and George Core. However, my choice for the best all-around critical discussion of Warren's poetry is the essay "Robert Penn Warren as Hardy American," in *American Ambitions* (1987) by Monroe K. Spears.

II

It is time to mediate on what the season has meant.

—Robert Penn Warren, "Fear and Trembling"

In general, the present critical consensus is that the vital center of all of Warren's work is to be found in his poetry. It is hard to fault this perception; since, no matter how wide-ranging his literary adventures—and he seems to have tried everything once at least—and accomplishments (especially in the novel and most especially in *All the King's Men*), he began as a poet and continued, with some interruptions, as a poet until his final year. Warren's first published poems appeared in *The Fugitive* in 1923, at a time when, Louis D. Rubin, Jr., reminds us (in "R.P.W. 1905–1989," *The Sewanee Review,* Spring 1990) that "Thomas Hardy, Joseph Conrad, Anatole France, Henri Bergson, and George W. Cable were still alive."

In his review of *Selected Poems, 1923–1975* Spears points out that this third version of *Selected Poems* follows the example of the earlier two by its arrangement in reverse chronological order and revises the canon by adding and subtracting poems. The emphasis was always forward, featuring the newer poems. "Warren, in thus giving pride of place and preference in bulk to his later poetry, makes his sense of the shape of his own career very plain. More than five-sixths of this volume—268 of its 325 pages—dates from 1954 or later; it is work, then of the poet's middle and later years, from the age of forty-nine on." Even during his extraordinary, highly productive last decade or so, Warren's poetic enterprise included a constant recapitulation and revision of his work to date, a recreation of content, all with a subtle, if specific purpose. "Many of the poems in this volume have been revised, some of them drastically," he wrote in the "Prefatory Note" to *Selected Poems: New and Old 1923–1966.* "But in revising old poems, I have tried not to tamper with meanings, only to sharpen old meanings—for poems are, in one perspective at least, always a life record, and live their own life by that fact." The literary life he describes, the one he was living, was one in which change and discovery, the *new,* served to help understanding of the old, his own past. That is to say, there was coherence even amid the continuing change. Which is something we should keep in mind in examining Warren's achievement.

His view of how the future revises the present and the past should remind us that all the work of a man of letters of Warren's undeniable accomplishments is intricately related to all the rest (like his famous image of the spiderweb in *All the King's Men*) and that although one form, in this case the poetry, may prove to be most important, all his creation in all other forms, however slight or ephemeral, shares in the general meaning and significance of his work as a whole. Thus the reader (and many a critic) needs to be reminded that when Warren was busiest as a novelist, the narrative impulse was mostly directed there and that as he wrote less and less fiction, the storyteller advanced into the expanding frontier of his poetry.

It appears that Warren's final literary work involved the revision of all his poetry, first to last, with the general goal of preparing to leave behind a legacy of his *complete* poetry. Some of the details must, of course, wait upon the completion of Joseph Blotner's authorized biography. But this much appears to be certain, that, working together with his friend, the publisher and book collector Stuart Wright (who was also, at that time, still serving as Warren's literary executor), between October 1986 and January 1988 Warren examined and revised all his poetry written up to that point. Stuart Wright has written: "My initial task consisted in the textual collation of all printed versions of all poems, 1922–1985." Warren, himself, meanwhile began to work (again) with the published books. "In early 1987, probably in February," Wright says, "Warren began rereading and annotating his own copies of the poems, beginning with the *1944 Selected* and ending with the *1985 Selected.*" For three days in May of 1987 Wright and Warren went over every poem line by line. Warren incorporated the changes and revisions into the books: "Warren then marked each of these volumes 'Stuart's copy' or 'Corrected copy for Stuart' and presented them to me for preservation. All poems that contained substantial revisions were then typed up and submitted to Mr. Warren during the late summer of 1987 for his final authority on them."

Sooner or later a patient and knowledgeable scholar will have to go over all the changes Warren made and try to interpret their significance. By and large, as might be expected when the poems had already been subject to much earlier scrutiny and revision, the changes, though many, are small. Some cutting: two whole pages of "Synonyms," for example, from *Being Here* (1980) and two entire poems, from the same volume, cut out—"Tires on Wet Asphalt," marked "bad poem" by Warren, and "Eagle Descending," marked "cut/not good." Most of the revisions, however, are slight, aiming mostly, it seems, at a greater clarity and precision of image or syntax or grammar and often at a sightly smoother rhythm. This latter interested me most; for the rhythms of Warren's later poems have teased and baffled many of his best critics. According to Wright, when they went over the poems Warren would often bang out a line metronomically with any handy instrument and ask if it sounded "right." It has occurred to me that just as so many of Warren's poems are explorations by design, thus shifting and changing, so the rhythms of the later poems can be taken, perhaps appropriately, as *tentative* in character. Which, in a sense, is the strength of them as well as the signature of their individuality. The earlier and more conventionally formal poems of Warren work within relatively simple stanzaic and rhythmic forms. It may be that what could have been a weakness became a compensated strength, that, lacking the ear and the ease of, say, Wilbur or Merrill or Ciardi, Warren was forced to invent and compose his own kind of music. Since time, in all its mysteries, is one of his most urgent and recurring subjects, it seems right that he should work out his own sense of time and breath, like a performing jazz musician, poem by poem.

It is also a part of the general critical consensus that Warren's poetry began to take on its new and improved habits and directions sometime in his middle years. I, myself, contributed something to this view with a piece, published in John L. Longley, Jr.'s *Robert Penn Warren* (1965), "The Recent Poetry of Robert Penn Warren," which is mainly an essay reivew of *Promises: Poems 1954–1956* (1957) and *You, Emperors, and Others: Poems 1957–1960.* Of *Promises* I had this to say (which seems worth saying again here): "It is technically different, with new, rolling, long lines based often on stresses and speech rhythm, and new and interesting variations on traditional stanzaic forms. The *language* is different, able now in simultaneity to encompass the prosaic and the 'poetic' to create out of disparate parts a total effect of poetry. The earlier virtuosity is here replaced by the much harder trick of surface simplicity and an easy and familiar mastery of the whole range of the living language, from commonplace to 'highfalutin' rhetoric. Nothing, no subject, no work, no notion, is to be cast aside as 'unpoetic.' It is an explosive book and a bold one. A declaration of independence."

In general, the chief critical argument of late has been the point at which the newly revised poet, Warren reached his peak and prime. In one sense this speculative history is highly amusing; for, again and again, critics safely assumed, beginning twenty years ago, that Warren was more or less finished, had completed his oeuvre, only to discover, fairly soon, that the old man was still actively creating and doing better work than ever before. Some of the best critics (I think of George Core and Calvin Bedient as exemplary here) argue persuasively that the real "breakthrough" came with *Audubon: A Vision* (1969). Usually, the first published version of *Brother to Dragons* (1953) is credited with helping Warren begin to find his way forward. It does seem that dramatic and narrative projects and sequences served to reinvigorate Warren's whole creative process. If this is so, then later work, like the magnificent *Chief Joseph of the Nez Perce* (1983), is more important than has been fully recognized. At this stage I would, however, suggest only minor modifications of the critical view, fore and aft. I think it is clear, though, that we need to be more open-minded about the continuity and coherence of Warren's poetry.

It seems to me that most of the independent directions he took, the voices he exploited and developed, were already present in Warren's earlier work; that the fashions of poetry began to change and he changed, too, not following the fashions so much as helping to set them.

Certainly he began to favor forms of poetry that were much more open and inclusive, stressing the narrative, dramatic, even (*pace* T. S. Eliot) the ruminative, at the expense of the purely lyrical modes. The long and flexible lines he came to had precedent in Whitman; and, different as they are, I sense a kinship, if not an influence, in Robinson Jeffers. But the language and timing, the energy and syntax, the subjects and the themes were mostly his own and had been there, at least by implication, all along. These lines, climactic, from the early poem "The World Comes Galloping" (out of *Selected Poems 1923–1943*) possess many of the qualities of the much later Warren:

> Then at the foot of that long street
> Between the pastel stucco and the feathery pepper trees,
> Horse and horseman, sudden as light, and loud,
> Appeared,
> And up the rise, banging the cobbles like castanets,
> Plunged:
> Wall-eyed and wheezing, the lurching hammer-head,

The swaying youth, and flapping from bare heels
The great wheel spurs of the Conquistador.
Plunged past us and were gone:
The crow-bait mount, the fly-bit man.

Critics have generally done a first-rate job at outlining what is special and original about Warren's poetic form and content after the middle and late 1950s. As one might expect, their treatment of subject and meaning is more inclusive than their attempts at describing technique. Still, such characteristics as his often gnarled and knotty syntax (as if we were invited to share in the process of thinking and making the poem even as we read it), his compound words, his inversions and generally clotted texture have been highlighted. Less often appreciated, I think, have been his wonderful visual sense, free and easy movement along the whole spectrum of color, of light and shade; his highly sensitive and very precise evocations of weather; his constant use of the shape and flux of memory as a different kind of speech; his sense of humor, never quite absent even in the most serious poems, on the most serious occasions, manifesting itself so many ways, not least in surprising similes (carried over from his early "metaphysical" days?), as here, typically, in "Looking Northward, Aegeanward: Nestlings on Seacliff," from *Rumor Verified: Poems 1979–1980* : "And think how, lost in the dimness of aeons, sea sloshed / Like suds in a washing machine. . . . " Or the celebrated simile from "Homage to Emerson on Night Flight to New York": "My heart / Is as abstract and empty as a Coca-Cola bottle."

What we need now, all the more so since it seems to have been so important to Warren, is an extensive analysis of the coherence of his whole work. Beyond that a step or two, we shall need some serious and innovative critical study of Warren's influence on other poets and also the *interchange* of influence; that is, since he continued, not as a monument but as a living example, not an icon but still a performing creator taking his chances, we need to know much more than we do, more than anyone has been willing to consider, how new directions and movements in contemporary poetry, especially among the impressionable young, may have served to influence him and to help him continue to define and refine his own unique voice. For Warren, as an unabashed man of letters, was preeminently a literary person, aware, more aware than most, of the literary currents, the ebbing and flowing of the American literary tides. Professor by trade, often an editor and more often a judge of the work of others by dint of his position in the hierarchy, he could not have avoided exercising a strong influence, especially on younger poets. That influence is evident in Randall Jarrell's later poems, in the central work of James Dickey, overwhelmingly in the work (so far) of Dave Smith, whose poetry has been powerfully shaped by both Warren and Dickey. Perhaps, from a quite different aesthetic point of view, it can be seen in the growing body of poems by Charles Wright, who sees himself, with some irony, as the natural child of the union of Emily Dickinson to Walt Whitman; but whose long lines and easy juxtaposition of the high-toned and the colloquial, the tacky and the classy (with the latter usually predominant) show the distinct influence of Warren, the elder Southerner. Moreover, Wright's familiar philosophical meditations and ruminations owe a good deal to Warren's unflinching reintroduction of philosophical problems and at times, even in irony, of abstractions into contemporary verse.

All of these poets are Southerners, coming, one way and another out of the Southern tradition. As such they have a special obligation to Warren, as the leading Southern poet who broke free from the ancient and honorable tradition of the "poetic," of the lyric as our ideal form, reintroducing story-telling and public and private vernacular to Southern poetry. (Some critic will note, sooner of later, how Warren's poetry preserved half a century and more of Southern slang.) Faulkner, who also began as a poet, and almost at the same time, could not break free of the Southern mind-set, try as he would. Called himself "a failed poet" and wrote his poetry in his novels.

Sooner or later somebody is going to have to deal with the question of Faulkner's influence, both negative and positive, on Warren. In advance of that study, I propose the notion that Faulkner's overpowering achievement as novelist helped Warren (together with some personal wealth and security which Faulkner never enjoyed) to free himself from the novel and return almost exclusively to poetry.

And there are the others, poets directly influenced one way and the other by Warren, who are not Southerners and not part of that still-undefined literary tradition. Evidently, by choice, Warren did not teach the writing of poetry during his long years at Yale, lest it inhibit his own creativity. But he both taught or knew any number of young poets who passed through Yale. And, one way and another, he was helpful to them. One thinks of known examples—Mark Strand, David Slavitt, John Hollander. We need to know more about this.

And not to forget his own daughter, Rosanna Warren, who has published her poems, including a couple of volumes, over the past few years.

III

The world drives at you like a locomotive in an archaic movie.

—Warren, "Notes On A Life To Be Lived"

Finally, it seems to me that we shall, sooner or later, need to examine what parts of Warren's life and times, most of this century, "our present maniacal century" he called it in "What Were You Thinking, Dear Mother?," are *not* present and *not* to be found in his poetry.

Much that is directly out of headlines, magazines, and the blue-green flicker of television, is powerfully present, as here in these lines from "Function of Blizzard":

> Black ruins of arson in the Bronx are whitely
> Redeemed. Poverty does not necessarily
> Mean unhappiness. Can't you hear the creak of
> bed-slats
> Or ghostly echo of childish laughter? Bless
> Needle plunging into pinched vein. Bless coverings-
> over, forgetting.

But a poet, any writer, is to be known by his choices, what he chooses not to write about, what doesn't interest him enough. Except distantly, Warren never wrote anything much about the academic world he lived and worked in so much of his life, or about the gilt and glamor of the high-style literary life he enjoyed for many years. Elegant names appear in dedications, but not in person. Joy of many kinds is celebrated, but seldom with the (surely familiar) pop of a Moet-Chandon champagne cork. The speaker in so many of the poems is a plainer man, still something of a country boy, meat and potatoes man, one of us. Perhaps this comes from Warren's desire, noted by Monroe Spears, to be "a representative man."

Although at several times and in several places Warren called his work a "shadowy autobiography," and even though he tells us much that is inward and spiritual about himself—for instance the deep loneliness and the sense of what has to be named homesickness which haunt his poems, first to last—he is not free and easy with the outward and visible details. We may, with Blotner's biography in hand, be able to read between many somewhat enigmatic lines; but Warren's intention, clearly, was not to assume that popular overtly confessional mode.

Only a true literary celebrity could have written what he did when and as he did. But Warren did not act like a celebrity in his poems or in his life. Perhaps he was (as he must have been, moving among the great and greatly honored for most of his adult life) all too aware of the shabby illusions generated by a world which soon enough honored celebrity for its own sake and which, thus, in his lifetime more and more became a matter of image without corresponding reality, shadows without substance; and soon enough came to bestow honor not only upon ordinary mountebanks and confidence men (some poets among them), but also thieves, perjurers, murderers, rapists, perverts, etc. It may be that Warren's art and life were, at least in part, a constant and successful (in his own terms) rearguard action against all that.

Anyway, he is beyond wounds and blessings, praise and blame now. I like to imagine that he has passed beyond the wounds of memory— "Far back, scraps of memory hang, rag-rotten on a rusting barbed-wire fence" ("Antinomy: Time and Identity"). And is shaking his fist at the wind like the rhyming speaker of "Autumnal Equinox on Mediterranean Beach":

> . . . come bang
> To smithereens doors, and see if I give a hang.

III

From The Hollins Critic

Author's Note

Louis D. Rubin, Jr., created *The Hollins Critic* in the early 1960s (in the academic year 1963–1964, I think), and it is still very much in existence, going on today. I wrote for it for a while, co-edited it with John Rees Moore later, and have kept up with it ever since. The idea was and remains a good one—a new book by a good and serious writer is reviewed, usually in terms of the writer's whole career up to that point, in an essay of, give or take, five thousand words. The issue also offers a checklist of published books by the author in English, hardcover and paperback, together with a drawing of the writer by artist Lewis Thompson, and a few poems. The only significant change has been the addition, as a kind of appendix to the issue, of a number of shorter reviews of other recent books. It is worth keeping in mind that all these books were new, still in the marketplace, enjoying a shelf life in the bookstores, when they were reviewed in *The Hollins Critic*. The big quarterlies had a later, and maybe the last, critical word; but for the most part they were talking about out-of-print and remaindered books. Except for *The World & I*, the astonishing magazine for *The Washington Times*, which devotes an average of one hundred and fifty pages and more every month to essay-length book reviews, *The Hollins Critic* is unique and, I like to think, uniquely valuable.

John Cheever
and the Charms of Innocence:
The Craft of *The Wapshot Scandal*
(1964)

These stories were no worse than the stories of talking rabbits he had been told as a boy but the talking rabbits had the charms of innocence.

—John Cheever, *The Wapshot Scandal*

The first thing that should be said and not forgotten is that *The Wapshot Scandal* is a very good novel, an outstanding piece of work and craft by any known standard of judgment and it is the best book John Cheever has written. Since his earlier and first novel, *The Wapshot Chronicle*, received a National Book Award for 1957, this means that in the world of prizes and awards and in the circles where there is jostling for the laurel wreath of Success, a game as shrill and chaotic as Drop-the-Handkerchief, it is a book and Cheever is an author who must be taken quite seriously this season. Already *The Wapshot Scandal* has received very good notices and reviews and, what is more important, these have been in the most prominent and choice spots, as significant as the fire hydrant in front of a fashionable restaurant where only certain shiny limousines with very special license tags are permitted to park. In the front-page lead review for the *New York Herald-Tribune* (and other papers) Glenway Wescott, not only an artist himself but also an arbiter with charm, influence, and definite opinions, saluted the publication of the book with high praise, seasoned with just a mere soupçon of qualification. He found in the book many of the virtues which he at once celebrates and pleads for in *Images of Truth*: clarity, lucidity, decorum, a fine surface of sensuous aesthetic experience supported on the firm rock strata of meaning and implication. He saw it as tragi-comic, a book thus accurately reflecting the ambivalent feelings of a man of feeling in our time. Elizabeth Janeway in the front page review of *The New York Times Book Review* celebrated the book chiefly in terms of anecdotes she just couldn't resist retelling and by pointing out the extremely clever and "deceptive" use of symbol and analogy employed by Cheever to give the haunting resonance of deep meaning and wide implication. *The Washington Post* offered its highest compliment by stating that the cosmic view of the novel, unflinching honesty lifted by the wings of hope and wisdom, was a fine example of the working philosophy of our late president. Most recently Cheever has received the mixed blessing of a *Time* cover story. It remains to be seen whether or not the celebrated jinx will work.

If there is any justice in this world, *The Wapshot Scandal* is on its way. Whether or not it climbs to a place on the best-seller lists and endures there for a proper interval remains to be seen, is in the hands of Lady Luck and, of course, that vast, faceless, surging, restive mob, the reading public which, like the voting public and the razor-blade-using public, nobody really knows for sure and practically everybody mistrusts. *The Wapshot Scandal* may or may not sit in the spotlighted position of the best-seller list, but it does not take a gypsy to predict that the book and its author will be much discussed in the coming months, not only in cocktail parties and reading groups, but also in seminar and classroom. High time too. John Cheever has been producing honorable work for more than twenty years and from the beginning he has always threatened to become "a major writer." Perhaps he has at last earned that title. One thing we can be sure of. He has written a good book in a time when good books are few and far between. And that's a cause for celebration. It is, however, at once a better and a *different* book than his reviewers have allowed, and it is quite good enough to be subjected to the kind of inquisition, the rack of speculation and the thumbscrew of questions without easy answers, which only the strong and brave should be asked to endure.

II

She loves the fine, the subtle, the non-cliché . . .

—from an advertisement in *The New Yorker*

John Cheever is a *New Yorker* writer and may be the best of the bunch. Of course, we all know that both the editors and writers for that distinguished magazine would deny and have denied that a *type* exists.

Let us understand the reasons for the denial and ignore it. No use pretending Shakespeare didn't write for the Elizabethan stage. Any magazine worth its weight has a character, one which is partly created by editorial standards and equally by the relationship the magazine enjoys with its readers. *The New Yorker* has a third power haunting, if not dominating, the present, a history long enough already to be called a tradition. We know a good deal about the beginning and the early years of *The New Yorker.* The names—Ross, Thurber, E. B. White, Gus Lobrano, Gibbs, and so many others—are celebrated, have been recorded in many a popular, nostalgic reminiscence and have passed beyond mere household familiarity to stand, aloof but never lonely, bronzelike with a nice patina, in the cluttered museum of public mythology. By now at least two generations of Americans have thumbed through *The New Yorker* with pleasure. Didn't we cut our teeth on the magazine's own major contribution to our culture—the cartoons? Still, a popular magazine is a business. Just as the politician must get himself elected, so a magazine must turn a profit to insure its own self-preservation. We have seen magazines come and go, succeed and fail. *The New Yorker* has not only survived; it has prospered, bloomed. Which means, that no matter how adventurous the editorial policy and no matter how well it has been able to adapt itself to the facts of life, change and decay, there is still at heart a basic purpose, that of self-preservation. And thus the preservation of the status quo is not just an aim but a duty.

The New Yorker reflects all these things yet has a general history of its own. And there are a few general things about it which have to be said. One is that over many years *The New Yorker* has been a patron of many writers. More and more steadily than have foundations or colleges or rich old ladies with buzzing hearing aids and ropes of pearls. It is also true that it has specifically patronized the finest second-rate talents of our times. No use arguing. It is simply a fact that none of the acknowledged masters of the art of writing fiction or poetry from the first half of our century has been a regular contributor to the magazine. Maybe this will change, but a literary historian would not bet on it. The remarkable thing is that *The New Yorker* has always maintained a very high level of consistent quality and craftsmanship. Which, of course, is something even, perhaps especially, the masters themselves have not done.

John Cheever and the Charms of Innocence

The vintage *New Yorker* story became a model for the modern short story. Briefly it was the maximum exploration and exploitation of a single dramatically presented incident, more or less strictly observing the unities of time and place and rich in implication, both in depth of characterization and in a larger implied story which had a past and predicated a future. Plot, in the conventional sense, was largely absent, as were the middle-class moral dilemmas of slick fiction. In setting the stories were either regional—the East and occasionally the uncorrupted West or the passive and amusing South, or foreign and exotic. Naturally the stories reflected the general moral views of the magazine and its public—reasonably but not ostentatiously well-informed, perhaps a little snobbish, though united against the more common forms of snobbery, more or less liberal politically. It was never, not even in the case of certain religious writers, religious. Its moral fiber, its touchstone was a kind of secular humanism coupled with a gentle intellectual agnosticism. The virtues it honored were all civilized virtues, sedentary, sophisticated and rational, all defended by the curtains (never made of iron) of humor, irony, sensitivity, the skeptical intelligence, and a form of gentility which was au courant. Minor figures who entered wearing the white hat signifying a good guy were charming eccentrics, happy-go-lucky losers, cheerful outsiders. Members of the lower classes, those of whom it could be safely said they didn't read *The New Yorker*, and people from other older generations were permitted to display a healthy-minded vulgarity. Those worthy of attention from the class (let's face it—middle) of the readers themselves were usually attractive physically, possessed of charm, and perhaps distinguished by the blessing or burden of a little extra sensitivity and more intelligence than is average. The mortal sins in this universe were, inevitably: vulgarity without the redemption of eccentricity, self-pity, stupidity, hypocrisy, bad manners, complacency, excess of passion, and a lack of good health or physical attractiveness. In short, *New Yorker* fiction was a fiction of manners, and its purpose, classical from tip to toe, was to instruct as it delighted. Nature, of course, was neutral and basically good. It was, however, an idyllic nature, in its own way as formalized and stylish as an eighteenth-century pastoral. There was a kind of tourist's view of the natural world replete with the names of plants and animals, these, however, always shining like coins or rare stamps in a

---

collector's album. Still essentially progressive, still haunted by the last of the evolutionary analogies, *The New Yorker* viewed the worst excesses of modern civilization with distaste and sometimes with alarm, but never with despair. For, no matter how black the present, how fraught with peril the future, or how quaint the past, the fiction and poetry of *The New Yorker* walked forward hand in hand with the advertisements and "The Talk of the Town," always moving toward the vague but discernible horizon, the glow of which indicated at least the possibility of a Jerusalem of The Good Life somewhere up there among the Delectable Mountains and just beyond the reach of the clean fingernails of the Ideal Reader.

During World War II the form of the story began to change. And here we return to John Cheever, who had something to do with changing it.

III

We are no longer dealing with midnight sailings on three-stacked liners, twelve day crossings, Vuitton trunks and the glittering lobbies of Grand Hotels.

—*The Wapshot Scandal*

From the beginning with "The Way Some People Live" (1943) and on through the publication of "The Enormous Radio" (1953) the stories of John Cheever in *The New Yorker* (as of this date he has published more than one hundred there) have exhibited an independence of form. Perhaps it was inevitable that this would happen now that the "single event" story has been widely anthologized, taught in schools, and is somewhat less than chic. Anyway, for whatever reason, the stories of John Cheever and of some others who appear in that magazine, are now most often much less "dramatic," much more free in the survey of time and space. Cheever, for example, characteristically ranges widely in point of view and also in tense, sometimes past, sometimes present, occasionally even future and conditional. There is a much more positive exploitation of the narrator-writer of the story. He ap-

John Cheever and the Charms of Innocence

pears openly like the chorus of an early Elizabethan play, does his best
to establish an intimacy and rapport with his reader, and then cheerfully re-enters from time to time to point out significant objects or to
make intelligent comment. Like a cultivated and slightly superior museum guide, the narrator is clever and witty yet always *sympathetic* to
the reader because of his slight, pleasing smile, his gentle habit of self-
depreciation, and his wry, yet knowing shrug. The narrator is up-to-
date in his allusions, his knowlege of the *things* of this world, and can,
if necessary, but not without a wink of misgiving, use the latest slang.
His own language is exact, always a model of lucidity and decorum, free
from the unrefined extravagance of poetic frenzy, yet able from time to
time to reach a modest altitude on the slopes of Olympus, far from the
sweaty chaos of the laughing white gods, but anyway a place with a
view near timberline where a gourmet picnic might be spread.

Cheever has introduced a new freedom in the form. The meaning of
this kind of form is fairly clear. It wants to *say more*, not only about
persons, places, and things, but also about what these things mean,
what patterns they make. Cheever has, for example, from the beginning blithely and easily introduced the world of dreams into his stories.
His characters dream a good deal and they do it matter-of-factly. He
has also permitted them to digress, to reminisce, to imagine. And it is
one of his special abilities and triumphs that he can lead them (and the
reader) step by step credibly from a perfectly "realistic" situation into
the areas of farce or nightmare. Perhaps this is what one reviewer
meant when he wrote, "It is as if Marquand had suddenly been crossed
with Kafka."

Cheever is deeply interested in character and he knows his fictional
charcters by giving them depth, veils and layers of experience, and the
loose ends and untied shoelaces of living, breathing beings. One has
only to compare and contrast his treatment of characters with that of
Mary McCarthy. Her people are mannequins, shoved in a store window and stripped naked for the amusement of the reader. It would be
obscene if her characters were not wooden. It would be cruel if her
characters did not in the end seem to be lifted out of somebody else's
book or story she is criticizing. Cheever has a good deal of sympathy for
his people and if they sometimes fail, in spite of the latest methods of
resuscitation and artificial respiration, to breathe the breath of life, it

is apt to be because he becomes impatient, quite naturally, with the extremely difficult demands he has set upon himself.

On the early stories, probably the most intelligent critical remarks come from William Peden in his excellent notes to the anthology *Twenty-Nine Stories* (1960). First Peden makes an important comparison, calling Cheever "an urbane and highly civilized social satirist" like Galsworthy. Peden goes on to say, judiciously: "Few writers have depicted more skillfully than he the loneliness and emptiness of certain segments of contemporary society." And he points out that each and all of the stories have been chiefly concerned with "the corrosive effect of metropolitan life upon essentially decent people who are isolated, defeated, or deprived of their individuality in the vastness of a great city." If you wisely include the proliferating suburbs as a part of the great city and if you weigh Peden's words, that is about the long and the short of it.

But we are talking about Cheever the novelist. Even though both his novels have appeared in bits and pieces, slightly re-edited for formal reasons, as stories in *The New Yorker*. And even though his two most recent collections of stories—*The Housebreaker of Shady Hill* (1958) and *Some People, Places, and Things That Will Not Appear in My Next Novel* (1961)—are so constructed as to qualify as novels if the definition of that form is at last liberated from certain arbitrary restrictions. More and more *all* the parts of Cheever's work are clearly parts of a whole. What he has to say to the world has changed a little as the world has changed. But not so much as one might imagine. And not so much as *The Wapshot Scandal* intends.

One thing needs to be said here and now. Clearly it is more than difficult, it is a *feat*, to be a serious writer and at the same time to share without much questioning not only the standards, but also the whole set of rules and bylaws of a social club as cozy and intimate and proud as *The New Yorker*. It is hard not to end up sounding like a tape recording of clever cocktail party chatter. Yet John Cheever has achieved the delicate balance and done it with the bravado of the tightrope walker in top hat and tails, bottle in hand, who seems to stagger across the dangerous wire. No one can deny that he is a good serious writer. No one can deny the achievement he has already demonstrated. And this would be true if he never wrote another line.

John Cheever and the Charms of Innocence

The *Wapshot Chronicle* appeared in 1957 and won a National Book Award for that year. As in the case of all prizes, it was and will remain debatable whether his first novel was the *best* book of the year, but it was a fine one and it was a cause for jubilation in the circles of those who care. More important than prizes, praise, or blame, he created with economy and dispatch a lively novel which included a town, St. Botolphs, and its people, a family, the Wapshots, from the *Arabella* up to, almost, the present; a variety of characters and events, of anecdotes and parables and fables, and at least two thoroughly memorable and realized characters—Leander and Miss Honora. It was full of humor ranging from bathroom jokes (the Wapshot toilet was haunted and occasionally flushed itself in the middle of the night), to farce (the book *opens* with a runaway horse-drawn float bearing the Women's Club far from a Fourth of July parade), to moments of modern sophisticated comedy involving psychiatrists, crazy castles, and the style and tone of Leander Wapshot's journal, one of the happiest devices of the novel. That Leander has sinned grievously and has a truly nightmarish vision of a rutting hell before he drowns himself becomes at least modified by the fact that he is allowed to have the last word in his journal, a word of advice for those who come after him.

Advice to my sons . . . Never put whiskey into hot water bottle crossing borders of dry states or counties. Rubber will spoil taste. Never make love with pants on. Beer on whiskey, very risky. Whiskey on beer, never fear. Never eat apples, peaches, pears, etc. while drinking whiskey except long French-style dinners, terminating with fruit. Other viands have mollifying effect. Never sleep in moonlight. Known by scientists to induce madness. Should bed stand beside window on clear night draw shade before retiring. . . . Avoid kneeling in unheated stone churches. Ecclesiastical dampness causes prematurely gray hair. Fear tastes like a rusty knife and do not let her into your house. Courage tastes of blood. Stand up straight. Admire the world. Relish the love of a gentle woman. Trust in the Lord.

In his history of the Wapshots and St. Botolphs Cheever offers a history of the nation, its growth, bloom, and the question of its possible decay and corruption. The tone is tolerantly amused and nostalgic dealing with the past, lyrical about nature and especially about trout fishing in the unspoiled Canadian wilderness, a little sad about the decline and decay of a small town, satirical about the excesses of the urban and suburban revolution and the desperate impersonality, the flight from freedom and responsibility of modern times. A beautiful satirical point of view is created by sending Young Moses Wapshot to Washington and Young Coverly first to New York and then to a missile site or two, two young rubes against whose bemusement and bafflement the modern urban milieu could be measured.

The book is rich in implication, gained by the "tricks" Elizabeth Janeway so admires, the time-honored method of storytellers from Homer on of acquiring larger implication by allusion, analogy, the echo of an event or a myth. And, as one might expect, these allusions and echoes are chiefly from the wellspring, the pure water of our culture, the classics and the Bible, always used in such a way as to be *functional* decoration. Venus is the reigning deity, yet she is ambiguous, sometimes seen *in bono*, sometimes *in malo*. There are deaths, births, and entrances. It is truly a chronicle, giving the impression of sprawling largess, weight and size, whereas, in fact, it is not really a long novel. A virtuoso performance.

What does the book say? It says all men are sinners, but it is possible to be good, loving, and brave. It says the good old days weren't all that good, but that, indeed, something has happened to the American dream, that it is approaching nightmare. It says that the nightmare is there in the best of us, but it is still possible to hold up your head and "admire the world." For a book with much pathos and misfortune it ends on a positive note of instruction, made palatable by the sweetness of Leander's simplicity and Cheever's irony.

And that could be that. Except that he has chosen to continue the Wapshot history by continuing it into our time. The books are related, but not strictly sequential. Though some of the same people appear in both, they are somehow changed and modified by the times. They are not quite the same characters. And the world, even its history, is now different. The tone and style are different. (We miss the vitality of Leander's journal, which only appears once.) Things disintegrate, decay, blur out of focus, fall apart. The relationship is much like that of *The Rainbow* and *Women in Love* or, closer to home, of *The Hamlet* to *The*

Town. Which is to say the two books are Cheever's old testament, written of the time of myths, the law, and the prophets, and his new testament, beginning now on a Christmas Eve and ending, although on Christmas, with a curious last supper to be followed shortly by the last book of the Bible—the Apocalypse. The sins of *Chronicle* are original sin. *Scandal* moves inexorably toward the end of the world. Thus the two books must be taken together; but, as in scriptural exegesis, we must not gloss the new law with the old.

The difference between the two can be illustrated by a small thing. Cheever's writing has always been marked by its representative use of the five senses. But in *Chronicle* it is smell, the odors of the world, the flesh, and the devil which predominate. There are great patches and lists of good odors, rich savors. *Scandal* is, by contrast, practically odorless. Most of the odors are bad or sordid and linger to haunt us like ambivalent ghosts. The author-narrator makes this quite explicit, saying that "we leave behind us, in the hotels, motels, guest rooms, meadows and fields where we discharge this much of ourselves, either the scent of the goodness or the odor of evil, to influence those who come after us." In another place a character surveys fallen apples: "Paradise must (he thought) have smelled the windfalls." But in contrast to *Chronicle* the predominant sensuous patterns of *Scandal* are all black and white, the presence or the absence of light. " 'Light and shadow, light and shadow,' says old Cousin Honora of the music. She would say the same for Chopin, Stravinsky or Thelonious Monk."

IV

I want to put on innocence like a bright new dress. I want to feel clean again!

—*The Wapshot Scandal*

The Wapshot Scandal begins in St. Botolphs and somehow ends there, after following the young sons of Leander, Moses and Coverly, through many misadventures and following Cousin Honora to Rome and back, fleeing an investigator of the Internal Revenue Service, to her death by self-starvation. It is, however, principally concerned with Coverly, Moses' wife Melissa, and Cousin Honora. Moses, the favored and luckier of the two boys, was never fully realized in *Chronicle* and is really no more than a shadow in *Scandal*. Concentrating on these three characters, Cheever keeps the story happily bouncing back and forth, pausing now and then for a wonderfully relevant digression, moving across wide spaces and through patches of time as if waving a passport which reads "freely to pass." Now Cheever is for the most part on his old stamping ground, and Proxmire Manor, where Moses and Melissa exist, is a dead ringer for Shady Hill. The opportunities for satire of the present state of things are manifold and Cheever doesn't miss a trick. It's all there— suburbia, the economy of indebtedness, the religion of the churches, TV, space exploration, scientiests and missiles, drugs and cancer, repairmen, undertakers, drive-in theaters, superhighways, frozen food, computers, "the sumptuary laws," travel, indifferent clerks and airline stewardesses, a daring airline robbery, Congressional hearings, security clearance and the income tax, homosexuality, advertising slogans, doctors and the AMA, a male beauty contest, blue plastic swimming pools, outdoor barbecues, shabby and unsuccessful adulteries; oh it's all there all right, God's plenty of the outward and visible signs of a time when "standards of self-esteem had advanced to a point where no one was able to dig a hole," a wild, yet terrifying imitation of "a world that seemed to be without laws and prophets."

The full range of humor is there too. The basic slapstick—"Oh, the wind and the rain and to hold in one's arms a willing love! He stepped into a large pile of dog manure." The irony of character; a wounded veteran thinks: "He could have gotten a deferred job at the ore-loading docks in Superior and made a fortune during the war but he didn't learn this until it was too late." The author-narrator's special brand— describing Proxmire Manor as a village which "seemed to have eliminated, through adroit social pressures, the thorny side of human nature."

It is part of the irony and humor of this book that the whole plan of the story is told in capsule in what appears to be an irrelevant digression, the story of a woman, scarcely known by Melissa, whose ruin and downfall began the day the septic tank backed up. Step by step, we follow her into a nightmare of disintegration as, one by one, each of her appliances breaks down and cannot be repaired; she becomes a drunk and an adulteress and ends a suicide. (The book is full of suicides to underline the suicidal inclination of the age.) The pattern of this digression is repeated over and over again. Begin with a credible, typical situation, push it an inch or two into the realm of hilarious farce, then the farce all of a sudden becomes dream, and all dreams turn to nightmare. It is typical of Cheever that he backs into his moral plea to the world behind the mask of irony, permitting his mouthpiece to be a decrepit old senator on a congressional investigating committee speaking out to Doctor Cameron, a mad missile scientist:

> "We possess Promethean powers but don't we lack the awe, the humility, that primitive man brought to the sacred fire? Isn't this a time for uncommon awe, supreme humility? If I should have to make some final statement, and I shall very soon for I am nearing the end of my journey, it would be in the nature of a thanksgiving for stout-hearted friends, lovely women, blue skies, the bread and wine of life. Please don't destroy the earth, Dr. Cameron," he sobbed. "Oh, please, please don't destory the earth."

Yet the earth and the people in it seem inevitably headed for destruction. Even grand old Cousin Honora kills herself. But, like Leander, she leaves a legacy, not a journal but a Christmas dinner to which she has, as always, invited enough strangers to make the magic number twelve. It is Coverly, unlucky and so often defeated, who pulls together, picks up the pieces and keeps the last Christmas dinner in honor of his cousin. He attends a Christmas Eve service performed by a drunken, ineffectual Episcopal priest, and does his duty by staying alone in the church until the last *amen*. In the morning he collects what is left of the Wapshots and they await the arrival of Honora's eight invited guests. Who turn out to be all inmates of The Hutchins Institute for the Blind, only two of whom are identified, an Old Testament type muttering the wrath of God on the sinners and a sweet Negress who carries the simple message of love and mercy in a gesture. Of these guests Coverly thinks:

> They seem to be advocates for those in pain; for the taste of misery as fulsome as rapture, for the losers, the goners, the glops, for those who

dream in terms of missed things—planes, trains, boats and opportunities—who see on waking the empty tarmac, the empty waiting room, the water in the empty slip, rank as Love's Tunnel when the ship is sailed; for all those who fear death.

It is a profoundly moving conclusion and as close to an explicit statement of Christian faith as I have seen from a *New Yorker* writer, perilously close to religion. Venus has been ubiquitous in this book, too, but here she is clearly the old Venus *in malo*, whose rewards are folly and degradation, who is the first handmaiden of Dame Fortune who gives all who serve her a spin on the wheel. (If this sounds almost medieval, it is. There is even a mysterious archer, clad all in red, who fires an arrow at Coverly and, fortunately, misses.) In *Scandal* John Cheever makes a firm and definite distinction between false love (*cupiditas*) and the love that moves the stars (*caritas*). And he ends on the note we are now familiar with, for there is no other song or burden for our times, that "we must love one another or die."

For all these reasons *The Wapshot Scandal* is at once John Cheever's most ambitious work and his finest achievement. Because he is an artist with his own voice and because he has earned the right to speak out in that voice, it is a fine achievement in the art of the novel this year or any year.

V

It seemed incredible to him that his people, his inventive kind, the first to exploit glass store fronts, bright lights and continuous music, should have ever been so backward as to construct a kind of temple that belonged to the ancient world.

Johnson, an agent of the Internal Revenue Service, views a classic white-steepled New England church, *The Wapshot Scandal*

Now the quibbling begins. It will be brief. Yet there are a few things to be said—a few. They will not be exactly objective or fair, for ultimately critical judgment cannot be. It may be that if I break the rules and simply state a few personal prejudices and feelings, it will enable the *reader* anyway to judge for himself. First, I am Southern and from as far back as any Wapshot. The Southern background does make a difference. We have never rejoiced in the civilization Mr. Cheever satirizes. In fact it is none of our own. Deep in our hearts, if not in our heads, we feel, perhaps smugly, that it is the end result of all that grand, hypocritical spirit which erupted in New England and would not rest until it had destroyed ours. We feel New England and Mr. Cheever are getting what they asked for and deserved. Perhaps a little more rational is the notion, which is inevitably entertained by those who have had the historical experience of defeat, that disillusionment is a naive posture. There is an air of excitement, urgency and anger, an air of *discovery* about Cheever's treatment of human suffering, of its trinity of devils—poverty, disease, and ignorance. One must resist the temptation of the inner smile, the inner voice which says, " 'Tis new to thee."

People do not live like people in *The New Yorker*, try as they may, and they never will. The insulation of that world is foolish and as forlorn as the storm windows Cheever characters are forever putting up and taking down. There may well be a system of election and damnation, but the elect are not necessarily the charming, the gifted, the beautiful, the eccentric, or even the innocent. Nor are they necessarily children, cripples, Negroes, or victims. There is no text which says that God cannot look with love upon the stupid, the cruel, the vulgar, the hypocritical, and the guilty. It is these who need His love most, and it is these whom we have been commanded to love. And that is most difficult. I am not talking about Salinger's Fat Lady. (There's a Fat Lady seen briefly in *Scandal.*) After much trial and error Salinger's Glass family discovered that it is possible to love the Fat Lady. Cheever has come to that conclusion too. But in truth we are not advised to love the unlovable, we are *commanded* to. You don't get medals or merit badges for obeying orders. It is to the point that in medieval allegories most of the time the devil did not wear red at all. He came in green, camouflaged in the color of faith.

What I am saying is that although this book makes a plea for charity, it does not practice it. Sympathy, yes; compassion, yes, for some characters; and sentimentality is abundant and aplenty. For what is sentimentality but a deep concern for human suffering which disregards the human spirit?

Now a few quibbles in rapid, random order:

(1) historical—political—social

Historically the book is very inaccurate precisely because it exists in a vacuum. More obviously in *Chronicle* but also in *Scandal,* both of which intend to deal with the American experience, the *events* of that experience impinge almost not at all upon the characters. It is as if Cheever divided American history into two periods—the Quaint Period, from the *Mayflower* to the middle 1930s, and the Vulgar Now, the time of guided missiles and frozen food. Does he really believe that all the wars and the Depression had *no* influence on the American character? Or is it that "we all know all about that anyway"? Do we really? Have we progressed that far?

(2) moral-theological

Have already quibbled once. But we have been told, wisely I believe, by a pope, that to consider our own age as especially characterized by sin and corruption is a form of spiritual pride and also quite silly. We may be destroyed or destory ourselves, but it will not be because of our highly developed and high-powered immorality. Morally Cheever appeals to every sane human being. Nobody, even the men at the missile stations, wants to destroy the world or do away with blue skies, trout streams, butterflies, old houses, *The New Yorker,* or even the literary status quo. It is not likely, on the other hand, that Cheever's moral message will restrain one maniac from pulling a lever or a trigger.

(3) literary

Though an innovator of sorts, Cheever has made a *habit* of his innovations. They are altogether acceptable now and, it seems, that suits him fine. At times his method and virtuosity disguise a kind of carelessness and indifference. The verisimilitude he must start with, no matter how deeply into dream or farce he goes, is not always there just because he is able to hang out a list of *things* and current phrases (like the little flags on used-car lots). He drops characters who don't interest him and lets others exist in a realm of two-dimensions and cliché. Well, it is his world, isn't it? And one has to admire his bravado. Still, with all admiration, it would be a lie not to admit to the feeling that it

John Cheever and the Charms of Innocence

is very *safe*. The man on the flying trapeze with a good safe net beneath. The lion tamer cutting a caper in a cage full of toothless lions.

These quibbles don't add up to much. What should one ask of *The Wapshot Scandal?* It is a good book by a good writer, more than good enough and better than we deserve. It is just good enough to be judged against the ideal of greatness. Which may be asking too much.

To Do Right in a Bad World:
Saul Bellow's *Herzog*
(1965)

But the deadly earnestness with which they lower the boom! On what?
after all. On flowers. On mere flowers.

—Saul Bellow, Herzog

I approach this one with more than routine fear and trembling. Not just because *Herzog* has been out a while, has received attention from the top-paid, top-rated reviewers and critics in all the top places, has been almost uniformly liked and praised (except for a magazine piece or two where somebody with an eye on the main chance for critics tried to be different), has received the high compliment of being subjected to parody in *The New Yorker*, has climbed onto the best-seller list and hung in there too. Not just because everybody says Saul Bellow is an *intellectual* and the only honest-to-God intellectual I know agrees. Not just because Saul Bellow has been writing good books for twenty years which means he was a bona fide, card-carrying pro while I was still chasing fly balls in right field and didn't know a good book from third base. Not just because he has been written about in books and articles and has written articles about writing himself, so that anybody who comes racing into the game at this stage had better be clever or else maybe ignorant, or both. Not just because he is a Jew and a Jewish writer and I am not and even my grandmother wasn't. Not just because I admire his work, I envy his gifts and wish, secretly, that he would step down hard on a large, ripe banana peel and take a memorable pratfall, etc., over teakettle and end up writing anonymous dialogue for Soupy Sales, filling in balloons for *Little Orphan Annie*. Not just for these reasons but for all of them and more.

But herewith, having duly warned everyone, admitted some premed-
itated and accidental faults, confessed to a lack of proper credentials,
and no doubt already driven off a country fair number of readers with
an undeniable display of a serious lack of high seriousness, I seem to
have stumbled on a banana peel myself and landed smack upon—a
method. Obviously, then, the method will have to be personal with all
the limitations that implies. It will have to be appreciative and fragmentary. I hope it will be honest.

II

When Nelson Algren said, in *Conversations with Nelson Algren*, that
Saul Bellow has been writing *Herzog* all of his life, there was just
enough truth in what he said for the remark to be revealing, or misleading. Of course Algren's context was a statement of why he didn't
have to read *Herzog*, and *that* is extremely misleading. It is easy enough
to chide a writer today for writing the same book again, for creating
variations on a theme that he has claimed as his own, a claim he has
staked, like an old-time prospector, and mined for real or fool's gold.
One of the many things the writer of our times shares with the corporate and complex society he lives in is specialization. The successful
writer specializes, produces a product with his brand name on it. The
product goes to the marketplace, and he stands or falls by and for it.
Woe betide the purveyor of Brand X. And, ironically, it does no good
not to specialize.

I recall a story I heard Walter Van Tilburg Clark tell some students:
how his publisher was so pleased with the success of *The Ox-Bow Incident* that he told him, "Give me another *Ox-Bow Incident* and I'll make
you a rich man." I do not know if Mr. Clark is a rich man. I do know
that he wrote that book once and for all and hasn't repeated himself.
I also am aware that you need not look in the quarterlies and learned
journals, not even *The Hollins Critic*, this season for much discussion of
the work of Walter Van Tilburg Clark.

You see the paradox here. Specialization is disguised as a kind of originality. It is what one may call the General Motors kind of originality.

Same old engine, with "modifications," of course, but new chrome, new "lines," new accessories. Coupled with this notion of originality is the profound belief in progress. A writer must "develop" from one book to the next, "evolve," "grow."

The irony here is that all these things happen naturally anyway. We are born with most of our limitations handed to us on a silver platter. We put on a set of inhibitions with our diapers. So it seems redundant, to say the least, to ask a man to cultivate his inadequacies and call necessity a virtue.

The condition I have described applies to both subject matter and technique for a writer. It is a situation real enough and serious enough to explain, at least partially, the earnest and desperate threshings and writhings of young and middle-aged writers to break out of, to beat the system.

A personal example. I recently completed a novel I had been working on for some time. A principal character in the book is a tent-revival preacher. My own publisher (Little, Brown) rejected it outright and, at least in part, because of the subject matter. My editor, a kindly man, explained that to write about a revival preacher after *Elmer Gantry* was a little like writing a book about chasing a white whale. See what a writer is up against? Fortunately, my agent found an editor with a record of publishing books about preachers by Southern writers. So it goes.

What has all this to do with Saul Bellow and *Herzog*? First, that what Nelson Algren meant to imply is *not* true in his case. At a time when specialization, "the image," if you will, is force-fed to the writer and reader alike, he has not, in fact, repeated himself. Either technically or in subject matter. Within the given limitations of his knowledge and his interests, Saul Bellow has managed to escape the curse while all things conspired to tell him it was not a curse, but a blessing. He has achieved and held prestige, and now, after the usual minimum of twenty years of work for an American writer, he has even managed a measure of popular success. *All without pandering.* For the true prostitution of our time, the real "selling out," has nothing to do with genre, popular or unpopular. That writer is a prostitute who accepts the place allotted to him and the limitations assigned to him by others. That definition makes most of our writers, including the most highly regarded, prostitutes. It has always been so. How could our age imagine itself immune?

There is a final happy note about Bellow's story. While going his own way, he has been given credit for being a good boy. I have yet to read a review or an article of his work that does not take for granted that he is a specialist. A writer with as fine and broad a sense of humor as Bellow's must find the situation bitterly funny. Yet another example of "you can't beat them, they join you"?

III

A considerable body of criticism has been written about the fiction of Saul Bellow. Much of it is sympathetic and some of it is quite good. In large part it has been written by critics who have at least a common ground of heritage and experience with the writer—urban, intellectual, and Jewish. In this body of criticism there is a kind of consensus. It is generally agreed that Bellow's concerns are urban, intellectual, and Jewish, that he has a fine sense of humor, that he unites continental literary traditions with American experience, and that he has a certain kind of hero. The Bellow hero is most often seen to be a man alone, at odds with society, "alienated," an "outsider," with deep existential problems, one who must in the course of the presented action either accept or reject the world he has not made and the society he finds himself in. (For a well-written statement of the consensus view, see Ihab Hassan's *Radical Innocence: Studies in the Contemporary American Novel,* Princeton University Press, 1961, pp. 290–324. For a more recent statement of the same, see Frederick J. Hoffman, "The Fool of Experience: Saul Bellow's Fiction," in *Contemporary American Novelists,* Southern Illinois University Press, 1964, pp. 80–94.)

The trouble with a consensus is that it smooths rough edges. This one is a little like Nelson Algren's off-hand remark to H. E. F. Donahue and his trusty tape recorder. It is partly true, but. . . .

Only one of Bellow's heroes is by demonstration or definition an intellectual—Herzog. Some of the others, especially Augie March and Henderson, are aware of ideas, troubled by them, *use* ideas, but both Augie and Henderson are men of action and movement. The heroes are, indeed, Jewish, except for Henderson. (Leslie Fiedler has written most interestingly about Henderson as *goy* in *Waiting for the End.*) And the milieu is generally Jewish, though many well-realized minor characters are not Jewish. And each of the protagonists has a different background and moves in a different group. Joseph, the narrator of *Dangling Man,* is a Canadian citizen out of work by choice, waiting to be drafted, caught up in "a sort of bureaucratic comedy trimmed out in red tape," dependent on others for all his asserted withdrawal and isolation. Asa Leventhal of *The Victim* is a hard-working, reasonably successful editor of a trade magazine. He is originally from Hartford and his world is Manhattan, Staten Island, and Brooklyn, a world full of friends and relatives as well as a few persistent enemies. Augie March begins in the Depression and centers around Chicago and the near edges of poverty which Augie manages to skirt by unceasing hustling. His hustling takes him all over the country and the civilized world. Tommy Wilhelm of *Seize the Day* is an ex-actor, in his early forties, son of a doctor, living on upper Broadway. Henderson is vintage American, born rich. Herzog is, contrary to the impression given by reviewers, a fairly successful academic with a Chicago background. His father made money. His brothers are very successful and, whereas Moses Herzog is not a rich man, he can manage a divorce, a country house, a piece of property in Chicago, and the period of voluntary idleness which makes up the elapsed time of the story. Each is different, then, and set in a distinctly different economic and social situation. It is highly unlikely that any of his heroes would ever meet each other.

Urban? Yes, but. A large part of *Henderson the Rain King* takes place in Africa, the Africa of the imagination; Augie scoots all over the place; people, true to our times, are always on the move. Alone? Sometimes literally, but never for long. Bellow never allows a hero to live without family, wives and ex-wives, friends and enemies. It is an irony that none of his heroes, even Joseph who wants to be alone, can be alone. It is simply impossible. Lonely, yes. Sometimes. The other books are riddled with a wild and wide variety of characters large and small, and Bellow is marvelously effective in showing how these people *affect* one another.

And, yes, Bellow has a superb sense of humor, manifest in style, in gags and situations. What is surprising to me is that he has not been recognized as a *comic* writer in a larger sense. The basic framework and

---

situation of each of the books is comic, no matter how "serious" the situation may be and no matter how seriously the hero must take his predicament. The material is the stuff of comedy and the resolutions are comic. After his long wait, Joseph can write on his last civilian day: "Hurray for regular hours! And for the supervision of the spirit! Long live regimentation!" Even the deeply moving ending of *Seize the Day*, when Tommy Wilhelm stands in a chapel by the coffin of a stranger, out-mourning the mourners, weeping for himself, the world, and the tears of things, even this is a fundamentally comic situation, which Bellow underlines by playing it off against the reactions of the others. "It must be somebody real close to carry on so." Henderson's Africa, which Norman Mailer took seriously enough to wish in print that *he* had been allowed to follow the story to its deepest, darkest conclusion, is, let us admit it, a highly sophisticated fusion of *Rasselas*, Edgar Rice Burroughs, Hemingway, and the funny papers. The persecution of Asa Leventhal by the incredible Allbee is a virtuoso development of the familiar theme in Yiddish, and in a writer like Malamud, of the *schnorer*, the parasite and its relation to the host. In short, though mood and tone may and do change from book to book and though each book reflects a different world, all are bound together as comic, parts of a comedy. Which means that those, the majority, who see a change in Bellow's books in the form of a development from dark Kafkaesque views to "the irony of joy," or some such, didn't read the first works with any sense of proportion, did not manage to test situation and character against the standards of experience, did not, in spite of clear and explicit invitation from the author, bring their imaginations to bear upon his imaginary fictions. All along Bellow has been a sad-faced clown offering the world a bouquet of flowers. The flowers have been largely ignored and they keep trying to get him to exchange his baggy pants for a sturdy gray flannel from Brooks.

Bellow's work asks for humanity; it demands imagination and common sense from the reader. Which may be asking too much.

Which reminds me of a story. Bellow has written another version of this tale (see "Deep Readers of the World, Beware," *New York Times Book Review*, Feb. 15, 1959) from his point of view. There were other witnesses and this is their version. Who knows where the truth is? Bellow was teaching a seminar at Princeton. The subject for the day was part of the *Iliad*, and they got to the place where Hector's body is dragged around the walls of Troy. "What do you make of that?" Bellow asked. A clever and well-trained student swung into action, pointing out that it was terribly significant that Hector was dragged around Troy *three times*, that this was, then, a "key passage," that from it we could examine the whole structure of the *Iliad* and discover that it is an intricate arrangement of triads, etc., etc. During this (they say) Bellow's mouth opened, his jaw dropped, his eyes bugged. A condition which the speaker interpreted as a tribute to his dazzling critical performance. Until Bellow banged his fist on the table with the force of the late Sam Rayburn swinging a gavel. "Damn it, son!" he's reported to have cried out. "Doesn't it even make you feel sad when Hector gets dragged around the walls?"

Apocryphal or not, it makes a real point. If, while you are reading the fiction of Saul Bellow, you don't know when it's funny and when it's sad, if you can't laugh or cry and can't tell who's on first without a program, then you'd better pack up your kafka and your kierkegaard, stick your nietzsche under a few clean shirts and bug out on the first train for Marienbad. Bellow is a careful and thoughtful writer who gives you every clue and every chance, but you have to be with it. His invitation is like the proverbial country girl's—"Don't leave your coat and hat cause we won't be coming back this way."

Technically Bellow has managed to avoid the habit of repetition, too. The technical premise of *Dangling Man* is a journal kept between December 15, 1942, and April 9, 1943. This, of course, makes for a self-conscious first-person narration of the hero, a double removed from the event itself in that the narrator is consciously addressing an imaginary reader. It is a familiar and honorable form, but it is also one which critics seem to have trouble with. Naturally this kind of narrator takes himself seriously and will, like any human being, try his best to present his case in the most favorable light. Ultimately this is a dramatic form. Seek for the author and you will not easily find him. It is fatal to confuse author with narrator at any point, no matter how persuasive the narrator may be. *The Victim*, which Bellow once referred to, speaking to students, as "my Ph.D. thesis," is the most conventional form, if by conventional we mean the accepted, Jamesian third-person narration, built upon a linked series of dramatically presented scenes.

The trick of this form is to appear to stick to surfaces, to adhere to a distinct point of view, in this case Asa Leventhal's, and though sensation is permissible, one is expected to avoid dealing with thought process except insofar as it is rational, articulate, and directly relevant to presented action. This form has been highly esteemed in our time, but it is not necessarily more "dramatic" than a number of other forms or, in spite of Flaubert, James, and the whole Fugitive Syndrome, by definition superior to any other form. (It didn't take Wayne C. Booth to prove this, but his long labor did serve to remind the academic world that there are many other forms of rhetoric in fiction and that this form is, at least partially, a fraud.) Bellow plays this game with skill and makes it fit his subject with a good tailor's precision. The real work, of course, has to be done in the selection of significant, but seemingly random detail and in the realm of physical sensation. In both ways Bellow is master enough to break through the inhibitions of the form without seeming to.

The Adventures of Augie March takes off like a flight of startled birds in the grand tradition of the direct, first-person narration, in this case presumed to be spoken directly to a reader or listener without the subterfuge of a diary or journal. The first sentence sets a tone and manner which never break down. "I am an American, Chicago born—Chicago, that somber city—and go at things as I have taught myself, free-style, and will make the record in my own way: First to knock, first admitted; sometimes an innocent knock, sometimes not so innocent." And away we go. The advantages of this form are, basically, the immediate and direct credibility of the testifying witness and great freedom in time and space without strain. Moreover it permits a maximum exploitation of the richness and variety of the *spoken* American language, though this condition can be honored strictly or loosely. Bellow chooses the loose convention, letting his energetic, hustling narrator, self-educated and always "free style;" mingle high and low, rhetoric, slang and idiom in the same sentence. It fits perfectly again with his subject. It is wild and woolly, yet at the same time conventional and decorous. The style is the man and the man is the book. *Seize the Day,* which was first of all a long story (or short novel), then part of a collection of stories before it became a separate unit in itself, is in part a return to the tight form of *The Victim,* even tighter for its unity of time and limitations of space. A careful reader, however, will notice that Bellow had some fun with the form this time. There is more use of first person than *The Victim* permitted and there are crucial sudden places where he tosses the strict adherence of point of view overboard and, in effect, reverses the pseudocamera eye to play on the hero and to gain *reaction*. This is done so skillfully and subtly that it merely happens, without fanfare and never breaking the spell. *Henderson the Rain King* goes back to the straight first-person manner of *Augie March*, but the style is quite different to fit the character, and it is used for a different purpose. The purpose in this case is the time-honored one, to give the candy coating of credibility, to help the reader suspend his natural disbelief in a completely incredible story. When we get to *Herzog* we will see Bellow using a little bit of everything he has done so far and making it work.

There are some conclusions one can draw from Bellow's technique. He had never invented a form (if this is possible), that is, never pretended to be inventing an original way of telling a story and thus called attention to form itself. Rather he had used ancient and honorable forms in his own way. So did Chaucer, Shakespeare, and Milton, you say, and so what? Get back to the time we have to live in. Novelty is highly prized. Writers go to great lengths to appear to be presenting a brand new, "improved" form. Just like makers of detergents, deodorants, and toothpaste. Not Bellow. He has escaped the Madison Avenue madness. He reveals himself as a conservative, if we can even use that word without pejorative or laudatory connotations. He also reveals himself, long before Booth, interested in the rhetoric of fiction, in the reader and his responses. And, finally, he shows that he is not in the least interested in the "poetic" novel, by which is usually meant the adaptation of the methods and manners of modern poetry, chiefly a lyric mode, to the problems of prose fiction. He is clearly interested in preserving and defending the precincts of prose. In this view, at least for a long time, he must have found himself in a distinct literary minority.

His success is, therefore, all the more remarkable. It must be attributed to his great skill and craftsmanship, his choice of subject and his commitment to it.

IV

There is something funny about the human condition, and civilized intel-
ligence makes fun of its own ideas.

—Herzog

The story that Herzog tells is fairly simple and you can be easily
fooled by it. Moses Herzog is alone in the wake of a ludicrous and unhappy divorce and is on the verge, he feels, of losing his mind. It is a
good mind and it is important to realize this fact. Most reviewers, enchanted by the comedy, don't seem to have recognized the fact that
Herzog is well trained, quite successful in his profession, even though
he has tasted failure and frustration and wonders where he is going
from here. Herzog keeps a kind of intellectual journal throughout and
at the same time is writing real and imaginary letters to people living
and dead. (It is this device which gives Bellow the best of both first-
person and third-person narrative techniques.) His comments and
questions are often enough amusing in style, which may put some readers off. They are nevertheless real and serious concerns. Herzog is nobody's crackpot. He is a gifted and intelligent man, a civilized man, a
good man in many ways, and he demonstrates a capacity, a potential for
wisdom. He has done and continues to do some foolish things. He
learns through his folly. Ideally, one should laugh with Herzog not at
him; for he is the real thing, and Bellow has been able successfully to
make drama and entertainment out of the plight of the intelligent man
who wants to do right in a bad world. I can't think of anyone else who
has done this except maybe James Gould Cozzens. And that's a horse of
another color.

The point is that when Moses Herzog writes Spinoza or Nietzsche a
letter on the chatty level of equality, that's no joke. Or, rather, the joke
is on those who do not recognize that Herzog can, indeed, hold his own
with intellectual heavyweights living and dead.

What's his problem, then? Of course he has been kicked around, but
he is quite intelligent enough to understand what has happened and
why. His problem is the intellectual's problem. He is almost crippled by
distrust of his own feelings and instincts. Knowledge has made him a

stranger to himself. He is lost until he can stand the burden of self-knowledge, can trust himself. Ramona, his mistress, for reasons of her own, tells him this quite clearly and it is all there including the truth of it, proved by his reaction:

> She told Herzog that he was a better man than he knew—a deep man, beautiful (he could not help wincing when she said this), but sad, unable to take what his heart really desired, a man tempted by God, longing for grace, but escaping headlong from his salvation, often close at hand. This Herzog, this man of many blessings, for some reason had endured a frigid, middlebrow, castrating female in his bed, given her his name and made her the instrument of creation, and Madelaine [Herzog's ex-wife] had treated him with contempt and cruelty as if to punish him for lowering and cheapening himself, for lying himself into love with her and betraying the promise of his soul. What he really must do, she went on, in the same operatic style—unashamed to be so fluent; he marveled at this—was to pay his debt for the great gifts he had received, his intelligence, his charm, his education, and free himself to pursue the meaning of life, not by disintegration, where he would never find it, but humbly and yet proudly continuing his learned studies. She, Ramona, wanted to add riches to his life and give him what he pursued in the wrong places. This she could do by the art of love, she said—the art of love which was one of the sublime achievements of the spirit.

Herzog's reaction? "He, Herzog, overtake life's meaning! He laughed into his hands, covering his face." Yet operatic style or not and regardless of her motives, it is Ramona who tells him the truth about his dilemma and himself. The truth of heart, soul, spirit which his fine mind will not allow him to accept at that point. He must go through the actual adventures of the book, chiefly a disastrous return visit to Chicago, and he must follow through his intellectual quest before he can accept Ramona and her truth.

Near the end, in a letter to Professor Mermelstein, who has written a book in the area of Herzog's studies, Herzog lowers the boom on certain fancy and rather abstract modern notions, popular existentialism, and takes his stand with humanity.

> Let us set aside the fact that such convictions in the mouths of safe, comfortable people playing at crises, alienation, apocalypse and desper-

ation, make me sick. We must get it out of our heads that this is a doomed time, that we are waiting for the end, and the rest of it, mere junk from fashionable magazines. Things are grim enough without these shivery games. . . . You see how gruesomely human beings are destroyed by pain, when they have the added torment of losing their humanity first, so that their death is a total defeat, and then you write about "modern forms of Orphism" and about "people who are not afraid of suffering" and throw in other such cocktail party expressions. . . . We love apocalypses too much, and crises ethics and florid extremism with its thrilling language. Excuse me, no. I've had all the monstrosity I want.

It doesn't take an expert in semantics, even in my broken quotation, to see the key and okay words going down like clay pigeons. And behind those okay words are real and formidable people, thinkers and artists, in this year 1965. Herzog, having had a bit of heaven and a bit of hell, can give them hell. I resist the critical game of making Herzog Bellow's mouthpiece, but I think there's no denying Bellow gives them some hell too.

I try to picture Herzog's expression. I remember, then, Wesleyan University, where I taught, in the ferment of Norman O. Brown's discovery of Freud, Nietzsche, Dionysius, and the life of the body, of Ihab Hassan's wrestling with "radical innocence." It was a funny time when sedentary faculty members suddenly took up arm wrestling, dancing lessons from Arthur Murray's, and necking with each other's wives in parked cars. Some of them discovered exercise and put on sweat suits and trotted around the track. I remember the faces of the athletic coaches as they watched from the shade of the gym. I remember especially the battered face of a young coach who had, until recently, taken his lumps with the Green Bay Packers. I see his face dissolve into the imaginary face of Herzog.

It rings true.

At the end Herzog returns to his white elephant of a house in the Berkshires to await the arrival of Ramona. Nearing the end, he had written a fury of notes and letters, a fever of straightening out the errors of the world. That is suddenly behind him. Walking back to the house (which a slatternly neighbor is cleaning up for him), he picks some flowers for the table, and the moment is the miracle of the change he has been struggling toward.

But then it struck him that he might be making a mistake, and he stopped, listening to Mrs. Tuttle's sweeping, the rhythm of bristles. Picking flowers? He was being thoughtful, lovable. How would it be interpreted? (He smiled slightly.) Still, he need only know his own mind, and the flowers couldn't be used; no, they couldn't be turned against him. So he did not throw them away. . . . Perhaps he'd stop writing letters. Yes, that was what was coming, in fact. The knowledge that he was done with these letters. Whatever had come over him during these last months, the spell, really seemed to be passing, really going.

There it is, all wrapped up, done with the magic of art by a skilled artist. But he isn't done yet. Watch him, the artist, top it by *showing you* in the last few simple lines, finding exactly the right image, the right words for the happy fade out, in a truly happy ending.

Walking over notes and papers, he lay down on his Recamier Couch. As he stretched out, he took a long breath, and then he lay, looking at the mesh of the screen, pulled loose by vines, and listening to the steady scratching of Mrs. Tuttle's broom. He wanted to tell her to sprinkle the floor. She was raising too much dust. In a few minutes he would call down to her, "Damp it down, Mrs. Tuttle. There's water in the sink." But not just yet. At this time he had no messages for anyone. Nothing. Not a single word.

Crazy to try to follow *that!* To come on with words of one's own after the marvel of a fine craftsman writing a finis to his finest work so far. But even heavy-weight title fights are followed by a walkout bout. I owe my reader, whoever he may be, the courtesy of a conclusion. A recapitulation and conclusion. Recap: Bellow's career as a writer ought to be a joy to anyone who cares about writing. He's a winner from the word go without ever once being a prostitute. He would be anyway, whether the fat boys, who hand out laurels and winner's wreaths and don't know which end of a horse to feed sugar to, whether they knew it or not. But, *mirabilis!*, he managed to hypnotize them too. Enjoy the spectacle. It's not likely to happen again for a century.

Now Bellow has capped that long career with a daring and great novel. He has escaped the cliché. He has successfully overcome the catastrophe of his success. Bless him. Where he goes from here, who knows? There are many other kinds of novels and many of them still and always to be written and rewritten. Maybe he'll write some of them. Meanwhile all of us readers—Jew or Gentile or Eskimo—owe him a toast and our deepest gratitude.

11

Morris the Magician:
A Look at *In Orbit*
(1967)

With a gesture, no more, this boy makes old things new.

—Wright Morris, *In Orbit*

What has to be said first of all is that there are precious few if any novelists alive and working who are as able as Wright Morris to make both sense and art out of the brute, raw, flashing, shifty facts, the material of the American present. Which is what he is up to in *In Orbit*.

Of course many other writers, young and old, talk about doing this a great deal. Like the hucksters of soap, soft drinks, patent medicines, cigarettes, and underwear, they talk a great game and let their lives depend on it. Not that it matters very much whether they ever really deliver. At a time when the *image*, almost any image, is more important, even more "real" than any truth it may reveal or deftly conceal, it is only natural that your successful image-maker should be deeply appreciated. He is the fascinating sleight-of-hand magician and, thus, an image of the times himself. The things he can do with a deck of cards are only tricks, but we all know that, don't we? It's curiously reassuring. We know the deck and the names and suits of the cards, and we are comfortable with the game. There are no wild cards to worry about except the inevitable Joker, and we know all about him too. We are ready for him. Shuffle and riffle. Bright tricks in two dimensions. We can admire the learned dexterity. And he, the smiling or poker-faced card sharp, is really just one of us after all. Art-smart!! It is a relief to be reminded that, talent or not, the artist is just another hustler. It is more fun to read about Norman Mailer's antics in the newspapers, to hear what Gore Vidal is saying about the Kennedys, to turn on the television set, *educational* television, and to look at John Updike's extraordinary profile etched against the wind and surf of Cape Cod than it is to read their novels. Even Ginsberg, wrapped in something like a stained bed sheet, banging gongs and muttering the old mumbo jumbo, is finally just one of the boys. Buy the kid a drink, anything he wants. He talks a lot but he talks a pretty good game. He can make you laugh. And, you know?, once in a while he can make you think about different things. We can afford to pay for a little culture these days. The fast-talkers, the hustlers, barkers, the image-makers get what they deserve. Which happens to be a share of the white meat and good gravy, albeit after the grown-ups have left the table.

Here and now, in this context, ours, it would seem that Wright Morris has practically everything going against him. For one thing he works so hard. Fifteen novels since *My Uncle Dudley* in 1942. That comes perilously close to being, pardon the expression, *prolific.* Which is not a good thing for a serious novelist. What is he trying to prove? What does he want? He doesn't even write journalism or instant history. He has had a few grants and they gave him a National Book Award for *The Field of Vision.* Of course, as serious as he is, he's never hit it with a real best-seller. But even that can be arranged. The publishing houses are full of bright young editors with all kinds of ideas. If it's money he's after, there's money, at least enough for all the good guys, the reliable ones, to have a piece of the action. You do have to be cool, clean, discreet, keep your ear to the ground, and above all be patient, though. Morris won't stand in line. He can't stand still. Take a look at the checklist of his published books. Note how he goes from publisher to publisher. Whatever else that may mean, it's a sure sign of a troublemaker, an agitator. Maybe even a sore loser. And all the time he keeps writing these books. He comes from Nebraska, a rube, and maybe nobody told him the novel is dead and art is for kids.

All that activity is embarrassing. For one thing, it makes it tough on the critics. They have a hard time keeping up anyway. So many books are published every year. Mostly trash, of course, that you can skim or ignore. Even a real *reader* like Granville Hicks can't begin to deal with them all, as he is the first one to admit. The big trouble with Wright Morris is that he keeps writing and changing. You can't get a line on him. He won't stand there and let them put a name tag on his lapel. By now, already, he has worked up a regular *canon,* just like a decently dead writer. And still he keeps on. It's some kind of compulsion or something, the kind of thing that can ruin a man's reputation.

On top of which the books, all of them, aren't exactly easy reading. He couldn't turn out some light summer reading if his life depended on it. He can be funny, sure. In fact he is one of the funniest writers around. But there is some kind of an edge to all his jokes. He can go for the gag line with the very best of them, and you can't help laughing. Then later on you may get the suspicion that the joke is partly on you, too. Just when you think you have somebody or something to *laugh at*, he comes along and spoils everything by making you wonder, *think* even, why you are laughing. He has the same problem with his plots and characters. Things start out comfortably enough, even though he likes to play around with time and point of view and won't put it all down *straight*, and he can be as neatly and tightly schematic as you please. Then just when you settle down to relax and let it all happen the way it usually does, he has to get cute. Blink a couple of times, rub your eyes, and next thing you know you can't tell the good guys from the bad ones. Morris is no *New Yorker* writer. It is like he wanted to disturb the peace.

Think of it. What a thing, to step out into the light and bow politely, holding an ordinary deck of cards, riffling and shuffling and then all of a sudden for no reason at all the cards turn into marvelous brilliant birds flying off and away in every which direction. That's not a trick. There is no trick to it. It is purely and simply magic.

Which is why so many people, professed readers of good books, haven't read much Wright Morris. And which is why the critics, for the most part, have chosen to ignore him. It is ever so much easier to write about the mythopoeic world of, say, Reynolds Price.

And there are many other things going against him as well. For example, there is the fact that even though his novels are individual and separate, they are also built upon each other, as intricately and subtly related in their own way as Faulkner's. In one sense more so. In *After Alienation: American Novels in Mid-Century* (World, 1964) Marcus Klein points this out, indicates how it works up through *Cause for Wonder* (1963). Sometimes it is an explicit relationship of place or character in directly linked novels like *The Field of Vision* and *Ceremony in Lone Tree*. Sometimes there is a variation, another version of place, character, or event, and in this sense all the books and stories become complex variations. The result is that the books keep getting better. The more you read and follow the design, the better, richer they get. Very self-conscious, someone might say. Besides which he is a frankly *literary* writer. He not only admits to having read a book or so and, when it suits him, alludes to same, but also he uses his reading in an odd allusive way to give more dimension to the story at hand. It's all right, of course, to use the old standards—the classics and the myths, the Bible, Shakespeare, etc.—but what about a modern writer who uses *The Sun Also Rises* or *The Great Gatsby* or *Finnegans Wake* quite openly as grist for his mill. He is not often exotic and esoteric in the functional use of this device. The books and stories he echoes and uses are, after all, all books and stories that we have read, or anyway ones we are supposed to have read.

Not that he sees those books exactly as everyone else does. Not that he reads and criticizes by consensus. Back in 1958 he decided to do some talking himself, and he put together a book of criticism, *The Territory Ahead.* It seems to have baffled a good number of people. Instead of the conventional and acceptable pitch about how tough it is to stand in the huge shadow of the Masters, he seemed to go out of his way to point out their flaws, faults, and failures as he saw them. He dealt with a good many writers, principally with Thoreau, Whitman, Melville, Twain, James, Hemingway, Wolfe, Fitzgerald, and Faulkner, and these artists were treated as intelligent, sentient, dedicated, and responsible men. They got full credit and with it full responsibility. He did not concern himself much with the role and function of the critic, except to demonstrate it gracefully. He did not address himself directly to the critics. He spoke more to that probably extinct breed—the intelligent reader. He did not even use the usual jargon of contemporary criticism, let alone the respectable conventions of manner and method. He used his own language and words, words which, in fact, show up in his fiction, so that *The Territory Ahead* has to be taken as part of his whole body of work too.

Those who troubled to read *The Territory Ahead* seemed to get two or three notions out of it. Morris seemed to be against a kind of backward looking and dreaming that, he said, has possessed American writers from the beginning, a characteristic he incorporated under the label of

Nostalgia. He also seemed to indicate that there has been a little too much unrefined, unprocessed experience, "raw material," and not enough art and technique in the American novel. And he was obviously annoyed by the prevalence of clichés. Aren't we all? Find a writer or critic who is willing to come on strong in favor of bigger and better clichés. Like Calvin Coolidge's preacher, they are all against the cliché.

What people missed in *The Territory Ahead* is quite a lot. One of these days a clever young critic on the make or the ascendancy will glance back at that book and notice the *prophetic* quality. He will see how well it predicts and describes the direction that much American fiction has indeed taken in the past decade. Somebody also may notice that the book is really about a kind of *balance*, about holding opposites in your hands at the same time. That he isn't just against something as natural as the urge and need for Nostalgia, but that he doesn't see any future or virtue in an *art* based solely on doing what comes naturally. Someone will observe that he isn't just *against* the cliché in the abstract, in general. He wants something else. He wants to know what the big and little clichés are, to identify and name them, and finally to *use* them, to transform them into something else by means of intelligence and imagination. An alchemy of the cliché. It may be seen that he is not attacking the past, but instead is talking about the present and the future in the sure and certain hope that both exist too and matter. But above all Morris pleads a case for an art of the deeply involved imagination, for intelligence, technique and conceptual power as absolutely essential to any truly living imagination. What he is against are all the easy ways out, all the artistic cop-outs. Just when practically everybody, assured of certain certainties, was ready to settle down and wait for the death of the novel, just when many a working novelist found himself almost enjoying the genteel pleasures of twilight and demise, along came Wright Morris saying that we have only just begun, demanding more, not less, of every artist. Considered this way, *The Territory Ahead* is a literary offense, a book of hard sayings.

Other things that seem to have hurt Wright Morris's chances? (Never mind, for the moment, that his bold assault on the dwarf and giant clichés of our life and art has led to the exposure of the heart of phonus balonus in much that is dear. Many a sacred cow has been shown to be a creature of plywood, plastic, and epoxy. Never mind, for the moment, that much of what Morris has to show and tell must surely annoy all kinds of people, especially the professional *sages* of the times, who put their hats over their hearts every time a cliché marches by.) A big fault, Morris won't stay put in any *decade*. Starting out when he did, he is supposed to be a writer of the 1940s. Maybe, looking back, we could allow him a slot in the 1950s. But the 1960s? By continuing to create, by writing here and now at the peak of his energy and power, Morris thumbs his nose at one of the most sacrosanct and convenient clichés of contemporary literary history—the Decade. You would think that, if nothing else, the normal wear and tear, the adversity, the relative public neglect and indifference to all that he has done, would have slowed him down a little.

And then there is the undeniable fact that he has so much talent, such great and various gifts. He has a superb ear, none better. It is exact, right, and surprising. He has a trained eye. Which is not surprising, for he is a first-rate photographer and in two books, *The Inhabitants* (1946) and *The Home Place* (1948), he used his photographs integrally with the text. As a photographer he knows, no doubt, the frustrations of that art, so well expressed by Cartier-Bresson in *The Decisive Moment:* "We photographers deal in things which are continually vanishing, and when they have vanished, there is no contrivance on earth which can make them come back again. We cannot develop and print a memory." Except, of course, in a novel. Morris has always shown a rich and various power of close observation, a memory for detail. His fiction is full of *things*, not just the names, but the look, feel, and texture of them. The surface is dazzling. In view of which his emphasis in *The Territory Ahead* on the necessity of overcoming the tyranny of raw material and memory is important. Unlike the image-maker, he is not trying to disguise a weakness. He is trying to train and control a powerful strength.

Using that strength and his talent, he could easily have gone a long, long way, maybe a much easier way, and nobody would have noticed the difference. But Morris has other things he can do very well, too. He can create characters of all kinds, shapes and descriptions, young and old, men and women, lots of them; and having created them he can keep them alive and kicking. He stays with his characters, letting them have time and space to grow, change, become until finally the best of them are suddenly all there, as solid and three-dimensional as bronze figures. And like great sculpture they are finally and forever mysterious. They appear first of all as people do in life (and art), veiled in familiar and gauzy clichés. Morris gets the music going, and they start to dance and peel the veils away and down to skin and bones. When the striptease is over, we see human nakedness, but it is a nakedness infinitely more mysterious and beautiful than any veiled figure. Only a very few of our writers have ever been able to create characters like that. It is commonplace, easy enough, and often just right for the modern reader to have a character stripped in scorn and exposed in shame. Morris has great compassion for his characters. He gets it without permitting himself or the reader one faint whiff of sentimentality. Which may be defined as the bogus gesture, the cold comfort, of allowing the reader to try on a character's ill-fitting shoes for size. He gets it, too, by being a master of every aspect of *point of view.* Which really means that no matter who is telling the story or how he is telling it, you don't cheat. When you are with a character that's where you are.

A lot of writers can write pretty well. Fewer by far, but still a fair number, live long enough and learn enough to be able to create some real characters. And then there are a very, very few, the great ones, who have taken one more step. They take story or plot, or whatever you please to call the *fable* of fiction, and they make it mean something in and of itself. Not say something. It is easy enough to say things and write messages. De Mille (or was it Sam Goldwyn, Sr.?) was right. Western Union is the medium for messages. To mean something is something else.

The structure of a fiction becomes a world, a meaningful and deeply mysterious pattern, and in that sense it can become, however small and broken by comparison, a creation mirroring the Creation. Morris has come this far. He does it in the individual book. He has done it and is doing it, intricately, when you consider the design of his whole work. Of course this has great risks too. In general this abstract and probably arbitrary scheme of a writer's development—from words to characters to the pattern—can be attended by a diminishing of interest in (and thus ability with) the primary stages. The earlier qualities are refined away, and we expect this to happen, believing as we do, that growth is as much loss as gain. Somehow (by magic again?) Wright Morris has managed to keep all three qualities alive at once, in suspension, in near perfect balance. And this puts him up at the very top where the air is thin and where a man and his work can be judged by the highest standards we know of, past or present. When he writes a book and it is published we who profess and call ourselves readers had better read it.

II

After some time she said, "You ever feel you're in a friggin movie? You ever stand up in a movie and tell the friggin hero which way to run?"
"That's right, Daughter, and this is the movie."
"The friggin moonlight made me think of it," she said.
And that was all.

—*Ceremony in Lone Tree*

The brute, flashing, shifty facts of the American present. Told mostly, except for brief memories and recollection here and there, in the present tense. And working fast, in a brief span of condensed time, the time of a day, as in the larger and more expansive novel which immediately precedes this one—*One Day*. *One Day* deals with a day in the nutty California community of Escondido, a wild and woolly day for the restless natives, a day on which, almost as a by the way, the president of the United States was killed in Dallas, Texas. *One Day* is a tough book, because, since Morris wrote it, he doesn't have to and won't remind the reader of the national pathos of that day. He can and does take for granted the elegiac mode. He sticks to his characters, their zany, absurd, bollixed up personal tragicomedy. He is fearless even of the cliché reactions to the assassination, and he is fearless of satirizing the clichés of the human means toward worthy goals, such as Civil Rights. *One Day* and *In Orbit* are very closely related in general and in details. *In Orbit* tells of one memorable day in the town of Pickett, Indiana. It's the day when a twister roared through town raising all kinds of hell. It is also the day on which a kind of human tornado,

Jubal Gainer, wearing a crash helmet and a J. S. Bach sweatshirt, came barreling in from Olney County on a stolen Suzuki and ran out of gas. He hits town, it seems, like the twister, like a plague. He is involved in a rape (of sorts), an assault (of an odd kind), an ambiguous robbery and stabbing, a brief "reign of terror," and before he can get out of town and on his way to nowhere in particular again, he and the twister meet and he takes a ride on the wind. All the principal characters, an odd and entertaining bunch, survive, and in a curious way get what they deserve or wish for. In what happens and in the way it is told, the main line of the story is comic, then. People get clobbered by the twister, all right. There is plenty of damage. But not Jubal or the principals. Not anybody we *know.* They have their own wounds and troubles, but they are still alive, living with them, at the end. As the distant murder in *One Day* can be taken for granted, so also the twister, no joke, can be *assumed,* but not forgotten.

If Marcus Klein is right—and I am not at all sure he is, or, better, that it is all as neat and schematic as he makes it—the arrival of Morris on the *present* scene was "signaled by *Love Among the Cannibals*" (1957). He can cite the authority of the author in any case, Morris's statement in a published interview (Sam Bluefarb, "Point of View: An Interview with Wright Morris, July, 1958," *Accent,* 19, Winter 1959). There Morris said: "*The Cannibals* is the first book in which the past does not exist. We begin with the present, we live in the present, and it is an effort to come to terms with the present, in terms of only the present." True enough for that swinging story of two Hollywood songwriters and their girlfriends; except that, even there, there is an implied past. From then on the main interest and surface of the stories may be the present, but always Morris is careful to give his places and his people a past which is at least present to them. It can be extensive in a large novel like *One Day,* or it can be beautifully sketched without interruption of the forward rush of a tight story like *In Orbit.* There are as many pasts as there are people, characters, and places. And in just the same way there are as many varied *present* times. But all those become part of two not distinct, but related histories, layers of time, the history of the land, America, and the cumulative history of the work of Wright Morris. The day of the twister, the day when Jubal Gainer, looking like some kind of a spaceman and taken for one, too, by those who have the luck to encounter him, hits Pickett, Indiana, also the day on which the Beatles movie *Help!* is playing, is the day when an historic elm (a lone tree) is cut down:

> Through the window, shaded by an awning, he observes the day's major event: the felling of an historic campus elm. Small fry stand in a circle anxious to be hit by falling branches. A rising wind sways the branch supporting the man with the saw. This elm is special. It is known to have been there when the Indians scalped the first settlers, hardy stubborn men who worked like slaves to deprive their children of all simple pleasures, and most reasons to live.

The American past is there and except for Jubal and the chance of the twister, the cutting down of the elm would very likely have to be "the day's major event."

The past of Wright Morris's novels, the cumulative family history of his work, is very much present in the present of this book. It is also very complicated to talk about in detail, like trying to explain a joke to a humorless inquisitor. But it can be suggested with examples. *Item:* in *One Day* Alec Cartwright, a free-swinging, freedom-riding chick who opens the events of the day by leaving her mulatto baby in the arrivals slot at the animal pound, wears a Brahms sweatshirt. Jubal Gainer wears Bach, alike but different, as Kashperl, who runs the army surplus store in Pickett, is quick to note: "Best-sellers all, but here in Pickett, Brahms edges Bach, thanks to his beard." Evelina Cartwright, Alec's mother, loves and pampers cats. So does Charlotte Hatfield, the faculty wife, in *In Orbit.* That biracial baby: well, Jubal Gainer appears to be an odd mixture of races, thanks to a cigar butt and stove paint job done on him by an erstwhile buddy.

> The helmet framed in the window seems to have no face. An amber visor screens the eyes, out of the shadow a nose slowly emerges. Is it of pewter? The color is fading around the wide mouth. It is like nothing Haffner has ever seen, but it does not go beyond what he has often imagined. A white man emerging from a black man, or the two in one. A man who makes the most, or is it the least, of a color-fast situation. Better yet, a man whose colors, madras-style, are guaranteed to bleed. Haffner can only laugh: he laughs in the boy's dark two-toned face.

They are trying to *save* redwoods in the Escondido of *One Day* with the SPARE THAT TREE CLUB; they are cutting down the campus elm in

In Orbit. People imagine headlines to cover events in both books:

(a) *One Day:*
INFANT LEFT AT POUND
Prankster Suspected

(b) *In Orbit:*
VISITING SPACEMAN
ASSAULTS
HOLLY STOHRMEYER

When an ice machine goes berserk in *One Day* and Evelina Cartwright's car rolls away down a hill, Evelina races after it, calling the car
to come back. Here is Haffner of *In Orbit:* "Not infrequently Haffner
will forget about the handbrake and the car will idle down the street,
Haffner trailing, calling aloud *Here! Here!* as if to some unleashed pet."
After all the disasters of the day in Escondido, the Fuzz, represented by
Sheriff McNamara, is mostly worried about *what else* is going to happen. The Fuzz in Pickett appears in the form of Sheriff Cantrill. "He
doesn't smile. It is clear that the events of the day are beginning to
weigh on Sheriff Cantrill. Particularly the events that have not yet occurred." There are dozens of such parallels between the two books.
They are not accidental.

If *One Day* and *In Orbit* are close kin, we have to recognize that,
exactly in the same way, *One Day* and *In Orbit* incorporate a variety of
bits and pieces from all of Morris's work so far. Again some simple examples will have to do. Italy and Greece (*What a Way to Go*, 1962) are
important to a greater or lesser extent, used or alluded to in both novels. So is Austria (*Cause for Wonder*, 1963). So is the Mexico of several
past novels, evoked at considerable length in *One Day*, swiftly handled
in *In Orbit* during an inventory of the extraordinary contents of
Haffner's pockets, at the top: "The first item proves to be a snuffbox
made of horn, stamped *Hecho en Mexico.*" Alan and Charlotte Hatfield
recall with nostalgia, and in a way reminiscent of *Love Among the Cannibals*, the beaches of the west coast. And so it goes. It can be a matter
of vocabulary. Characters keep thinking *what next?*, which was not only
a recurring question but also a song title in *Love Among the Cannibals*.

Morris the Magician: A Look at In Orbit

The movies and movie stars, the way people are *like* some movie star, the way events are *just like the movies*, are significant *motifs* in these novels. "Key" words, sparingly used, leap off the pages in *In Orbit*. Example: "Avery speaks eagerly but a little hoarsely: the disaster has aroused his *nostalgia*" (italics mine). And isn't Jubal's crash helmet very much the same as that of young Lee Roy Momeyer in *Ceremony in Lone Tree?* Miscellaneous and random examples. They could be multiplied many times. The point is quite simply that they are functional in a very special way. They do more than just "link" the works of Wright Morris together. They allude to and evoke the *past* of those works, to the extent that the reader is familiar with them. But turn it around another way. They give a sense of all the novels progressing forward, too, building to the latest. Which in this case is *In Orbit*. *In Orbit* will no doubt dissolve into the next book, carrying the whole evolution forward again.

What is happening, in a sense, and we can sense it happening, is a grand and total *design*, complex and organic, built upon "real" history and literary history and the history and experience of his own work. It is, by now, a very large design, and it is more a gesture of honest self-appraisal than bravado when Morris suddenly and briefly alludes to *Finnegans Wake* (discussed brilliantly in *The Territory Ahead*) near the end of *In Orbit*. This grand design is like other ambitions literary designs of the past, yet different. He uses all the conventions and methods we know of to keep his work together as a whole, but the effect is completely his own. His hand of cards is once and for all his own. It hasn't been dealt before, and the same hand will never be dealt out exactly again.

III

What he seeks lies just beyond the flickering, rain-screened beam of the car lights, the twilight zone that is neither light nor dark. In this light some things are seen at their best. Such light as they have they seem to give out.

—In Orbit

In *In Orbit*, in and of itself, the relationships between events, people, and things are as close and complex, as similar and different, as the suggested quality inherent in all of Morris's work. The words are there, and always interesting and well-realized characters are there, but the *design* is crucially important and superbly achieved. Every *thing* comes to work for the design. For as widely different and separate as the characters are, and quite unbeknownst to each other, they keep seeing and feeling and experiencing the same things, and not just in "fact" but in imagination. They make the same metaphors and similes, same and different. They live through the same weather, one and all. Their separation from each other, the fragmentary character of their individual lives is heightened by a virtuoso exercise in rapidly shifting point of view. The principal characters all see different things and reflect upon them and are forever unable, it would seem, to communicate these things and reflections to each other. Yet they all *share* a common experience, in general and in close detail. All things, all events, become symbols then, by a process of cumulative association. One thinks, for analogy, of Malcolm Lowry's *Under the Volcano.* And then one realizes that Morris has achieved a similar effect in a very short novel.

There is a difference. He carries it a step beyond; he wants something else. Lowry did it in terms of a single tortured consciousness known in depth. Morris does the same thing using half a dozen points of view, all seen briefly, swiftly. Ordinarily, and we all know it, this method is used to demonstrate what we cannot know. The cliché of the method is that the reports of many witnesses establish that there is no design, no "truth." Yet each of these witnesses does in fact and within the context and confines of his or her very specific limitations, faults, and hang-ups, see the same thing without knowing it. Who knows it, then? The reader does. The reader has all the pieces. The reader is therefore privileged to be aware of the outlines of the design, though the Design it reflects, the Creation, remains enigmatic, beyond simple answers. It is a glimpse of the working out of that ineffable Design in time, a flashing view of what was once called Providence. Chance is terribly urgent, but Chance (like Dame Fortune of old) is part of the Design. When all things come together, as they do, we the readers discover that the characters are not so different as they dream they are and they wish to be. In a profound sense, in spite of rape, stabbing, violence, and a terrible twister, *In Orbit* is a human comedy. A black comedy? Not quite. It's more like the boy, Jubal Gainer himself, with his madras face. He didn't *mean* anything. But—"As luck would have it"—fleeing the draft, his past, lunging into an unknown future on a stolen motorcycle, he happened to hit the town of Pickett and to run out of gas, happened to run into enough eccentrics and mischief to last a man a lifetime, happened to get lifted into literal orbit by a twister he didn't see coming from behind him, and in the end is back on the road, gassed up, and rolling . . . well, *somewhere*. Looking much as he did before; described in fact in the same terms and with the same analogies. With a difference.

> On his chest J. S. Bach dries in a manner that enlarges his forehead, curves his lips in a smile. Is that for what looms up ahead, or lies behind? This boy is like a diver who has gone too deep and too long without air. If the army is no place for a growing boy, neither is the world. . . . There is no place to hide. But perhaps the important detail escapes you. He is in motion. Now you see him, now you don't. If you pin him down in time he is lost in space. Somewhere between where he is from and where he is going he wheels in an unpredictable orbit. He is as free, and as captive, as the wind in his face.

Morris has created, with elegant precision, control, and condensation, a comedy of doom and destiny. The wounds of comedy are real enough, but laughter helps to ease the pain. Nobody else we have around could have done this book. It took a lifetime and twenty-five years of professional writing to do it. *In Orbit* makes the image-makers look like what they are—bush league. It makes the novel seem brand new again. It ought to make those who are trying to write novels and those who are trying to read them happy. Like Jubal we've got something to look forward to. Unlike Jubal we know that whatever it is it will be good. Meanwhile here in *In Orbit* we have as much of the magic, as much of the joy of art as we could ask for.

IV. Afterword (1971)

Following *In Orbit* came an extraordinary book by Wright Morris, *A Bill of Rites, A Bill of Wrongs, A Bill of Goods.* Fifteen closely related essays on the perplexities and absurdity of the here and now, put together, *constructed* as Morris at the peak of his powers puts a novel together, the same devices, large and small, working in consort together to create a cumulative effect; the same dazzling ability to keep mixed and complex feelings alive, by the power of intelligence and the eloquence of art; the same result of savage honesty, of open-minded energy.

It is a remarkable book, demanding of the reader not cleverness, but care; not selling yet another bill of goods, but daring the reader to test his own fragile certainties in a trial by ordeal.

It is rather common these days for poets and novelists to turn their sensible attention to the areas, the manner and matter, once reserved for "nonfiction." At worst they produce inferior journalism. Or, perhaps, the grand and frozen gestures of the sage descending from the mountain top to tell us all. And those few who have managed some degree of excellence seem to have done so at the expense of their other work, which, weighed against the separate achievement, seems somehow shabby and inadequate.

This is not the case with Wright Morris. Just as with *The Territory Ahead, A Bill of Rites* has a place in the whole of his work, grows naturally out of his work in fiction. All is changed and altered slightly; for being an artist and involved in the energy and change which we name Creation, he will not stand still this side of rigor mortis. All is changed, yet nothing, neither the matter nor its essential energy is lost.

All of which adds up something so extraordinary that we ought to celebrate. In his new book Morris has demonstrated (again) that a man, an artist, can intelligently, rigorously deal with the mixed feelings of a shattered time without settling for the simplistic, without accepting self-division as inevitable, without joining the chorus of salesmen and telling lies in the name of the presumed truth. His achievement here, as in the sum of his novels, seems to me unique, yet at the same time exemplary.

It is ironic, but not surprising, that this new book received, relatively, very little attention from reviewers and that, when reviewed, it offended and confused them. The more subtle and clever were, of course, proportionately the more annoyed.

The new book is important in and of itself, a true report and record of the times. In a larger sense it is an important addition to the lifetime

---

labors of a great writer. The final twist, the best irony, is that it *cannot* be ignored.

My essay on *In Orbit* was inadequate from the start. A slight appreciation of something wonderful. It is a pleasure to admit that, though. Faced for once with the real thing, the rare thing, the critic has the privilege of standing at attention, offering a salute, and, for once, meaning it.

At the moment of this writing there has just appeared a beautiful book by Morris in the genre he has named "Photo-Text"—*God's Country and My People*. Returning to the method he earlier used in *The Inhabitants* and *The Home Place*, but on a grander scale and with the advantage of an elegant format and reproduction, he has combined his own photographs and text to present a coherent aesthetic experience.

As one might expect, Morris understands as well as any man alive the proper relation of the word to the photographic image, that is, the *difference* between the two. He does not subordinate text to image by, for example, making text mere expository caption or comment on the presented photograph. Nor is the photograph used to "illustrate" the text. Rather, separate and equal, they relate to and react to each other in such a way that the sum of the two is more than its parts. The cumulative effect of this living relationship, this wedding of distinct expressive forms, is that once the reader-observer's imagination, awakened, has become engaged, it is impossible any more to imagine the one without the other.

This is, then, *multiart*, not mere "multimedia," and a natural, seemingly inevitable outgrowth of this whole lifetime of work, directly related to all his work.

Though a marvelously executed print, almost an abstraction of roots and dry soil (it almost *might* be a contoured aerial view from a receding moon-bound rocket), has the last word, the last *words*, even out of context, form an impeccable conclusion: "Our talent is still for dreaming, and out recurrent dream is flight: a few hours away the luminous fueling stop of the moon. House or ark, sea or plain, shimmering mirages or figures of earth, God's country is still a fiction inhabited by people with a love for the facts."

Facts and fiction, taken together until the two become one. And the name of that one is art.

12

An Amoebaean Contest Where Nobody Loses: The Eclogues of Virgil Translated by David R. Slavitt (1971)

> They are only poets dressed up as farmers, or you and
> I, got up as poets in farmer suits. But departures are
> real enough and loss is nothing new.

—David R. Slavitt, "Tityrus" (Virgil's First Eclogue)

Publius Vergilius Maro was in his early thirties when the *Eclogues* appeared in book form. He was living near Naples then, just north along that sunny, almost seasonless, beautiful coast where, with a favored group of young scholars, he was studying philosophy under the Epicurean Siro. And he was writing poems. In 39 b.c. this sequence of ten related pastoral poems was published. Virgil was a long way from home, a greater distance than the time and space separating the "new city" of Naples and the village of Andes in the north where he was born and the town of Mantua he called home. He had left early to study, first in nearby Cremona, in sight of, in the shadow of the Alps, next in Milan, then at Rome for rhetoric and law. The fields and vineyards, the swift, clear, graveled streams, the pastures, the sudden changeable winds and weathers coming off the mountains, beyond which lay the dark, barbarian, tribal world, all were far behind him. In Naples also he was spared the worst excesses of the civil wars which tormented and ended the Roman Republic; and the aftermath, including the seizure of land (perhaps even his own family farms) for discharged soldiers, he obviously heard about and worried over, suffered with and for, but did not have to witness. Out of memory and nostalgia he summoned up his native landscape, peopled it with literate and literary shepherds bearing Greek names; and, basing his work on

The Eclogues *of Virgil Translated by David R. Slavitt*

---

the models of Theocritus and earlier Greek bucolic poets, he created a slender and delicate structure, a sequence of songs and evocations, sophisticated and rustic, allegorical and actual, at once, as Horace would classify the art of the *Eclogues*, "molle atque facetum," supple and witty; a method by which, as Tityrus puts it in the first eclogue, a real poet could play what he pleased on an imaginery shepherd's pipe.

Others were pleased, and quite suddenly Virgil's life changed. He gained recognition and more. As E.V. Rieu describes it in the introduction to his own prose translation of the *Eclogues*: "The *Eclogues* were even recited or sung in the theatre—by no means a regular by-product, in those days, of publication in book form—and their author received such acclamations as were generally reserved for the ruler of the Roman world." Virgil became an "official" poet. And he went on to write the *Georgics* and to devote the rest of his life to the definition and celebration of *pietas* through his masterwork, the *Aeneid.* When he was dying, Virgil requested that the epic, still unfinished, be burned; but the emperor intervened, interposing final and absolute authority, and ordered it published. Virgil's life found direction with the publication of the *Eclogues.* And so was all Western literature changed as, ever after that, generations of new poets turned to the *Eclogues* for inspiration and example in much the same way that Virgil had begun himself, turning to Theocritus, Bion, and Moschus, who themselves had looked back to others, to the poets of Cos, for example, whose names are lost but whose words live on, modified, transformed, and renewed by others. Virgil managed somehow to preserve and to make new again an ancient tradition which was apparently dying with its language and culture; and his work became both the source and the standard measure for nearly two thousand years of European versions of the pastoral. The pastorals of Virgil's friends have been lost to us, but there are the manuscripts of later Latin pastoral poets like Calpurnius and Nemesianus. And there are the Christian poets of the late days of the empire and throughout medieval times, especially in the brilliance of the Carolingian renaissance. The roll of poets, indeed of *great* and well-remembered poets, who created pastorals built around the model of the *Eclogues* is beyond any listing. But a very few names can suggest something of the story—Dante, Boccaccio, Petrarch, Giovanni Battista Spagnoli (Mantuan), Ronsard, Du Bellay, Spenser, Sidney, Marlowe, Ralegh, Milton, Dryden, Pope, Shelley, Tennyson, Arnold, Edith Sitwell, and Robert Frost. In short, ever since their appearance the stances and strategies of the *Eclogues* have been translated, imitated, adapted, transformed, revised, and renewed.

In our own century (beginning, perhaps, a full century before) the ways and means of the pastoral gave way to more direct and literal-minded modes. Ever foxy, Robert Frost might don a rustic costume, but he saluted his ancient master indirectly, by allusion. In 1910 James Holly Hanford, the great Miltonist, felt compelled to defend Milton's *Lycidas* from the charges of a literary establishment which had turned against the old pastoral tradition. In his brilliant essay "The Pastoral Elegy and Milton's *Lycidas*," he was willing to admit at the outset "that we have today all but forgotten the pastoral tradition and quite lost sympathy with the pastoral mood. The mass of writing to which this artificial yet strangely persistent literary fashion gave rise seems unendurably barren and insipid; to return and traverse the waste, with its dreary repetitions of conventional sentiments and tawdry imagery, is a veritable penance." Hanford had to defend one of the great poems of our language from the charges of "artifice" and "conventionality," qualities which (until very recently) in our time would be automatically listed as obvious flaws in any literary form. Even writing today, he would be hard put to make the pastoral "relevant." The pastoral poem, as such, has almost vanished, though it thrives in disguise in much contemporary American *lyric* poetry and more than once has ghosted a contemporary novel, sometimes even a great novel like Faulkner's *The Hamlet*. But, suddenly, here and now we are presented with a brand new, freshly done, unconventional, utterly contemporary version of Virgil's poems, done directly by translation and not in disguise. And in this version by David Slavitt, Virgil's poems are alive again, not archaeological shards, but as though new-minted, cast and molded, shining in the currency of the late-twentieth-century American language. The commercial publication of this handsome and handsomely illustrated edition is a remarkable occasion, an event worthy of celebration at a time when such events are few and far between.

The Eclogues *of Virgil Translated by David R. Slavitt*

II

No one reads poetry anyway now, except
other poets—which is quite distressing.
They cannot be much as readers, being inept
as rhymers (those that can rhyme), while
confessing
to mental illness, or listing girls they've slept
with (those that like girls) . . . But I am
digressing.
In a time of tastelessness and epic slaughter
we need some of your hock and soda water.

—David R. Slavitt, "Another Letter to Lord Byron"

Where to start? Fiction? That was where he was standing. Sabatini, Sartre, Silone, Stendhal, Sutton, Swados. . . . Or, no, he had read novels. Not all of them, surely, but he knew what a novel was, and it wouldn't be adventurous enough, he thought, to start out with a novel. Poetry? Garrett, Gay, Graves, Gregory, Hall. . . . He opened a rather smart-looking book with shiny sprinkles in the white binding and read, "Oysters are jails. Half wits / And frightened people too afraid to move / Drown in an oyster's keep." No, not poetry either. Spangled bindings and "oysters are jails" indeed. He realized that his bladder was full.

—David R. Slavitt, *Feel Free*

In 1970, in sunny Florida, by account of his own preface, David Slavitt, poet, novelist, dramatist, critic, and something of a celebrity under another name, with some leisure time at hand, began to fiddle with the idea of translating the *Eclogues*. At first glance and with easy, instant reaction, this seems outrageous. It seems absurd that in this day and age anyone would want to translate, much less to publish, a new version of Virgil's pastoral poems, replete with piping shepherds, rich with a mother lode of pathetic fallacies. Talk about irrelevance! And with second glance and wince, look who's doing it—David Slavitt, a bright and clever fellow to be sure, known for turning tidy profits under the pen name of Henry Sutton. Say what you will, pro and con, about Slavitt-Sutton, he's no Erich Segal. After all, Segal is (or was until the wounds of fame and the weariness of jogging to and from the bank became too much for a slight body to bear) a Classics professor. He can conjugate a Latin verb as good as anybody. And Segal never claimed (or admitted as the case may be), as he made the regular rounds of the selfsame sequence of TV talk shows and appearances Sutton had earlier toured, that he wrote his popular novel for *money*. Sutton made no bones about it, not on television, nor in the (separate and unequal) articles he wrote about the experience of creating a best-seller, one for the *Kenyon Review*, one for *Esquire*. No, Sutton called it *schlock*, written for *sheckels*, and thus anticipated, single-handed, the game of *Naked Came the Stranger*. And then, as if to compound offense, he defended his goal as proper to our times and, further, pointed out that the pop or trash novel, to be well done, demands a reasonable degree of literary sophistication on the part of both the writer and the reader. No part of this public stance can be called respectable. The beautiful pop-up people—Irvings, Arthurs, Jacquelines, Erichs, and Rods—insist ad nauseum that they write the way they do, like all great artists, because *they really feel that way*. Henry Sutton gave them a *zatz* and a Bronx cheer, refusing to embrace such a bald untruth even for the sake of respectability. He admitted he did it for fun and for money, and he could write in other modes and voices than that one. Which was bad enough. But to go further and to point out that the pop mode, the trash genre, demands much craft and craftiness, a good measure of clever artifice, this was to add insult to injury. In short, on the basis of first glances and winces, Slavitt seems an entirely unlikely candidate, to say the least, and an arrogant barefaced knave, to say more, to offer up a new translation of Virgil's *Eclogues*. If only it had been Robert Lowell . . . ah, *well*, that would be another matter. Lowell has earned his cheverons and medals, his public place as translator and imitator. He has translated far and wide, even some Virgil. Perhaps, on the other hand, it might have been Richard Wilbur, whose translations of Molière sing clean and clear on the page and in the theater, and whose lyrics contain many of the pastoral moods with grace and natural elegance. Or perhaps it could have been some combination, poet and classicist, out of one of the well-funded translation centers here and there. We live in an age of translation, as busy at it as Elizabethan England. If the *Eclogues* had any interest, any real merit, surely one of the tried-and-true translators would have done the job, on a grant or fellowship, long before now. Moreover, we live in an age of specialization. Though every poet alive may dream of writing best-selling novels to support the habit of writing verses, and though many have given it the olde college try, they have not been so vulgar as to succeed. David Slavitt, who has received no fat grants or fellowships to tide him over, went out into the heart of darkness of the literary jungle (and not blindly, for he knew it well enough from his days as book editor and movie editor of *Newsweek*), took aim, bagged trophies, and came out, laughing and scratching, to tell his tale. Since Ford, Rockefeller, and the federal government wouldn't, why, then, he'd fund himself. And with the leisure his loot earned him, he proceeded to write poems and to translate the *Eclogues.*

The very idea of Slavitt undertaking the *Eclogues* is an offense. It hits right to the solar plexus of clichés we live by. And that stunning blow is reason enough to back away, to question the validity of first glances and instant reactions, to look a little deeper and see what we can find. Some things are easily accessible. The facts are available, not secret. Some facts, then: David Slavitt began his study of the classics in the best classical program available in this country at the time, at Andover, studying under one of the most influential (and demanding) classicists in the country—the late Dudley Fitts. Slavitt continued his classics at Yale, formally and on his own, under the freedom offered to a Scholar of the House. At Columbia he wrote his M.A. thesis on Fitts, and he has continued reading in Latin literature ever since. He also learned a great deal about poetry from Fitts, and it was as a poet that David Slavitt was first published with *Suits for the Dead* (1961). Since then he has published two other collections of poems, as well as three Sutton novels and two Slavitt novels, prior to this occasion—the simultaneous publication of the *Eclogues* and of a new Slavitt novel, *Anagrams.* He has also written screenplays, and two of his plays—*King Saul* and *The Cardinal Sins*—have been produced Off-Broadway and in England. In brief, then, he is a rare bird in our times, a genuinely multitalented and productive writer, and evidently is as untroubled by his popular success as he has been undeterred, uncrippled by the frustra-

---

tions of being a good, original, overlooked poet. It is as poet that he appears here. But, still, a few things ought to be said about his novels, in particular his own David Slavitt novels. They are, as one might expect from a poet, brilliant and diverting in language. Slavitt has not found it necessary to inhibit his verbal gifts in order to make an arbitrary distinction between prose and verse; for, unlike most novels by poets, Slavitt's novels are marvelously constructed. And each offers a particular kind of narrative problem and then solves it. *Rochelle* is a kind of Restoration comedy in modern dress, structured just so, and is told by a first-person narrator who is deliberately "unpleasant." That is, the narrator comes on strong and, at times, offensively. Since he is presenting both the story and himself, we might be expected to suspend judgment at least, if not to anticipate an obvious charade. And sure enough, at precisely the right time and place in the story, the narrator drops his guard briefly, long enough for us to see that he is not so cynical, sophisticated, or wicked as he wishes us to think. Only a few critics noticed that, the rest assuming that the author had inadvertently produced an annoying protagonist. They also missed much of the comedy of this tale of "virtue rewarded," literally and figuratively. Next, in *Feel Free*, Slavitt told the story of a lovable bankrupt, Bernie Lazarus. The third-person viewpoint was Bernie's. Lovable Bernie caused all kinds of trouble, and some of it real misery, to people all around him. The situation and the treatment of it served to satirize many of the clichés of the "urban Jewish novel." Practically everyone managed to miss the point of *Feel Free*, funny and satirical, but a black comedy if comic at all, by taking Bernie at face value, from first to last. *Anagrams* is a virtuoso literary novel, omniscient in point of view, built around a pair of college poetry readings; and the big showdown is a game of anagrams; it is a very funny and very sad book, which probably says as much as any novel can about the inner workings of a poet's spirit. It is a tour de force, with levels of fun and games that could please Nabokov. It will richly reward any reader who's willing and able to play the game himself.

But David Slavitt has remained primarily a poet. Like many first books by good poets, *Suits for the Dead*, in retrospect, shows much of what the poet could and would do. The range in forms, tones of voice, and subject matter is wide and various. He shows that he can handle all kinds of tough, tricky forms, and that he *likes* forms. He is perfectly at home in many rhythms, formal and syncopated. The language is brilliant, the range almost complete (from Ronald Firbank to Lenny Bruce and Dave Gardner). He can be witty or can crack wise as the occasion demands. Above all he can *think* in verse, thus inviting the reader to use his intelligence too. And he is not afraid of the "literary" subject, making it as near and palpable as the weather of today, as, for example, when he chooses sides with "A Person From Porlock" for interrupting Coleridge's compositon of "Kubla Khan":

> Still, let us delight
> that the world of Porlock—or Jackson Heights—
> impinges
> a little on Khan, on Coleridge. The metaphysical
> Fullerbrush man's knock, though sometimes hated,
> is somehow right.

In his introduction to *Suits for the Dead* John Hall Wheelock noticed something more, something deeper than surface virtues and pleasure. He saw Slavitt's poems as "a way of knowing, as a revelation which interprets, thus brings order out of, the multiplicity and chaos of experience—by means of selection and synthesis giving it form, and thereby increasing our knowledge and our understanding of it." Wheelock took special note of "one of the outstanding characteristics of Mr. Slavitt's work, his use of tone: either to mask an inner seriousness, which is then gradually permitted to assert itself, and with all the greater force, as the poem goes on; or . . . to yield us an experience on two levels." The poet is masked, then, speaks through characters and personae; the forms will be dramatic, will have meaning, mingling delight with instruction, according to the classical prescription.

The demanding subtlety which Wheelock recognized is more evident in *The Carnivore* (1965). The range of this collection is, if anything, wider, more extravagant than in the first book: from the classic pastoral elegy of "Elegy for Walter Stone," to the jazzy rhythms and zany rhyme schemes of "Half Fare," written for one son, his firstborn, and "Nursery Rime," a version of Bo Peep which Gene Krupa might profitably study, for his youngest child. There are also a number of odd,

---

epigrammatic poems, derived from his interest in ancient history, poems like "The Enigmatic Death of the Emperor, Alexius—A.D. 1081," "In Defense of Arcadius—A.D. 396," "On Realpolitik and the Death of Galba," "Stauracius," "The School of Athens," "Theodoric," "Belisaurius"; and these are intermingled with such others as "Planting Crocus," "F.A.O. Schwartz," and "St. Patrick's Day: 47th St." *Day Sailing* (1969) offers units of poems, built around place or theme or both—a series constructed around the title poem and the place where the poet lives, Cape Cod; a series on art and the art of love (which contains the first version of Virgil's tenth eclogue); the virtuosity of "Another Letter to Lord Byron," in the proper Byronic stanza and properly set off by itself; and finally a grouping of long poems, beginning with the startling and moving "Exhortation to an Arab Friend (1965)."

A general (and inadequate) observation: by the age of thirty-four this poet had demonstrated an extraordinary range and depth, a combination of baroque virtuosity and brute strength which few, if any, of his contemporaries could match. Though inadequately recognized, his singular gifts did not pass unnoticed by some critic-scholars with a long, large view. Irvin Ehrenpreis and Louis Martz are two of these who are on record as ranking Slavitt's poetry among the best we have. Clearly he possessed the capacity, the sophistication, and the courage to undertake the challenge of translating Virgil's *Eclogues* anew, and not in any disguise, but by joining his own voice with Virgil's.

III

> *Knowing better,*
> *we listen and even we believe for a moment,*
> *as Virgil did, and Theocritus, and Daphnis.*
> *Professionals, but they believed they could feel*
> *those rocks getting ready to sing, even taking a*
> *breath,*
> *a stronger breath than any of yours or mine.*

—David R. Slavitt, "Daphnis" (Virgil's Fifth Eclogue)

There are any number of good reasons why Virgil's *Eclogues* have been so influential.

The Eclogues *of Virgil Translated by David R. Slavitt*

(1.) Because they were magnificent poetry. But many great poems, in languages living and dead, have survived only to gather more motes of dust than readers.

(2.) Because Virgil lived to write the *Georgics* and, above all, the *Aeneid.* But the minor and early works of many other great poets are long gone or are recalled only in bits and pieces by a few scholars.

(3.) Because of Fortune, the tricks and turns of time. Virgil lived a good life, endured his own time as a successful poet. As Slavitt puts it in his preface: "It is necessary first of all for an artist to survive, and survival is never easy. That Virgil died at the age of fifty-one, leaving an estate of something like half a million dollars in modern money seems to me delightful." And the work itself (literally) managed to survive times when so very much was lost. The manuscripts were carefully copied and recopied, in good times and bad. Which was partly pure luck, but also a sign that the poems remained *useful*.

(4.) Because the *Eclogues* have been useful, then, to alien poets in strange languages. Even as he was conserving an old Greek form, toying with it, Virgil was expanding the territory, acting as a pioneer of possibility. After his example, the pastoral could include great themes and subjects—the elegy, the love poem, the satire and lament, and the subject of poetry, of art itself. The *Eclogues* opened new trails for future poets to follow and to explore. But many of these—the masque, the pastoral romance—proved dead ends early enough.

(5.) Because Virgil added a dimension which was the greatest innovation in the form. He married the "real" and the personal to the artificial and the allegorical just as, in the *Eclogues,* he describes the native elms of his country as "married" to twisting grape vines. He showed how the general and allegorical could be joined to the particular, to a time, a place, one man's experience. And this, in turn, extended rather than limited the possibilities of figurative meaning, of all that medieval poets meant by *allegoria*. From the Greeks Virgil inherited the figurative tradition for the pastoral. One part of this was the use of the shepherd as the figure for the poet. But this figure belongs, as well, to the Judeo-Christian tradition. There is the logical figure of the shepherd as king, as leader, culminating in the figure of Christ the Good Shepherd, and still found in the living language where a priest is the *pastor* of his flock. And David, who was king, was also the psalmist, the shepherd-poet. In the Christian story the news of the coming of Christ came to the Wise Men in a dream and by the stars, but an angel spoke directly to "certain shepherds." For them, real shepherds, the angel did not need to be imagined. So it was easy for the Christian to take over the classical figure of the shepherd-poet, simple but divinely inspired, chosen to receive and to body forth in language, in song, the eternal verities. It is hardly accidental that the Venerable Bede cites Caedmon, an illiterate herdsman, as our first, archetypal poet in English. An angel came to Caedmon and ordered him to sing the story of Creation. And, like the demigod Silenus, in Virgil's sixth eclogue, he sang that greatest subject half-drunk, half-dreaming.

Another allegorical characteristic of the Greek bucolic poems was the dream of Arcadia, holy home of Pan, the shepherds' god and the inventor of pastoral music. Arcadia was a close analogy, a figure for the lost Eden of the Jews and Christians. Against that timeless example of perfection and loss could be set *any* specific time and place in the changing world. Thus time, change, mutability became basic themes of the pastoral; and so, also, these were set against the age-old dreams of all that is unchanging.

Clearly, for the sophisticated Romans of the Augustan Age, though the landscape of the *Eclogues* was real enough, the shepherds and their songs were figures intended to direct attention to other meanings—specifically to moral, physical, and historical truths. Virgil's method allowed him to deal with specific historical and personal situations, most of these lost to us as in the same way, for example, the context of specific historical allusion of Spenser's *The Shepherd's Calendar* is gone for all but graduate students. But this source of pleasure for his contemporaries in no way detracted from the other, more universal and general truths he dealt with, truths which allowed fifteen hundred years of Augustinian poets and scholars to turn to Virgil almost as often as to Scripture for delight and instruction. By blending the "real" with the figurative, by mingling the particular with the general, Virgil pointed the way for other poets to do the same thing. The *Eclogues* are, then, among all other things, an invitation to future poets to make their own pastorals, out of their own times and places and languages. if they are able, if they dare. . . . For in the invitation is a challenge to an amoebaean contest, a ritual singing match between poets, and always to be between the living poet and Virgil's ghost.

The Eclogues *of Virgil Translated by David R. Slavitt*

It insures the persistence of Virgil's sequence, but, by the same to-ken, it is a challenge to be accepted only by the very brave or the hope-lessly foolhardy.

IV

Sixth formers read it now, sweat out the
grammar,
furrow their smooth foreheads to get it right,
but cannot know what we know, you and I,
Tityrus says it all: "Fool that I was,
I used to think the city they call Rome
was like our market town, but bigger."
It's not.
A little later on, you can hear him groan,
Dead, the Latin dead, his groan is alive,
aloud, along the fields he saved for a while:
"What else could I do? There was nowhere else to go!
There was nobody else to turn to, no other way . . . "

—David R. Slavitt, "Tityrus" (Virgil's First Eclogue)

It is fitting that Doubleday should bring out *Anagrams* simulta-neously with this new version of the *Eclogues*; for it is the literary as-pect of the *Eclogues*, the views of the art of poetry and "the literary life," which Slavitt has chosen to stress in his translation. Much of this aspect has been ignored by our critics and scholars, the bad ones wres-tling with the order of composition of the *Eclogues* and the specific al-lusions, the best working on text, on the sense of overall structure, and the general allegory. Slavitt goes for the clear, but much-ignored im-plications of the *Eclogues*. "Indeed," he writes in the preface, "the lit biz is a primary concern of the *Eclogues*. No writer who has ever raged at agents, editors, publishers, critics, other writers, or the public can fail to recognize in these extraordinary poems the anguish Virgil felt, the compassion, or the hope." Slavitt's method, neither adaptation nor imitation, would have been immediately recognized as valid by any lit-erary critic from Virgil's time up through the time of Dryden. Slavitt does not offer a "literal rendering" of the *Eclogues*, though, in fact, the crucial lines, the sound, sense, and the modern equivalent of the

---

rhythms are all there. "To keep that double vision of the originals," he writes, "I have worked out what might be called a series of meditations on the *Eclogues*. The fluidity is such that the voices of the shepherds, of Virgil, of Virgil's editors, and my own voice can all comment on each other, and in the end produce the kind of harmony that characterized the original poems." And so we have a slender, elegant edition of the *Eclogues*, brightly decorated with the drawings by Raymond Davidson, the illustrations in perfect decorum with the words even to the deliberate wit of anachronism. Anachronism is basic. As Virgil used it, mixing the alien and the familiar, the marvelous and the common, so Slavitt cuts cinematically from ancient Rome to modern New York, from Greeks and Romans to the poet, any artist, among his friends and enemies:

> Then Lycidas
> tells him another, and Moeris . . . Moeris sighs
> for the way it was when there was nothing else
> to worry about but spring and a sprung line.
> But it closes in. The reception rooms are waiting
> with blondes behind blond woods of expensive desks,
> and further back the offices of villains.
> The babble of song has turned to the last glug
> of water down a drain. The plug is pulled.

Toughest for the translator are the most serious *Eclogues*. And none is more difficult to handle than the fourth, "Pollio," which celebrates birth and a new beginning. This one was, quite naturally, taken by later Christian poets as a prefiguring of the coming of Christ. But what did it mean to the pagan poet, this dream of a future as fair as Arcadia? And what can it mean to skeptic, secular modern man who has many idols and few gods? The question must be asked in the poem and the historical facts faced, and to be true, to translate Virgil, the high seriousness and hoping cannot be dissipated by irony.

> No plows,
> but the earth will offer up crops. No ships on the
> sea

The Eclogues *of Virgil Translated by David R. Slavitt*

risking the savage storms, but every land
will produce all things. No tints and dyes for wool,
but sheep will be blue and purple and yellow and
green.
The dreams are familiar, but then the need is
familiar
and always with us.

Here, with the poem's last lines, a poet of many masks and moods set-
tles for the purest (and most difficult) simplicity:

Let there be no child
who comes into the world without some hope,
some joy in him. And we shall have begun . . .

What does it all add up to for us, a book two thousand years old,
brought out in new translation by a tough-minded, tough-talking modern poet, a book undeniably great, but undeniably troublesome for the
reader who mistrusts the ancient artifice, who finds imaginary shepherds too difficult to imagine and therefore imagines them as irrelevant
to his real concerns, who acknowledges that his imagination is atro-
phied, but argues that the world of hard facts now taxes even credulity
to its limits? When the visible world is absurd, more fantastic than any
dream, who needs the recollection of invisible times too distant to be
believed? David Slavitt could have stressed the historical relevance of
Virgil's time, assassinations, civil broil, the end of the Republic. But he
chose not to, choosing rather to celebrate the poet himself (who alone
survived those times intact), and in the figure of the poet to suggest a
definition of what poetry is now, as it has always been, the marvel of
sentient human consciousness and the ceaseless quest to find forms to
tell (each new beginning being as old as Adam's) how it seems to be. It
is well put, by both Virgil and Slavitt in "Pharmaceutria":

None of us plays the game
for the money or the fame, but for that trick
of vision. Yes, it's all of it done with mirrors.
A man can look at himself and not quite be

the man he sees, because part of him is looking,
noting how it feels, how interesting
love or grief or hate can be, how slow
time seems to move, how the mind will wander
at moments of great joy, and how it could work
in a poem, say.

Afterword:
Review of The Tristia of Ovid, Translated by David R.
Slavitt (1989)

With the death of Horace in 8 B.C., Ovid (Publius Ovidius Naso, 43 B.C.–A.D. 17) earned recognition as the foremost living Roman poet at a time which happened to be the age of the emperor Augustus and included some of the outstanding and most influential of the classical poets. Although he had a different patron and, thus, belonged to a different literary circle, Ovid was friends with Horace and Propertius, and he was at least acquainted with the great Virgil. He was also a close friend and an admirer of the gifted poet Tibullus, who died young. (And who has also been recently translated by David R. Slavitt, *The Elegies To Delia Of Albus Tibullus*, Bits Press, 1985.) A well-to-do member of the equestrian class, Ovid kept a country estate in his native *patria* of Sulmo, about one hundred miles from Rome; and he owned a town house and an orchard in the heart of Rome. He was married three times, the last time for love and for life; and we know that he had at least one daughter. Urbane, witty, gifted, and, from what we can tell and guess, good-looking, Ovid loved the good life in the great city at the center of the empire. In A.D. 8 for mysterious and mostly secret reasons (then and now) he was suddenly *relegated* by Augustus to the far thin edge of the empire, the frontier town of Tomis near the Black Sea in what is now Romania. This specific form of exile allowed him to keep his citizenship and his poetry. It also allowed him to write and publish his work; though evidently his books were removed from the public libraries. It left him hope and left him dangling. For the emperor was able to bring him back home with a word whenever it pleased him to. It pleased neither the aging Augustus nor his successor, Tiberius, to end Ovid's exile. In spite of every kind of scheming and planning that the poet could muster, he died out there in the deep boonies, alone and

The Eclogues *of Virgil Translated by David R. Slavitt*

far from home and hearth, wife and family. It was, to be sure, an experience which gave him another subject for poetry. The first things that he wrote were verse letters to Rome, pleading and making his case by every means he could contrive. Over several years he managed to put together and send home to Rome the five books of poems which form the *Tristia.* These poems are fascinating, troubling, and brilliant. Fascinating in their autobiographical detail and picture of the lost life of Augustan Rome and the rude life on the frontier. Troubling in their necessary rhetorical stances of whining self-pity, servility before and flattery of authority. Technically brilliant (and enormously influential) in their felicitous mastery of the hexameter elegiac couplet. Probably, all things considered, no other classical poet has exercised such a persistent influence on our literary culture; and our great poets, from Chaucer, Spenser, and Shakespeare on up to Ezra Pound, have been deeply influenced by Ovid. But since the early seventeenth century the *Tristia* has seldom been translated until now, now when we are, alas, all too familiar with the literature of exile and the implacable power of the powers that be.

This is, far and away, the finest translation of the *Tristia* I have ever seen, a perfect matching of poet-translator with his material. Author of nine books of poetry of his own, a graceful master of metrics and forms, well-educated in classics at Andover and Yale, already established as a skilled and innovative translator (his version of Virgil's *Eclogues* was the subject of an earlier *Hollins Critic*), Slavitt is also, like Ovid, urbane, witty, intellectually energetic and daring, deeply involved in the literary scene, and painfully aware of all the injuries and exiles the world yokes and burdens us with. The result is a handsome book, beautifully illustrated by Raymond Davidson, and arriving with the jacket presenting enthusiastic supporting words of two of the most distinguished living classicists—Bernard M. W. Knox and Gordon Williams. Poets X. J. Kennedy, O. B. Hardison, Jr., Karl Shapiro, and Richard Wilbur are lavish with their praise. Wilbur writes: "Tone and personality, so often lost in translation of whatever kind, are captured here; someone clever, passionate and heartbroken comes very near us, and I think it is Ovid." For two thousand years Ovid has been somebody worth knowing. Slavitt's version of the *Tristia* offers the best introduction I can think of.

IV

Southern Literature
and William Faulkner

Author's Note

The life and works of William Faulkner have been on my mind for a long time. In my first year at Princeton University (1947–48) I encountered and immediately invested in the Viking Portable Library, that brand new series of fat, squat, pocket-filling, wonderful and wonderfully crammed little books. One of them was Malcolm Cowley's celebrated *Portable Faulkner.* I also had the Hemingway and the Fitzgerald. The big difference was that I had already heard of them and had even read a little of their work at home and in school. I had never heard of William Faulkner before, though I soon learned that various readers in my family knew of his work and had read some of it; and some of them, a greatly gifted Texas cousin, for example, knew his work well.

I cannot begin to convey the excitement (it was delicious and almost illicit) with which I "discovered" and devoured the work of that great writer. I read everything I could get my hands on. Which was quite a lot and not too hard; because in those days, even first editions of William Faulkner were just *sitting there* in a row in the regular stacks. And, anyway, nobody else, at least at Princeton in those days, was checking them out.

When I went in the army—to the Free Territory of Trieste, to Austria and Germany—I took the Viking *Portable Faulkner* with me. It fit perfectly in the pockets of my field jacket and a little less neatly and well in my fatigue trousers back pockets. Later on, still, I found myself in graduate school on the G.I. Bill. And because I was still a weight lifter in those days and always available for any kind of lifting and toting, hefting and hauling of things, I went up to New York City in a van from Princeton's Firestone Library, together with the young Faulkner scholar (he was one of the very first of that breed except, of course, for Carvel Collins) James B. Meriwether. From the basement of Random

House at the old Fifth Avenue address we lugged two large steamer trunks and loaded them into the van and drove them back to Princeton. Then in the basement of Firestone Library we opened up those trunks and found them to be chaotically packed with papers, letters, and manuscripts of William Faulkner. Most of all I recall his tiny, delicate, almost indecipherable handwriting. And his talented doodles and drawings. Meriwether sorted out everything and then organized an elegant exhibit of these things at Firestone. I should add that once, as Meriwether was sorting papers, I took some notes for him on long sheets of yellow legal paper. Years later I was astonished and amused to find those selfsame yellow sheets under a glass case at a Faulkner exhibit in the Alderman Library of The University of Virginia, together with a card attributing them to William Faulkner, himself.

Our paths criscrossed, here and there, but I never met William Faulkner outside of his books.

All of this is simply to explain what you can see for yourself in the pieces that follow—that the work of William Faulkner has meant a great deal to me as a reader and as a writer. He was and is a powerfully influential author. But there is no escaping him except by embracing ignorance. And, as I have argued here and there, his good influence is, finally, liberating, not inhibiting.

Some of these pieces are dated, of course; for massive and irrepressible scholarship, a genuine industry, has turned up troves of new information, new manuscripts, revised texts; and critical judgments are constantly changing and being revised, for better and worse. I have chosen to let my own efforts stand as they were and are, as a record of my own pleasure in discovery and learning by example.

13

Southern Literature
Here and Now
(1981)

*Without any censorship in the West, fashionable trends of thought are care-
fully separated from those that are not fashionable. Nothing is forbidden,
but what is not fashionable will hardly ever find its way into periodicals or
books or be heard in colleges. Legally, your researchers are free, but they
are conditioned by the fashion of the day. There is no open violence such
as in the East; however, a selection dictated by fashion and the need to
match mass standards frequently prevents independent-minded people from
giving their contribution to public life. There is a dangerous tendency to
form a herd, shutting off successful development.*

> —Alexandr Solzhenitsyn, address at Harvard University's
> commencement, 1978

In the following discussion it will be more than a contention, it will
be more a matter of firm and unquestioned assumption that in this particular observation, as in so many others, Alexandr Solzhenitsyn said
what is purely and simply true. Serious consideration of a wide range of
serious subjects is severely restricted in these times by "fashion," by
"mind set," by all the elements of a fairly uniform liberal intellectual
consensus (and its consequent intellectual rigidity) in contemporary
America which so startled Solzhenitsyn.

It is difficult even to try to describe the contemporary South and its
literature without departing from the boundaries of that fashionable
consensus. To deviate from the consensus, in public and in print, is an
exercise of bad manners which most Southerners would as lief avoid.
As Lisa Alther, a Southern novelist now living in Vermont, wrote in
The New York Times Book Review ("Will the South Rise Again?"):

"Most Southerners have strong and cranky opinions yet know that it's not polite to insist on one's own point of view or to dispute someone else's."

As a compromise, I shall do my best not to insist on my own point of view. However, I reserve the right to dispute anyone else's.

I

Lisa Alther, given a prominent position and an opportunity to ask her perennial question, produced a lively and entertaining article which arrived at no firm or startling conclusions beyond the casual observations that there are still some basic distinctions between the practice of good manners, and the emphasis upon them, in the North and the South; that the Southerner seems naturally to fall into the structure, language, images, and idiom of anecdote when sending his messages and communicating his thoughts and feelings; that, in a strictly literary sense, there have been some Southern writers in our times who are widely acknowledged to have been masterful and profoundly influential literary artists; that there appear to be a good many gifted new writers still coming out of the South, but that "the Southern Renaissance writers are a tough act to follow, however inspirational their example." She duly noted the signs of the much-discussed "New South," and she wondered (as have so many others) whether the South can possibly survive this season of transition from old to new, enduring all the apparently homogenizing and standardizing forces of the culture, both good and bad, and yet still somehow or other manage to preserve at least some of the region's distinct and admirable qualities of daily life, qualities which have given rise to some of the distinctly admirable qualities of Southern literature. This is not, as indicated, a new question; and her answers to it (being inevitably and in large part the kind of "answers answerless" which Queen Elizabeth I once so favored) are familiar enough also.

None of which is to fault Lisa Alther. Who, knowingly or unknowingly, has found herself, for whatever reasons, allowed simply to reiterate both questions and answers already often proposed by many others within and outside of the South. Her views are based upon and, indeed, elucidate a great many of these commonly held assumptions about the South, its way of living, and its forms of literary art. These *assumptions* of and behind any critical and intellectual consensus must be at least tested and explored before we can even pretend to move toward any kind of description of things as they may be and of things as they may well come to be in the foreseeable, imaginable future.

Another recent, and more relevant, item is the excellent introduction by Guy Owen and Mary C. Williams to their *Contemporary Southern Poetry: An Anthology* (Louisiana State University Press, 1979). Brief as it is, this essay is riddled with insights and fresh and accurate views of the present state of Southern poetry. Yet here, too, the essay must necessarily begin by discussing (questioning, anyway) the validity of the notion as to whether or not "the region has lost its distinctiveness and has been absorbed into the mainstream of America." Thus one major question troubling most critics of Southern literature is the extent to which the overwhelming weight of our national culture has so far changed the literature of the South. There seems to be no question in anyone's mind that, outwardly and visibly, Southern *life* and styles are being submerged in the American "mainstream." No one who trusts the reports of the senses and the records of memory can doubt that the South, with its growing cities and its sprawling miles of standard suburbs, has become all too much like most of the other urban and suburban parts in the United States. Same tricky maze of interconnected highways. Same shiny, noisy, busy airports. Same motels and tacky shopping centers and fast-food franchises. Same festering and decaying inner cities. Same chain stores with pretty much the same products. And many of the same national and evidently insoluble problems—high taxes and poor services, pollution, crime, the idleness of so many of the ill-educated young and the loneliness of the forgotten and exhausted old, the shrugging indifference of the powers that be, the brutal, yawning impersonality of our bureaucrats, the primitive ignorance and irresponsibility of our politicians. It is as if the worst of the Fugitive nightmares had now come to pass. On any given day in, for example, Atlanta or Richmond or Raleigh or New Orleans or Birmingham or Houston, it would be easy to believe not only that the South thoroughly lost the War, but that since then it has been effaced, ploughed under, and covered with asphalt. Has vanished forever in a total and final Yankee triumph.

Still, most sane Southerners, however much they may be offended by what is new and seems to be wholly alien, however much they suffer nostalgia for what seems to have left so little behind, are willing to admit that there have been at least some improvements, if only technological ones, in the quality of day-to-day living. Even so, much that was admirable, amiable, amenable, honorable, and even beautiful looks to be gone for once and for all. By now there is probably no corner of our South rural and remote enough to have been spared an infectious dose of the products of "today's mass living habits" in America, which Solzhenitsyn cited as "the revolting invasion by publicity, by TV stupor, and by intolerable music."

The long and the short of it is that a great many of our most sensitive and intelligent observers perceive, indeed, now assume, that most of the things which made the South distinct within the larger national culture are going or have already gone. To many thoughtful Southerners it seems a great pity; to others it may seem high time. But it is quite possible that neither the friendly nor the hostile view is more superficial, that this hasty perception of the present is, at the very least, out of date. It has been well argued, on the strength of some very solid evidence, that, throughout the entire world, the high season of centralization is over and done with. The dominant and characteristic worldwide trend in this last quarter of the twentieth century is toward the breakdown of all large and unwieldy political units; we are already witnessing a breakup so thorough and powerful that it may soon spell out the end of the whole concept of the nation-state as we have known it. (In which case, the South would prove to have *won* the War after all. Finally!) In many places this is taking place amid a context of war and revolutionary upheaval. Here in America it is (so far) more peaceably manifest in what René Dubos has called "regionalism by choice." Each census seems to indicate that Americans are now more and more *choosing* the places where they want to live. It seems not to be merely a matter of climate and comfort; for even though there is, inevitably, a major nomadic movement toward the Sun Belt, there is also a surge of settlers moving into the West and even into upper New England. The phenomenon, as it is developing in America, appears to be based as much upon popular perception of and affinity for a regional "lifestyle" as anything else. It follows that these new settlers will desire to protect and defend the qualities and characteristics which led them to their new homes in the first place; or, in the case of the native born, qualities which led them to choose to remain there. So, in this sense, very powerful forces for conservation, if not strictly and conventionally conservative, seem already at work. The irrepressible anxiety and nostalgia shadowing much contemporary literature and literary criticism can be seen not so much as the last trumpet calls of a lost cause (no matter how much we Southerners, by nature and in art, rejoice in the celebration of forlorn hopes), but instead as the expression of some of the deepest and, yes, even the *latest* trends in the culture.

It may be noteworthy that *each generation* of modern and contemporary Southern writers has responded in much the same way—lamenting the dimming of many bright things and the falling away of familiar certainties. Allowing for the fact that this is a traditional Southern trope (itself probably directly descended from the alliterative poetry of the Anglo-Saxons, who seem to have been happiest and easiest in the elegiac mood long before their own vital culture gave them any serious need to cultivate it), it is mildly strange that much of what the very youngest generation of Southern writers laments and regrets the passing of had to be, in fact, among the crowd of *new things* whose arrival and presence on the scene was roundly deplored by the previous generations. One of the things shared by these generations of Southern writers, masters and apprentices alike, is this very general yet essential sense of loss. Which, in turn, may be taken as an attractive characteristic of the Southern spirit, one which draws others toward the South and one which Southerners, wherever they may end up, by choice or out of necessity, always carry with them. Surely the knowledge that changes, whether for good or ill, always include some losses grows out of the bitter Southern historical experience and is a valuable corrective contribution in a society which not so much seeks to make a virtue of necessity by accepting change as to embrace all change on principle and, wherever possible, to manipulate it to advantage.

To begin, then, it is at least possible to doubt that the South as we know it, with its various people and its diverse culture, is in any danger of vanishing from the scene.

II

The most formidable fact which the working Southern writer must face (not really a *problem*, mind you, though it may be taken as one by many writers) is the recognition of his coming after at least one generation of Southern master artists. Of all these masters, some still living and a few (like Robert Penn Warren) still vigorously creative and actively influential, none casts a longer shadow than William Faulkner. All of the newer Southern writers—by which I mean to identify all those (and they are many and various) who have produced work since World War II; thus, by the old-fashioned reckoning, at least a generation and a half—have to live with the overwhelming example of William Faulkner and must come to terms not only with his great body of work, but also with his ghost. For his influence and example are now personal as well as artistic, thanks to Joseph Blotner's biography, and to the published selections of his letters, speeches, and interviews. Perhaps, ironically, more so than if he had not so zealously and successfully defended his privacy during his lifetime; that is, the *personal* influence and example, being suspensefully delayed and likewise partaking of the fresh impact of discovery, can be seen as stronger and more immediate, more like "news" than like history. Of course, it is worth remembering that the influence of Faulkner's work, of his purely artistic example, was also long delayed, deferred by the unconscionable length of time that passed before he earned any widespread recognition in establishment literary circles. In fact, his recognition began to occur almost a generation after he had earned it.

The contemporary Southern writer must also, and simultaneously, contend with many other powerful, pervasive influences and examples coming from the worldwide generation of masters. And Southern writers must now seek to find some form of accommodation with the larger, the *national* American literary situation, the "scene," insofar as it exists and infringes upon their capacity to create and to be recognized. There is nothing precisely new about this. William Faulkner and our other masters have always had to make the same kind of accommodation, at least ever since the Civil War and Reconstruction ended (for all practical purposes) for a long time the serious potential of the South as a center of publishing as well as writing.

That particular topic—the relation of the contemporary Southern writer to the larger context—will be treated in a separate section of this essay. But it is useful, here and now, to bear in mind that it is not a truly abstract or separate situation. For example, in addition to the undesirable inner and regional pressure, the *family* feeling, as it were, felt by every Southern writer that his efforts will be measured against the standards of achievement of the masters (thus, inevitably, against those of Faulkner), there is also an outer pressure coming from Northern critics and scholars and book reviewers, a good many of them alien and even indifferent to both the Southern experience and its literary traditions. It is, at the very least, an intellectual convenience for most of these people to maintain the notion that Southern literature began and ended with the prominent masters of the Southern Renaissance; that its greatness began and ended with William Faulkner, against whom every apprentice writer can be judged and found wanting in a way that, say, a Jewish first novel would never be strictly measured against the standards of Bellow or Singer or Malamud.

The Southern writer today must contend with a discouraging double standard when he ventures outside his region and traditions, as venture he still must until (and if) small presses, university presses, and Southern trade publishing and bookselling become, again a viable alternative.

As to the influence and example of Faulkner, and of the other masters whose present influence differs only in degree and not in kind, everyone is familiar with Flannery O'Connor's often-quoted image of the overwhelming influence of William Faulkner on all subsequent Southern writing: "Nobody wants his mule and wagon stalled on the same track the Dixie Limited is roaring down." Cited by Guy Owen and Mary C. Williams (in slightly different form) in *Contemporary Southern Poetry*, it is used by them to distinguish between the special position of today's Southern poet in comparison with other Southern writers. "One reason many of our poets may feel free to be southern, rather than simply American," they write, "is that they are not competing with predecessors of towering reputations as southern novelists are." Of course, Flannery O'Connor was partly fooling; it would be hard to imagine any way in which William Faulkner's achievement served to inhibit her own artistic development. Her wisecrack was addressed, in part, to the aforementioned Northern literati, who no doubt needed to be reassured that she was writing out of a different experience, creating her own world.

The contemporary Southern writer must be unusually self-conscious about the whole matter of literary influence. For some it may take the form of a flat denial of any influence, as in this comment by Reynolds Price (in *Kite-Flying and Other Irrational Acts*): "I can say, quite accurately, that Faulkner has been no influence, technical or otherwise, on my work. I admire the work of Faulkner that I know—by no means all—but with a cold, distant admiration for a genius whom I know to be grand but who proved irrelevant to my own obsessions, my own ambitions." Another stance, perhaps more credible, is that taken by Shelby Foote in any number of interviews. Foote, who knew Faulkner personally, simply *assumes* the influence of Faulkner on any contemporary Southern writer. But he clearly indicates that the major influences on his own fiction have been other modern masters: Proust, Joyce, and Mann.

Calder Willingham, a wonderful and outrageously comic Southern writer, has taken a much more aggressive and highly exaggerated position. In his *Transition* interview, he calls Faulkner (among other things) a "nitwit," a "half-educated village philosopher," "a total fool and a very bad writer." "If this man is a great writer," he adds, "shrimps whistle Dixie." Willingham contends that the best Southern writer is Erskine Caldwell. I mention Willingham's hyperbolic fooling around because, absurd as it is, it represents the lengths a gifted writer is willing to go to in order to dissociate himself from the reflexive critical dismissal of much of the work of contemporary Southern writers as no more than shabby imitations of the achievements of their predecessors and betters.

It is ironic that there should be pressures on the Southern writer to forfeit—to offer up, as it were—one of the qualities which has served to identify this work and to distinguish it from a great deal of other contemporary American literature: namely, a deep awareness of his own literary traditions and a sense of blood kinship with the past. It remains a part of the knowledge (and spirit) of the Southerner that the experience of the present is continually informed by the living past; that the past cannot be ignored or denied; that the result of acting upon any assumption that the present can somehow be lived in isolation from the past is both a crippling spiritual inhibition of the present experience and a destructive prospect for the future; that, thus, to embrace the present, with all its novelty and flowing sense of change, without being mindful of the past, is a grotesque distortion of reality and a fundamentally self-destructive enterprise. In short, for the Southern writer to deny, ignore, or pretend to be free of his own literary past would, in fact, mean the death of Southern literature.

A good deal of recent criticism and scholarship demonstrates that, despite their unquestionably innovative achievements, the works of the modern masters of Southern letters—and most centrally those of William Faulkner himself—were deep rooted in the traditions and conventions of both the literature and the historical experience of the South. The consistently dazzling virtuosity of Faulkner's style (which is idiosyncratic enough so that it cannot be discreetly imitated) has, as he perhaps intended, served to divert attention from the often classically traditional elements of this fiction. Frequently there is a dramatic opposition between style and substance, creating comedy or a stormy sense of tension. But even as Faulkner was in some ways a profoundly traditional writer, he was also a pioneer. No two of his books employ the same kind of narrative strategy. It is true that the celebrated style, voice, and certain deliberate and habitual personal tropes and techniques (as well as, in many cases, links of subject matter and characters, etc.) bind his works intimately together, but none of his novels is designed in quite the same fashion. He simply did not choose to repeat himself in this way.

It is important to realize the considerable courage involved in Faulkner's artistic strategy. All of the conventional pressures of the times, and especially those emanating from the commercial heart of America's popular culture, are designed to force the artist in the opposite direction. Artists of all kinds are discouraged from the risks of cultivating variety and are strongly encouraged to exploit any limited areas which, by popularity or critical recognition or (rarely) both, have come to be acknowledged as their provenance. In that sense it may be that Faulkner was fortunate to have been spared both popularity and extensive critical recognition until later in his life. Otherwise the pressures to conform might have been, as he ironically indicated in his introduction to the Modern Library edition of *Sanctuary* and more directly stated in the unpublished note on *The Sound and the Fury,* too overwhelming to resist. Even so, it is clear that he was much more interested in pioneering than in settling for one kind of fiction and then developing that to its limits. It was always Faulkner's *intention* to be a discoverer, which means that a part of his complex intention was to open up new vistas and directions for future writers. Whatever his intent—though I do believe it can be properly inferred, from many things in his published speeches, interviews, and letters, that Faulkner was consistently concerned with the art and artists of the future—it is certainly the effect of his example. That example, not precisely his literary "influence," can be at once liberating and inspiring to be contemporary Southern writer.

There are other ways in which Faulkner's work and his life (which become, more and more, inseparable from the work) can be exemplary to the late twentieth century Southern writer. One way, of course, is in his exemplary exercise of what has been called "the conservation of literary material." He was fearless in returning to a subject or situation when he felt it could sustain the force of further exploration. This tactic, of course, breaks both the critical mind-set and the rule against treating with anything but apparently new directions and new materials. Just as he broke the habits of our times by continually seeking new *techniques,* new and different ways of *telling* his stories, so he broke the other conventional attitude of at least professing that *the subject matter* is always new and different.

At the very least, then, Faulkner's work offers consolation and direction to the contemporary Southern writer. It offers a challenge as well: the writer is dared to divorce himself from easy habits of thought which are prevalent in the overall culture. Dared, by that towering example, to cultivate his art without regard to present systems of praise or blame and, indeed, without embarrassed or inhibiting reverence for the immediate past, the past which includes the achievement of William Faulkner, of Thomas Wolfe, of all of the Fugitives and other masters. By example, he demonstrates that the Southern past is not dead or disposable and cannot be ignored. It is and remains a resource to be wisely *used.*

Finally, and not least important, the life of William Faulkner offers a model for bedeviled contemporary Southern writers. The world has changed in many ways, some sharp and startling and some very subtle, in the almost twenty years since the death of William Faulkner. As noted, the South has also changed greatly, at least outwardly. The American literary situation is now quite different from that faced by Faulkner and the others of his generation. The whole publishing industry has changed drastically in the last two decades, so greatly altering the status and importance of the serious writer that the writing of poetry and fiction has almost become a different kind of enterprise. However, the situation is, on the whole, no less formidable or difficult for the serious writer.

Faulkner's great courage and patience and unceasing productivity are inspiring. The absence of recognition and reward did not silence him, nor did his belated triumph. Perhaps this was because, very early in his professional career, he came to terms with frustration and neglect, turning them both into positive energy. As indicated in his "unpublished preface" to *The Sound and the Fury*, Faulkner experienced great discouragement with his first three novels. After *Sartoris* was repeatedly turned down: "One day I seemed to shut a door between me and all publishers' addresses and book lists. I said to myself, Now I can write." (I have written elsewhere that Faulkner's statement is something every aspiring writer should have tattooed on his skin, so as never to forget it.)

His career is usefully emblematic in other ways also. There is the relevant fact that, without considerable financial resources, he still managed to survive, to do his work and to maintain a place and a family. He did this in part by writing short stories for the popular magazines, when that was still a possibility, and chiefly by his stints as a salaried screenwriter. His letters show that money was a serious, often urgent problem for him almost up until the very end of his life; he never really had a secure financial base. This may have caused him much anxiety, and there is no denying that the time spent in Hollywood, for instance, was time lost to his real interests and best gifts. Yet neither anxiety nor lost time could deter him. It is hard to imagine a more productive serious writer.

With the exception of a couple of *New Yorker* regulars, no one today could possibly earn more than pocket money by writing short stories. The movie studios no longer produce films on the same grand scale and no longer employ whole stables of writers. (However, it should be noted that the financial rewards are generally now much greater for the working screenwriters. And it is noteworthy that a good number of serious and highly regarded contemporary Southern writers—Calder Willingham, James Dickey, Larry McMurtry, and William Harrison, for instance—have made a mark on and a contribution to the development of that special narrative form.) By and large the Southern poet and fiction writer today earns some or most of his living by working for another kind of institution: the academy. Much has been said, and no doubt remains to be said, both for and against this affiliation, which is a fairly recent national phenomenon; but this is not really the place for that kind of discussion. All that needs to be said here is that if William Faulkner did not find the brutal institutional world of the film studio completely stultifying, then the working Southern writer can be allowed to hope that exposure to and labor for the academy (which is, after all, ostensibly dedicated to the preservation and dissemination of our best cultural myths and artifacts) is not necessarily a negative experience.

Here, also, the contemporary Southern writer can find many examples among the Agrarians, who in fact did so much to make a place in the academy possible for the poet and the novelist. Donald Davidson, John Crowe Ransom, Allen Tate, Caroline Gordon, Robert Penn Warren, Andrew Lytle, and others demonstrated that it is possible to maintain a serious literary career while actively associated with institutional education. Not only that: they also proved that it is, likewise, possible to make a major contribution within the context of the institution, as a teacher-scholar. Just as Faulkner managed to write some memorable and artistic screenplays, against the odds and even against his own expectations.

The real significance of all this, however, lies not in the possible influences of academic institutions on contemporary writers or vice versa. Rather, it is important that the contemporary Southern writer who has rarely, until very recently indeed, come out of a situation which allowed for much leisure to cultivate fine (and usually unprofitable) arts can now do so, earning and paying his own way. Ever since the Civil War and until very recently, the South has been *actually* as well as statistically poor. Yet serious poets and novelists, black and white alike, have flourished in that society and are still flourishing. The results are (though utterly unprovable, still and all undeniable) a literary art which is, as it has always been in theory and practice, close to the lives and the common experience of Southern life and history. It is a literary art which may or may not be difficult or obscure but which, in any case, is only rarely elitist. It is a literary art which is both democratic and populist in spirit and which is very seldom (except in occasional lapses into imitation of national intellectual fashions) created from a stance of haughty alienation from the quotidian world and the concerns of others. There is often hatred and anger in Southern literature, but one seldom sees the more usual contemporary contempt for all who are stupid or ignorant or unwashed or invincibly ordinary. Faulkner could find and celebrate the humanity (and the divinity) in the idiot, the pervert, the criminal—not, as in more fashionable contemporary literature, as antiheroes or any such, but as fully delineated characters. There are plenty of villains in Southern stories, and, because the South remains a predominantly Christian culture, evil, sin, and folly are hardly ever absent from the Southern vision. But the Southern writer has not set himself up as judge and overseer of a hostile and absurd universe. In fact, even the minor alienation of the artist (such a popular subject in our national culture and throughout contemporary European writing) has seldom figured very importantly in Southern writing. Tennessee Williams, Carson McCullers, and Truman Capote have all written minor works on this theme, and the major "portrait of the artist" by a Southerner is to be found in the work of Thomas Wolfe. But the artist Wolfe depicts, himself, though misunderstood and often ignored or rejected by others, is an artist with a communal and social spirit and function, anxious to be part of the community and to serve it.

III

Recently John Leonard, former editor of *The New York Times Book Review* and still chief cultural correspondent for the daily *New York Times,* and Harvey Shapiro, Leonard's successor as editor of the *Times Book Review,* an enormously influential publication (the more so in the absence of any serious regional competition), spoke, on separate occasions, to staff and students at the Bennington Workshops. Although each was very gently, very gingerly critical of the other (Leonard: "I found the sixties a more interesting decade than Harvey did"), they were largely in agreement about the goals, ways, and means of the *Review*. Both insisted that it is at least as much a part of a newspaper, therefore concerned with "news," as it is a popular organ of literary criticism. As John Leonard put it, "I am as much a reporter as I am a literary critic."

This explanation seems simple and straightforward enough, yet it camouflages some complex problems. For one thing, the insistent claim that the book-reviewing function is merely a part of the larger function of the press brings us quickly back to the special situation of the press in America today. Returns us to the thoughtful and coherent criticism of Solzhenitsyn's Harvard speech, in which he called the press "the greatest power within the Western countries, more powerful than the legislature, the executive, and the judiciary," adding, "There are generally accepted patterns of judgment and there may be common corporate interests, the same effect being not competition but unification. Enormous freedom exists for the press, but not for the readership, because newspapers mostly give emphasis to those opinons that do not too openly contradict their own and the general trend."

It needs to be noted that contemporary journalistic theory, denying the possibility of any truly "objective" reportage, allows that all good reporting is, in a sense, "advocacy journalism." Thus, though journalism may (or may not) seek to be fair, it nevertheless takes moral and political and social stands and choices. To the extent that *The New York Times Book Review,* and the reviews of books in the daily *New York Times,* are considered to be journalism rather than criticism, they are licensed to practice advocacy and to take the opportunity to make moral, political, or social points. Which can be very dangerous (for the writer, in any case) when the critic starts from a certain stereotypical hostility toward all things Southern.

Leonard, speaking at Bennington College on July 28, 1979, put it another way, but in no way contradicted Solzhenitsyn's impression and judgment. "There is something peculiar about the New York literary community," Leonard said, "and it might as well be spelled out." While he was quite emphatic that there is no organized conspiracy among the

New York literati—"There is no conspiracy. There is no literary Mafia"—he nevertheless allowed that there is "an undeniable coziness" among critics and reviewers in New York, and he acknowledged that, as a reviewer, he regularly depends upon "a whole network of signals from people I have come to trust." In short, then, there may not be any "conspiracy" among the critics and reviewers of New York; but there is strong evidence of precisely the kind of consensus which Solzhenitsyn saw not only as stifling any "new ideas," but also as eliminating the kind of serious debate which must accompany political and social free choice.

Second, the emphasis on *The New York Times Book Review* as being more a part of a newspaper than anything else ties it closely to the editorial positions of *The New York Times*. Which, like the city it serves, views itself sometimes as a national center and sometimes as only one region among others. The city is losing business and industry and tax base; even if the Census Bureau is allowed to count illegal aliens, the city is losing population. Statistics continue to show an alarming rate of increase in violent crimes committed in New York City. The independent Citizens Crime Commission, in a six-month study, reported that violent crime is "more serious and widespread than statistics indicate and is worsening." The city is now compelled to depend on federal money (i.e., tax money raised in other regions) to provide its essential services. In all the practical areas, except as a headquarters for mass communications and as a cultural center, New York's power and influence are steadily declining. Even in the area of culture the city must depend upon extensive federal support to maintain its apparent cultural preeminence.

In the business of commercial publishing, such as it is, New York remains the center it became early in this century, largely overcoming nineteenth-century competition from Boston and Philadelphia. Even so, the publication of poetry, short fiction, and serious novels by university presses and small independent presses, found nationwide, is beginning to prove that these firms can do as well with literature as can the large trade publishers. The situation is already changing, which breeds a certain testy defensiveness on the part of the self-interested custodians of "official" culture. For example, in the "Letters" section of *The New York Times Book Review* (January 6, 1980, p. 27), the Southern poet and novelist Guy Owen politely questioned the statement by James Atlas, in a piece about Thomas Wolfe, that Alfred Kazin is "the only well-known defender of Wolfe." Owen mentioned the significant work of Louis Rubin, C. Hugh Holman, and Richard Walser. To which the *Times's* Atlas replied: "I wrote that Alfred Kazin's was 'virtually the only sympathetic criticism' Wolfe has received since his death. Of course there have been other critics who admired him, but I would dispute Professor Owen's claim that the three he cites are 'well known.' " Translated, that can only mean: *One Kazin, our Kazin, is worth three of yours. We determine who may be called well known and who may not be.*

This is what Southern writers have been up against for more than one hundred years, but it is exaggerated and exacerbated now that New York is falling into decline and knows it. Under the circumstances, it is only reasonable that those who profit most from the status quo should strive to protect their enlightened self-interest. Unquestionably, the salaries of the professional book reviewers, earning them far more than all but a small handful of the serious poets and novelists they review, make them, together with the employees of commercial publishing houses, among the very few who actually *profit* directly from contemporary literature. They have a considerable inducement toward the preservation of the status quo, if possible.

I do not wish to deal with the speculative subjects of integrity and corruption, the presence or absence of either—except to say that one day, in some form or other, they will have to be dealt with seriously, even as a purely literary matter. Except to say, therefore, that a thorough discussion of integrity and corruption, at the center of the American literary establishment, would prove to be neither digressive nor irrelevant. And except to argue that the commercial literary culture, being part and parcel of the overall commercial culture, the *whole* society, offers as much (or as little) evidence of integrity as the latter and manages to maintain roughly the same levels of personal and institutional corruption.

IV

Closely coupled with practical considerations (and corollary considerations of self-interest and self-service) are many elements of a social if not ideological consensus. Most of it has, in fact, proved to be sub-sumable under the rubric of "radical chic," an epithet created by a Southern writer, Tom Wolfe, to satirize the complex duplicities and hy-pocrisies of the New York artistic and intellectual elite. Wolfe was one of the first and is certainly the most successful writer to see contem-porary New York City, itself as a region susceptible to the kinds of satire that used to be reserved for other regions. That his stance is both Southern and traditional may not yet be so widely recognized because of the dazzling flash and fire of his prose style, and because his usual mode has been ironic and satirical. But his most recent book, *The Right Stuff*, points up values he presents positively, as do such well-known articles as "The Last American Hero" (about Southern stock-car driver Junior Johnson) or "The Truest Sport: Jousting With Sam & Charlie" (dealing with Navy pilots during the Vietnam war). Perhaps Wolfe's most explicit and detailed picture of the prevailing "liberal" intellec-tual consensus, and its (deliberate) separation from the thoughts and feelings and perceptions of other Americans, is to be found in "The Intelligent Coed's Guide to America" (in his *Mauve Gloves & Madmen, Clutter & Vine*), in which he deals with the style and substance of "the literary notables of the United States" who are busy "giving lectures at the colleges and universities of America's heartland, which runs from Fort Lee, New Jersey, on the east to the Hollywood Freeway on the west." "Giving lectures," he adds, "is one of the lucrative dividends of being a noted writer in America." One of his chief points is that what these intellectuals think and say, and even prefer to believe, *is not true*: it flies in the face of the evidence, of all the facts. By and large, he suggests, these people know this very well; but it is comfortable and profitable and companionable to maintain the myths as a consensus of opinion. Here is his one-paragraph summation of the standard lecture colleges and universities were paying these "literary notables" for:

> Sixty families control one half the private wealth of America, and two hundred corporations own two thirds of the means of production. "A small group of nameless, faceless men" who avoid publicity the way a werewolf avoids the dawn now dominates American life. In America a man's home is not his castle but merely "a gigantic listening device with a mortgage"—a reference to eavesdropping by the FBI and the CIA. America's foreign policy has been and continues to be based upon war,

assassination, bribery, genocide, and the sabotage of democratic governments. "The new McCarthyism" (Joe's, not Gene's) is already upon us.
Following a brief charade of free speech, the "gagging of the press" has
resumed. Racism in America has not diminished; it is merely more subtle
now. The gulf between rich and poor widens daily, creating "permanent
ghetto-colonial populations." The decline in economic growth is caus-
ing a crisis in capitalism, which will lead shortly to authoritarian rule
and to a new America in which everyone waits, in horror, for the knock
on the door in the dead of the night, the descent of the knout on the
nape of the neck—

Speaking of Solzhenitsyn's arrival and tour of the nation in 1975,
Wolfe writes that "the literary world in general ignored him completely." He argues that they could not bear the public exposure and
subsequent dissipation of certain deeply cherished sociopolitical assumptions:

> In the huge unseen coffin that Solzhenitsyn towed behind him were not
> only the souls of the Zeks who died in the Archipelago. No, the heart-
> less bastard had also chucked in one of the lost great visions: the intel-
> lectual as the Stainless Steel Socialist glistening against the bone heap
> of capitalism in its final, brutal, fascist phase. There was a bone heap, all
> right, and it was grisly beyond belief, but socialism had created it.

The Southern intellectual tradition has not been especially hospi-
table to the theory and practice of modern corporate capitalism. But
neither have many Southerners rushed to embrace the rigid, bureaucratic schemes of modern corporate socialism. Populist or elitist (and
some even socialist), of whatever political persuasion, Southerners
have tended toward unity in the defense of individual civil liberty.
And, in general, Southerners take intellectual integrity very seriously;
thus intellectual hypocrisy is seen as particularly despicable. (A certain
gentle *social* hypocrisy, on the other hand, may be a form of good manners.) One of Wolfe's chief and regular targets for satire has been the
hypocrisy of the New York intellectual-literary establishment. Which,
taken together with their constant search for more signs and tokens of
personal status, their desire for ever more privilege and honor, and
their bad manners and deep streak of lightly disguised vulgarity, is a
large and vulnerable target indeed.

Since the beginning of his journalistic career, Wolfe has been satirizing the bad manners of New Yorkers (and once he even dared to ridicule *The New Yorker* itself). Probably his most devastating single piece on the subject, "Tom Wolfe's New Book of Etiquette" (in *The Pump House Gang*), distinguishes two forms in which, in New York, "the entire Book of Etiquette is being rewritten." He defines these two forms as "*The rationalization of politesse;* i.e., the adapting of social etiquette to purely business ends," and "*nostalgie de la boue;* i.e., the adoption by the upper orders, for special effect, of the customs of the lower orders." It is all illustrated with lively examples.

Because it was done in fun and with accuracy, if exaggeration, most critics and reviewers seem to have missed the darker indictment in Wolfe's satire. Most often he has been treated as a bright, eccentric, and amusing dealer in trivia, a pedant of the superficial. Such an assessment, equating manners with triviality, tends to confirm Wolfe's thesis and is certainly at odds with Southern assumptions about manners. Lisa Alther was right: manners *are* more important in the Southern tradition. They mean something. In a theoretical sense, good manners are conceived of as a mean between brute savagery (barbarism) and frivolous foppery (foolish oversophistication). In a practical, literary sense, good manners represent the mean between the utterly idiosyncratic (mannerism) and the tediously conventional (the cliché and the stereotype). In both life and art, the Southern emphasis upon manners and amenities derives chiefly from an assumed, a *given* view of the nature of Man, and thus from a view of the quality and nature of Man's history. The primarily Protestant, and certainly Christian, base of the Southern social structure—and thus, also, of the social fabric of Southern life—begins with the assumption and acceptance of the universal equality of original sin. This is one area, perhaps the only one, and at the anagogical level, where Southern assumptions are unabashedly egalitarian. (The Southerner is more or less democratic in *secular* spirit. But not exactly egalitarian.) All men are immortal souls, equally fractured by sin, equally and mysteriously loved by a loving God. Equally liable to enjoy grace and salvation, chiefly by and through faith. That faith may or may not manifest itself in good works. Therefore, for the Southerner, there is an unspoken and unquestioned religious, and often theologial, basis for the importance of good manners. Manners represent a formal obligation to one's neighbor (who is always Everyman) and the ritual recognition of the love of God and for the presence of the Holy Ghost in all of one's fellow creatures. Therefore an act of bad manners may well be, to the Southerner, an act of violence. A violation of the code of manners may well be taken as at least *meaning* the same thing as a fist in the face or a blade between the ribs.

It is a cliché of intellectual criticism of Southern literature and society to say that both are permeated by violence. It is a cliché of the intellectual establishment to assume that violence derives from social causes and is therefore reparable. The Southerner is baffled by this assumption. At his deepest level of knowing, the Southerner expects this world—filled as it is with fallen fellow creatures, creatures who are, to a greater or lesser extent, depraved—*expects* the world to be a violent place, as brutal and savage as conditions will allow. The secular-liberal view believes that violence, insofar as it is really present in the world at all, derives from social conditions. The Southern, more fundamentally Christian view is that conditions can only serve to check or to release the natural and inevitable energies of violence. Thus—as a part of those social conditions—formal manners become urgently important. Under certain circumstances a shrug, a raised eyebrow, a rude tone of voice can become clear acts of violence.

The very least that can be said, then, is that Tom Wolfe's satirical assault on both the intellectual hypocrisy and the bad manners of the New York scene, under the label of "radical chic," is just about as violent an attack as he could make, short of tossing around a case of fragmentation grenades.

"Celebrity," which is so closely associated with "radical chic" in Wolfe's definition, is usually frowned on by Southerners. Perhaps because it can be just as easily derived from notoriety as from good report, fame which is dependent upon celebrity is usually seen as false. For instance, the North Carolina novelist and poet Fred Chappell, in a review of *Contemporary Southern Poetry*, notes with pleasure the fact that the better-known Southern poets, "the Big Reputations," do not, in truth, stand out as obviously and inherently superior to the other poets included in the anthology: "the big guns make no grander bangs than the smaller ones." Taking James Dickey as an example of an unquestionably well known contemporary Southern poet, Chappell arrives at a skeptical conclusion, questioning not Dickey's serious gifts but the source of his wide *celebrity:* "Crowded in with his peers, Dickey is simply an equal among equals, and one begins to realize how much his personal flamboyance has contributed to his national acclaim." Chappell's observation is accurate both in terms of the anthology and in the larger sense of the literary scene the anthology represents.

The South has a wonderful and wonderfully various crop of contemporary writers. The reasons for this are many and complex, but not the least of them is the example of the earlier generation of masters (and many of these teachers as well) of the Southern Renaissance. Thus, ironically, there is a full precedent for the *concept* of the master artist. It is a concept which teases and troubles the contemporary writer until (and if), like Fred Chappell, the artist finds an occasion to perceive the richness, variety, and complexity of the whole literary scene. So the writer has the model of mastery, of extraordinary artistic adventure by an exemplary few. And the scholar accepts the image, knowing it to be an oversimplification and indeed a distortion of history, yet knowing also that it is the only way to imagine and understand the literary past. The critic accepts the notion of a few masters, surrounded by a crowd of apprentices and journeymen, because it makes public criticism, as it is understood, possible. The masters of the earlier generation become more than models of excellence; they become also, paradoxically, standards of measurement against which the newer work of contemporaries is to be compared. Teachers have found the concept extremely helpful ever since modern and then contemporary literature became a part of the institutional educational curriculum. Within the boundaries of classroom times and academic calendars, it is feasible only to deal with certain significant, representative and *teachable* examples.

Southern writers, scholars, critics, and teachers are all, in one way or another, supportive of the creation of contemporary literature. Yet each is necessarily also at least a tacit supporter of a system of artificial celebrity which no longer describes a real condition in the literary world. If it ever did. Unfortunately, this outmoded concept coincides with the commercial and self-serving aims of publishers and the whole periphery of professional intellectuals around them. Which, in turn, is an evidently inextricable element of the national economy.

V

Among the nationally oriented anthologies published during the last decade, Edward Field's *A Geography of Poets* offers more work by Southern poets than any other of its general kind. I count 39 of the 228 poets represented in this anthology as Southerners by birth or lifetime affiliation. A much more typical representation is to be found in *The American Poetry Anthology*, edited by Daniel Halpern, which presents work by only two Southern poets out of 75 in the anthology. (Actually there are 76 poets listed, but at least one of them is a completely fictional creation.)

Field, in the honest and revealing innocence of his introduction to *A Geography of Poets*, seems to feel that his own discovery of any number of reasonably intelligent and gifted and well-read poets out in America's provinces and hinterlands roughly coincides with their own arrival on the literary scene. Thus our history and traditions are seen as merely coincident with his. This is what all Southern writers have had to contend with (and *against*) at least since the mid-nineteenth century.

James Atlas, an editor of *The New York Times Book Review*, has published in *The New York Times Magazine* (February 3, 1980) an extensive article entitled "New Voices in American Poetry" in which only four Southern poets are mentioned by name: the late Randall Jarrell and the living Donald Justice, in reference to the bygone attitudes of the 1950s; Robert Penn Warren, as one of the "few older poets" still creating; and Charles Wright, not as a Southerner at all, but as a master of the school identified as the "New Surrealism." There is no indication, in this influential popular article, that any other Southern poets or writers might be an active part of the contemporary scene.

The South itself, even including the literary South, is another matter. Though many of our individual writers may be neglected and ignored, our magazines and institutions are not being left to their own fates and devices. Just as Northern industries have moved and are continuing to move into the South in search of various things (including the prospect of cheap and reliable labor), just as many Northerners are continuing to move to the South to live and to work—and thus *to earn their livings* within the economy and culture of the South—just as members of the Northern professions and services are following close behind this social event, in numbers and variety like the high heydays of Reconstruction, so a surprising number of the Northern literati, members in good standing of their literary establishment, have recently come to the South also. They have come to teach literature and writing at our colleges and universities, to become publishers at our university presses and, indeed, to edit many of our quarterlies and literary magazines. While the "nationalization" of many Southern magazines and presses has resulted in perhaps slightly more "visibility" for these institutions, it has, at the same time, deprived many good Southern writers of opportunities to publish their works, even as it considerably expands the publishing prospects and possibilities for Northern writers. It is, thus, in a literary sense at least, a classic example of colonialism.

This example is reinforced by the ongoing case of the National Endowment for the Arts. Not at all unusual is the picture presented by the 1979–80 Fellowships for Creative Writers ($10,000 each) awarded by the Literature Program of the National Endowment for the Arts. Of the 275 awards given, 33 went to writers listed as living in (or visiting) Southern states. Two Southern states, Arkansas and Alabama, were completely ignored. No Southern state received as many grants as, for example, California, Colorado, Connecticut, Massachusetts, or Vermont. New York (and chiefly, overwhelmingly, New York City), by receiving 78 of the grants, was a little more than twice as lucky and successful as all of the Southern states combined.

The Poetry in the Schools Program, though partially supported by the National Endowment for the Arts, is under the immediate supervision of local and state arts councils. This program presents another sort of problem for the Southern writer, an especially difficult one for the young or beginning writer. The program brings poets and writers into the public schools to teach and to read; it pays an adequate honorarium for the service, enabling a writer to earn a living at his craft and without losing all of his time and energy in the process. It also enables the often-neglected public school students to have some encounters with contemporary literature and the people who create it. On the whole a laudable idea. And yet . . . troubles began with the question of who should qualify, who should be legitimately "certified" as a poet worthy of being brought into the program. A difficult question, especially in the case of the new young writers for whom the program is most efficiently intended. Most of the state and local arts councils, ready and willing to defer to the honest judgment and expertise of others, choose to depend on official listings in *A Directory of American Fiction Writers* and *A Directory of American Poets* (together with revisions and supplements to both) published by Poets & Writers, Inc., a federally supported, tax-exempt organization based firmly in New York City. From the beginning until the time of this writing there have been a number of strong, probably valid complaints about the organization and its policies. Primarily the complaints have been that the outlying regions and states are underrepresented and underlisted, and that it is extremely difficult for a local or regional writer to win listing in the directories. On the other hand, a few large urban centers, most particuarly New York City, are both inaccurately overrepresented and overlisted. For the writer in New York City, for example, it is very easy to gain listing, even with a minimal publication record. The full "truth" of all this remains to be determined, but it is certainly perceived as true by many (probably most) Southern writers. One undeniable result of the listing system is that many Southern states have not been able to fill the vacancies in their Poetry in the Schools Programs with local writers, and it has been necessary for them to turn to the Northern states for candidates. Thus a surprising number of New York City poets have enjoyed warmer (and well-paid) winters working in Southern public schools.

Of course, abuses can be corrected and commonplace corruption can be exposed, but there is not much that can be done about the *attitudes* which permit both abuse and corruption at the expense of Southern writers and their culture. Not, at least, until they somehow feel independent and free and secure enough in their own good sense and judgment not to need any alien approval.

Finally, the very basis and strength of so much Southern literature, its *language*—its own version, alive and lively, of the English language—is itself under attack. Roberty Bly, a prominent and polemical (many would say, pontifical) figure in the national literary establishment, is quoted in the Atlas article as using the lingo of "radical chic" to attack both our language and our tradition: "We have to get rid of the alien English element. We're a colony of England, and you can't speak the languge of your conqueror." Bly may not see the irony of that in terms of our own American history, but it is clear, from his record as an editor and critic, that he has been mostly indifferent to Southern writing. Although he has devoted a good deal of time and attention to attacking the achievement of James Dickey, otherwise he seems, like so many other establishment editors and critics, largely unaware of the presence of any contemporary Southern literature. When that presence becomes (somehow) undeniable—as, for instance, when Walker Percy won a National Book Award for *The Moviegoer* and a good many years later Mary Lee Settle was awarded the same prize for *Blood Tie*—their outrage often lapses into shrill vulgarity. In both cases the writers were initially ridiculed by prominent reviewers for being previously "unknown" and thus apparently unworthy.

A perhaps even more outrageous example of what has to be called the vulgarity of ignorance was the failure to award any prizes to Shelby Foote's *The Civil War: A Narrative*. This trilogy, vast in scope and subject, occupying the complete attention of one of our most gifted novelists for a quarter-century, may yet, when it is at last read by the critics, be recognized as one of the very few truly great works by an American in this century. Like a good deal of the best Southern literature, it has not been completely ignored. But, on the other hand, it has yet to be really recognized.

VI

We have seen (I hope) some of the ways in which the contemporary Southern writer is beleaguered and isolated—by his religion in a defiantly secular society; by tradition in a society seeking to define itself as if it were without roots and traditions (at least as far as this nation and this continent are concerned); by their own highly developed idiom and dialect of and in a language which is at least fundamentally different from and often only a generation or two familiar to other American writers elsewhere; by a history which is at once rich and tragic and yet is (even as far as the facts are concerned, and never mind interpretation and any deeper understanding) unknown to others except within the terms of common misapprehensions and crude stereotypes. The South was different by being the most cosmopolitan and pluralistic part of this nation until the Civil War and then, following the great waves of immigration into the North, different by the label, if not the fact, of being uniquely homogenized, separate from the economic life of the rest of the nation by being dirt poor for a long, long time while the rest of the nation richly flourished. Now it is different because it is affluent and blooming while, for a multitude of reasons (a Southerner might say, a multitude of sins and errors), much of the rest of the nation, most especially the Northeast, is in swift and shabby decline. The South has been exploited and ignored, in a literary sense, by outsiders whose power (at least for the time being) is real enough, whose contempt and hostility are open and unembarrassed, whose indifference to the life and arts of the South is matched only by the weight of their ignorance about both. But what remain to be seen—what are, finally, far more important—are the actions and reactions of Southern writers here and now.

These actions and reactions depend on where these writers are and where they stand. Those mostly of an older generation who have been officially, nationally recognized, who have been awarded some place in the literary pantheon—I think, for instance, of Eudora Welty, Peter Taylor, William Styron, Reynolds Price, Robert Penn Warren, and Walker Percy—have certainly brought honor and distinction to Southern letters, and no less of both to themselves. But in a simple and serious sense they have been restricted, if not severely limited, by the very terms of the recognition afforded them. None of these people is apt to give any real criticism of the flaws and inequities of the literary status quo. (The exception is the rare occasion when one or more may rise up in defense of another when a perceived injustice has been committed: for example, when Styron's *The Confessions of Nat Turner* [1967] was savaged by various unhappy black writers and critics, or when some critics failed to respond warmly enough to Reynolds Price's novel *The Surface of the Earth* [1975] and Eudora Welty came strongly and publicly to his defense.) By and large, their position is what it has to be: that the status quo may have flaws, but that it is generally fair and equitable and that ultimately (look what happened to William Faulkner!) right, if not justice, is done. How else can the imagination perceive it? They are part of the literary establishment, and there is

nothing to challenge their happy assessment of it—indeed, no particular incentive (quite the contrary) to growl and bite the hand that
feeds them.

These people are exemplary to the younger Southern writers in perhaps the best way, by the example of their work. But the examples of
their lives and careers can hardly be of much value to the neophyte.
And though some of them, Warren and Price and Welty, for example,
have earned reputations as excellent teachers, none has been of much
practical help or assistance to younger or less fortunate writers. There
is no reason why it would occur to them to be so. In the absence of any
serious threat to the status quo, there is no pressure toward a communal
feeling.

There are those, like Willie Morris and Larry King and Tom Wicker
and Marshal Frady, who have gone North and have actively joined the
establishment, establishing their own impeccable liberal credentials by
denouncing Southern life (often confirming stereotypical liberal sup-
positions in doing so) while managing to preserve something of the
Southern style for themselves. This is, in effect, the ironic contemporary equivalent of the gesture called "pulling wool" or "pully woolly"
(in some part of the South), whereby certain sly black men ingratiated
themselves with their oppressors by acting out with gusto and enthusiasm the part already assigned to them. This example is not likely to
be followed by many younger Southern writers, if only because there is
no room for more than a very few "house Southerners" in the North at
any one time. Moreover, the influence of some of these Southerners-
in-residence *can be* pernicious in the sense that, since they are mostly
journalists (who would feel the need of co-opting a Southern poet or a
novelist?) and since they almost always say precisely what is expected of
them, they are regarded as experts and are influential not so much in
passing judgment on Southern actions and events as in enforcing conventional judgments already passed by others. Of course, it can be
justly argued that these writers are subtly "working from within the System" even as they honestly criticize and call attention to the many
faults and flaws of the South that they profess (as all of us do) to love.
And it may be that in their new and rapidly developing field of creative
writing, contemporary journalism, they are excellent models for young

Southerners. Certainly in journalism and nonfiction if one were today to take a different tack and approach than these Southerners-in-exile, one would not likely go far or succeed as well.

Unless, of course, one took the opposite approach, the strategy of head-on attack. Like Tom Wolfe and, to a certain extent, Truman Capote, and sometimes James Dickey, who, given an occasion, has been known to thumb his nose, figuratively, at Yankee expectations. Wolfe, Capote, and Dickey have enjoyed considerable success (in Northern terms) by and through satire, irony, sarcasm, and deft atttack on many of the clichés that the Northern establishment holds dearest. But it should be noted that Wolfe and Capote are not perceived as primarily Southern; that is, it does not yet seem to have occurred to the critics that the terms of the satire and attack rendered (differently, it is true) by Wolfe and Capote are conventionally Southern. Talent and virtuosity disguise the traditional stances of these writers. As examples for others they are, of course, limited. If you want to attack the enemy on his own ground and live to tell the tale, you have to be extremely gifted and equally clever.

What is left is something else, no less exciting for taking place somewhere else, far from the fading cultural centers, and probably far more valuable and lasting in the long run. There is some kind of explosion of talent and passionate interest going on in the South right now. There are literally dozens of good writers (perhaps it is not an age for *great* writers; we should be thankful, I believe, that so many are around who are very, very good), and they are scattered all over the South. They are in every part and in every state. No anthology of prose or poetry can begin to represent them or contain them. Though they belong to no school (and that quirky refusal to be part of an organized school or movement is characteristic of contemporary Southern writers ever since the Agrarians *had*, for a time, their school), there is a community of spirit which is noticeable and almost unique. (There is, of course, a sense of community elsewhere, within the context and confines of one school and another; but those groups are organized hierarchically, whereas the loose affiliation of Southern writers is generally egalitarian, as it has to be.)

The community of spirit of contemporary Southern letters extends elsewhere, to writers born and raised in the South who have gone away in body if not in spirit. It also extends itself fully and warmly to all of the other writers I have mentioned as being, one way and another, outside this large and (in the wide world) largely anonymous community. Throughout the South today good writers who have published fiction, poetry, and nonfiction (it is characteristic of many Southern writers that they do all three, evidently as it pleases and suits them) are teaching a large crop of good and eager students, mostly young, but also including adults, white and black, and often involving people from social groups which have not had, until now, any real voice in our literature.

This development of teaching modern and contemporary literature and creative writing in Southern colleges and universities, with working writers as faculty members, has grown most strongly in the past two decades, although it has its roots in earlier Southern traditions and attitudes. Many of the contemporary Southern writers were at least exposed to the teaching of earlier masters; and there were not only the well-known Fugitives, but also other teachers of great influence and distinction like William Blackburn of Duke and Jesse Lee Rehder of Chapel Hill, George Williams of Rice, A. K. Davis and John Coleman of the University of Virginia. Even before the Iowa Writers' Workshop began, these people and others in the South were teaching writing to young students. Often they did so under the guise of courses in rhetoric and composition; under whatever title, they taught and inspired any number of Southern poets and fiction writers. Their story, an important one in modern literary history, has been largely ignored and remains untold, but their influence is evident.

Insofar as the teaching of the craft of writing is concerned, the general attitude of the contemporary Southern writer seems to be chiefly positive and to be (again) special for being so. The most extensive discussion of this subject, *Craft So Hard to Learn: Conversations with Poets and Novelists About the Teaching of Writing,* edited by John Graham and this author, indicates what amounts to an almost uniformly positive attitude held by the Southern writers, each otherwise distinctly different from the others. Represented therein are William Peden, Fred Chappell, Henry Taylor, Michael Mewshaw, James Seay, James Whitehead, Sylvia Wilkinson, James Dickey, and William Harrison. All agree that a writer cannot be "made" by the experience of creative writing courses, though all likewise agree that the experience can be very helpful in developing the skills of the writer with natural talent. But all these writers insist that there are positive values for students who study the craft of writing and of close reading. They become better readers and a possible future audience, to be sure; but there is also the effect of the experience on the awakening imagination. As Fred Chappell puts it, "I have seen persons come alive to themselves in writing classes in a way they never have done before." The results of all this activity are beginning to be evident in the magazines and anthologies, in collections of poems and stories by new writers, in first novels. Even as literacy is steadily and dangerously declining in the United States (and the South is not immune to the general trend), there is a whole new generation of Southern students coming along. They seem eager to learn reading and writing, and they are lucky enough to have good writers to work with, writers who teach by example as much as by any precept.

The two great dangers of formal study of the craft of writing (and both of these are strongly evident in the more prominent programs *outside* the South) are the imposition upon beginning talent of the rules and rigidity of a single school of writing and the development of an uneasy, self-conscious relationship with the tradition; that is, either too slavishly following traditional examples or, on the contrary, seeking to ignore and escape tradition. Somehow the most recent generation of Southern writers seems to have escaped both dangers. In Fred Chappell's thorough and thoughtful review of *Contemporary Southern Poetry*, he makes note of various changes which seem to have taken place in Southern writing during the generation since the Fugitives. At the same time, he recognizes that the masters of the earlier generation would not be incapable of appreciating what is done now, though they might never have dreamed of doing the same thing:

> Gone with the wind are the gentle strategies of our elders and betters: tenuous literary allusion, velvet irony, historical immanence, latinate diction, veiled satire and the reverence for Europe. One has the impression, looking at the differences in the work, that the Fugitives might look upon the present lot of poets as a herd of wild-eyed sans culottes, but of course they were too wise and tolerant ever to be shocked.

Clearly, from Chappell's tone, the respect and tolerance work both ways. The tradition endures many outward and visible changes.

If one allows oneself even the least whiff of optimism, it becomes hard not to believe that something good, perhaps something quite wonderful for the future literature of the South is going to come from all this reservoir of talent, all this energy and desire. While it is too early to say what that future may be, it is certainly not too early to say that all signs indicate that Southern literature, far from being on its last legs and far from representing a falling off from earlier and better days, seems very much alive. Having come to honorable terms with its own past, it seems almost certain to grow into a future worth waiting for, worth witnessing.

14

An Examination of the
Poetry of William Faulkner
(1957)

In addition to the extensive body of his prose fiction William Faulkner is the author of two volumes of verse, *The Marble Faun* (1924) and *A Green Bough* (1933), and twenty-five other poems which appeared in print from 1919 to 1933.[1] Faulkner's verse has been largely ignored by the critics even though he began by writing poems and thought well enough of his effort to publish *A Green Bough* when he had already produced seven novels and almost thirty short stories. This is significant, for we know how rigorously he honored the inner gift which had created *The Sound and the Fury* and *As I Lay Dying*: he was willing, during a time of hardship, to pay for the privilege of rewriting *Sanctuary* in order to do justice to those books.[2] *A Green Bough* appeared later and one can assume that he felt no need to be ashamed of that work. Other than reviews the only notice which Faulkner's poetry has received is Harry Runyan's "Faulkner's Poetry," *Faulkner Studies*, 3, nos. 2–3 (Summer-Autumn 1954), 23–29. Mr. Runyan's article is chiefly useful in demonstrating the kind of judgment which has permitted critics to shy away from Faulkner's verse. He stresses the derivative nature of the poetry and concludes that the effect of the poems is "one of immature romanticism."[3]

It would be difficult to argue that Faulkner's reputation as poet would be great if he were known as a writer of verse alone.[4] However, this is a hypothetical situation, and the fact that he is a great novelist gives his verse importance. It is objected that the poems of William Faulkner are youthful exercises. In answer one may reply that the poems of the young are asked only to reflect the vision of the young; they cannot be wholly "mature" and they are apt to be imitative. If, however, they are true to youth's vision and imitate with taste, discretion, and vitality, they deserve to be heard by those who profess to take pleasure in poetry. If the poems happen to be the work of a man who has achieved great literary stature, they deserve to be treated as valuable documents. *The Marble Faun* is a highly complex literary exercise. The poems are, as Phil Stone says in his preface, "the poems of youth," but they are promising in more ways than it was possible to see then. The book fails, but the principal cause of failure is in the almost impossible task which the young poet set for himself. *The Marble Faun* is a cycle of nineteen poems, including a prologue and an epilogue, in the pastoral mode. The writing of serious pastoral poetry in our time has been restricted by the lack of an adequate pastoral idiom. This has always been the problem for poets writing pastoral forms in English, but it has been intensified by the decay of the literary language and the requisite quest for a new idiom, fitting for our time and place. Faulkner's attempt was unusual. He challenged directly, avoiding the alternative, the way of irony and the juxtaposition of past and present. He tried to make a mythological poem, composed in a language of echoes and innuendos and arranged in a kind of musical order. This was fixed in the formal context of traditional conventions of the English eclogue, using the cycle of the four seasons and the hours of the day to establish a relationship between separate poems. The effect gained by joining the evocative method of symbolist poetry with the highly developed patterns of the English pastoral is a unique conjunction. It could scarcely have been attempted by an unlettered, accidental poet. The structure of the book, separate poems joined together by common subject and both external and internal devices, indicates an early awareness of the problems of creating structural unity. Concern with form has marked Faulkner's work from the beginning and throughout a career noted for variety and subtlety of structural experiment.

The mood of the nineteen pieces is elegiac, though it is not death but a personal sense of loss that the poet laments. He speaks in the person of the marble faun, sometimes "marble-bound" physically in the space of "this gray old garden," more often the prisoner of interior powers which isolate him from the quick unthinking vitality of the idealized pastoral scene. His separation comes from knowledge, a sense of identity and loss, the memory of the dreamy past and a sense of the recurrence and repetition of all things, good and evil. The burden of his separation is awareness; its anguish is increased by the contrast between the impotence of knowledge and the thoughtless vigor of natural life, everywhere personified, or, more exactly, made animal, everywhere swaying and moving to a dance he cannot share. But he can hear the tune and be moved by it. The music and the gestures of Pan, model and original poet-shepherd of the pastoral scene, as well as the Greek original of Faunus, echo through the cycle, at once a torment and solace to the marble faun. The myth of Narcissus is repeatedly evoked. Time and again objects are seen in mirror image. All things, including Pan and the speaker, come to self-awareness in this way. The speaker, though, plagued by the knowledge of change, decay, mutability, and the rigors of rebirth, remains sad for "things I know, yet cannot know." The inner dialect of the poem is stressed by the struggle of opposing images, fire and ice, dancing and immobility, silence and music, youth and age, spring and winter, night and day. It is unresolved, ending as it began, the full circle implied by the device of the first two rhymes of the prologue matching the last two rhymes of the epilogue, "fro-go," "go-snow." Concealed in the guise of this pastoral cycle is one of the dominant themes of our literature, the struggle to identity, in this case defined in symbolic terms.

The achievement of a pastoral myth of such austere purity required a finished idiom, and it would have been a small miracle if the poet had possessed that gift at the start. The failure of *The Marble Faun* lies in the language and syntax. It is not entirely the result of the frequent archaisms, inversions, and old-fashioned poeticisms. These are tools and Faulkner used them to give the poem a timeless quality. He used the same devices skillfully in *A Green Bough*, and this kind of stylization, for a somewhat different purpose, was to become a characteristic of the highly regarded Fugitive verse, particularly in some of the poems of John Crowe Ransom. Neither is the failure of the poem the result of the apparently rigid stanzaic pattern. Except for the song of Pan, six quatrains in the sixth poem of the cycle, the poem is made up of stanzas of varying length, in lines of iambic tetrameter, rhyming in couplets. However, within this form there is considerable variation. The basic stanza is a unit of either twelve or fourteen lines, but there are fourteen different stanza units, ranging from six lines to twenty-six. Rhythm is varied by half-lines, run-on lines, and lines with shifted or added stress. Similarly, there is some variation in rhyme. The dominant music is of pure masculine end rhyme, but there are occasional feminine rhymes, some internal rhymes, and a few unrhymed lines. Faulkner was looking for a form rigid enough to confirm the abstraction of his theme, yet flexible enough to overcome the risk of monotony. It is not surprising that he had not mastered by labor the tools of language to accomplish this. It is remarkable that he was possessed so early by the idea of what he must try to do.

Ultimately the success or failure of the cycle depended on verbal texture, the conveyed sensuous values and relations of the sounds of words. In this poem the immediate sensuous affective experience is crucial. The verbal texture, however, is weakened by lack of sophistication: not, as has been supposed, by literary naïveté, but by the absence of the precision that comes only from the craft of making poems. The language Faulkner commanded would not stand the strain and he was forced to depend upon conventional "poetic" language. It is this weakness that has given some critics cause to dismiss the book as derivative in a pejorative sense. With the undeniable advantage of hindsight, we can see the importance of the fact that Faulkner's first great literary problem was texture. Like Joyce, he developed in his prose a dazzling variety and distinction in the use of verbal texture. Still, even in *The Marble Faun* there are moments when there appears, as Phil Stone suggested, "a hint of coming muscularity of wrist and eye." Faulkner had already achieved something of the French symbolists' ability to suggest correspondences by analogy, to describe the experience of one of the senses in the terms of another, a familiar device in his later fiction. And there are a few examples of the striking similes that were to become characteristic of his prose: the flight of blackbirds in a twilight sky "like shutters swinging to and fro," or again, like "burned scraps of paper"; silence is "like a hood"; lilacs are "faint as cries"; mist is "as soft and thick as hair."

Between the date of composition of *The Marble Faun*, "April, May, June, 1919," and its publication, Faulkner continued to write verse as well as prose. The verse published during this time indicates a consolidation of the interests evident in *The Marble Faun*. Of thirteen poems printed in *The Mississippian* during 1919–1920, four are "from Verlaine," and they show Faulkner's continuing interest in the abstract lyricism of symbolist verse. At this time Faulkner was studying French formally at the university, and we know that he did very well.[5] He was developing an increasing stylization of diction and syntax and a dependence on the controlling factors of formal verse patterns. It was not all apprentice work. Faulkner's first published work, "L'Après-Midi d'un Faune," appeared in *The New Republic*, August 6, 1919. Affiliations with Mallarmé's poem of the same title are vague, but the poem is of some interest as an intense condensation of the mood and argument of *The Marble Faun*.

During the years between *The Marble Faun* and *A Green Bough*, while Faulkner was busy with prose, he found some time for his poetry, and fourteen of his poems appeared in periodicals. Moreover he made use of his verse in his first two novels. The epigraph of *Soldier's Pay* was to reappear in *A Green Bough*, XXX, and verse quoted in *Mosquitoes* was also used, revised, in *A Green Bough*. In general this verse shows a refinement and development with some variation in kinds, a new hardness, some irony, and, in a few cases, satire. It is not surprising, though, that Faulkner's verse generally strives for a level of high seriousness. In "Verse Old and Nascent: A Pilgrimage,"[6] Faulkner's most explicit extended statement on the aims of poetry, he came out in favor of a formal and traditional poetry, one which he felt was under the obligation to convey "spiritual beauty." He described his progress through a series of early admirations which concluded at the point when he discovered the permanent virtues of Shelley and Keats. Contrasting these with what he saw as the main direction of modern poetry, he praised their "beautiful awareness, so sure of its own power that it is not necessary to create the illusion of force by frenzy and motion. Take the odes to a Nightingale, to a Grecian urn, 'Music to hear,' etc.; here is the spiritual beauty which the moderns strive vainly for with trickery, and yet beneath it one knows are entrails; masculinity." There are important implications in Faulkner's position. Poetry is the communication of spiritual beauty; its virtues are restraint, formality, and power to disguise, not dramatized. A poetry complementing this point of view would tend to avoid the light, the occasional, and, to a degree, the colloquial; it would tend to be exclusive. Faulkner's concept of the use of poetry is a lofty one, and, in a sense, an inhibiting one for the poet. For the full sweep and play of imagination and, perhaps most important, for the free introduction of humor, Faulkner would necessarily, if regretfully, depend on prose.[7]

Many of the poems in *A Green Bough* were written early, but, on the evidence of the poems which appeared in periodicals, Faulkner continued to polish his work. The question of Faulkner's revisions has been obscured by misinterpretation and casual scholarship. An excellent example of misinterpretation accepted as fact begins with Faulkner's remark about the composition of *As I Lay Dying* in the introduction to the Modern Library edition of *Sanctuary*. There Faulkner said: "I wrote *As I Lay Dying* in six weeks, without changing a word." Interpretation of this to mean that Faulkner did not at any stage revise the work was passed along until even so usually astute a critic as Olga Vickery confidently wrote that *As I Lay Dying* was "published without a single line of revision."[8] In *The Paris Review*, 4, no. 12 (Spring 1956) [32–33], there is a reproduction of the first manuscript page of *As I Lay Dying*. There are a number of revisions on this page and a comparison with the published version of the novel will reveal still other differences not evident on this manuscript sheet. Similarly, study of the short stories indicates many cases of revision occurring between the time that a story appeared in periodical form and the appearance of the same story in book form.

A number of the poems in *A Green Bough* further exemplify Faulkner's concern with revision. Of particular interest are the revisions of poems which had appeared in the Faulkner issue of *Contempo*, 1, no. 17 (February 1, 1932). It is likely that the verse dates from an earlier period, but there was revision between February 1932 and the publication of *A Green Bough* the following year. The poem "Spring" in *Contempo*, XXXVI in *A Green Bough*, shows how he worked over a finished poem in minor details to sharpen its overall effect.

Spring

Gusty trees windily lean on green
Eviscerated skies, the surging wind
Against the sun's gold collar stamps, to lean
His weight. And once the furrowed day behind,
The golden steed browses the field he breaks
And full of flashing teeth, where he has been,
Trees, the waiting mare his neighing shakes,
Hold his heaving shape a moment seen.

Upon the hills, clashing the stars together,
Stripping the tree of heaven of its blaze,
Stabled, richly grained with golden weather . . .
Within the trees that he has reft and raped
His fierce embrace by riven boughs is shaped,
While in the lonely hills he stamps and neighs.

A Green Bough, XXXVI

Gusty trees windily lean on green
eviscerated skies, the stallion, Wind,
against the sun's gold collar stamps, to lean
his weight. And once the furrowed day behind,
the golden steed browses the field he breaks
and full of flashing teeth where he has been
trees, the waiting mare his neighing shakes,
hold his heaving shape a moment seen.

Upon the hills, clashing the stars together,
stripping the tree of heaven of its blaze,
stabled, richly grained with golden weather—

Within the trees that he has reft and raped
his fierce embrace by riven boughs in shaped,
while on the shaggy hills he stamps and neighs.

The most obvious difference between the two versions is that in revision capitals are dropped as the insignia of individual lines. This is not accidental; of all the poems in *A Green Bough*, only six do not use capitals at the beginning of each line. Two, XXXVI and XVI, use capitals to mark the grammatical beginning of individual sentences. There is a distinct effect gained by this change: an increased run-on quality in the lines, making the individual stanza the unit in the sonnet, rather than the line. And movement, the movement and violence of the wind and the coming of spring suggested in rhythm, texture, and imagery, is enhanced. The breakup of the last stanza into two units tends to stress the coherence of the first octave, its development of a single complex figure. That figure Faulkner clarified and emphasized by replacing "surg-ing" with "stallion," and by capitalizing the metaphorical subject of de-velopment, Wind, separating it by commas. Similarly he eliminated two commas in line six which impede the forward movement.[9] The purpose of this kind of slight revision was to sharpen the original in-tention of the poem. Most of the other revisions are similar in purpose, the most drastic being the removal of an entire four-line stanza from the sonnet "Knew I Love Once" to form, with minor changes, the ten-line poem XXXIII of *A Green Bough.* Even slight changes are of some significance. For example, in revising "The Lilacs," *The Double Dealer,* 7, no. 44 (June 1925), 185–87, to make I of *A Green Bough,* Faulkner made a number of small changes, the most important being the elim-ination, as much as possible, of the poet speaker as singular, replacing him with a collective pronoun, thus increasing the dramatic conflict in the poem without the danger of the poet's being explicitly identified as more than a spectator.

A Green Bough appeared at a time when there was little sympathy in critical circles for an abstract lyric poetry chiefly concerned with the communication of "spiritual beauty." Most of the objections to the book are contained in a review by Morris U. Schappes, "Faulkner as Poet," *Poetry* 43, no. 1 (October 1933), 48–52. Mr. Schappes was bothered by the absence of pressing social issues in Faulkner's poetry and noted that in no poem had Faulkner come to grips with the problem of "the proletariat" in Mississippi. He was disturbed by the deliberate artifice of the poems and he criticized Faulkner for ob-scurity. There was another criticism, one based on the notion of art as a vaguely therapeutic gesture. "Inevitably," Schappes wrote, "there is driven home the impression that these poems are not the lyric definition of the relation of an integrated personality with the world about him but mere emotional poses." It was not enough that the poet write poems; he must also offer for inspection "an inte-grated personality." William Rose Benét, in "Faulkner as Poet," *The Saturday Review of Literature,* 9, no. 41 (April 29, 1933), 565, found the same fault and added to it the defect of incompletely assimilated "influences." Only a magician could assimilate all the forces Benét found at work in Faulkner's poems. Among the principals were Eliot, Housman, Cummings, Hart Crane, Rossetti, and Swinburne. "Mr.

Faulkner is an apt pupil in his poetry," Benét wrote, "choosing the most approved modern influences, but he can scarcely be said to have absorbed them." Peter Monro Jack's review, *The New York Times Book Review*, May 14, 1933, p. 2, stressed "lack of originality" and added H.D. to Benét's diverse gallery of influences. Only Eda Lou Walton's review in *New York Herald-Tribune Books*, April 30, 1933, p. 2, praised the book, treating the verse in terms of its own demands. A subtle kinship between the disciplines of his verse and prose fiction was suggested and a comparison made of his methods with those of Joyce.

> Although his poetry has by no means the absolute artistry of Joyce's "Chamber Music," one is reminded in reading him of the difference between Joyce, the novelist, and Joyce, the lyric singer. Faulkner, the novelist, is not Faulkner, the poet. But the two have one thing in common. Both have learned an art from conscientious study of various other artists' styles. Both have come through this discipline with something their own.

It is difficult to talk with certainty or assurance about movements in contemporary literature, and perhaps not really useful under any circumstances; but anyone who has followed the "trends" in little magazines and volumes of new verse is aware that the situation has changed enough during the last twenty years so that it is now possible to examine a book of verse like *A Green Bough* without being necessarily perturbed by deliberate artifice or the absence of current political and social issues.[10] We are not even so disturbed by "influences" any more. One of the things a half century of scholarship has taught us is that a wholly original poetic style is rare indeed. Now we are apt to think more of models than influences, and even the once honored term *imitation* is regaining some of its prestige. In superficial aspects certain poems in *A Green Bough* are distinctly imitative, but in a deeper sense there is much that belongs singularly to Faulkner. In a casual way the first poem of the volume has suggestions of Eliot. It begins with a tea party and moves into mythology. There is some dialogue and, on occasion, an echo of the rhythmic patterns of the early Eliot. The second has with less justice been compared to Eliot's "Portrait of a Lady."[11] Similarly XXVII, in quatrains and treating the myth of Philomel, calls to mind "Sweeney among the Nightingales," but the differences are important. Faulkner's poem begins where Eliot's ended and has no satirical comment on present reality by means of the myth. It is a pure lyric. Poem XV suggests Housman, it is true, with its repetition of "bonny," and four poems suggest the manner of Cummings in the absence of capitals at least. These eight poems, which make no attempt to disguise allusions to the work of other poets, represents the main evidence for those who have complained that Faulkner's verse is unduly derivative.

The poems of A *Green Bough* show a considerable variety of form and subject matter. They range from the lyric for song to the most intense and compressed imagery. The second stanza of XIX, describing a swimmer in sun-filled water, shows the more traditional music he was capable of.

> Within these slow cathedralled corridors
> Where ribs of sunlight drown
> He joins in green caressing wars
> With seamaids red and brown. . . .

The concluding stanza of XIV indicates the economy and clarity in Faulkner's suggestion of the world of the folk song and ballad. In this poem a young man has been hanged.

> Being dead he will forgive you
> And all that you have done,
> But he'll curse you if you leave him
> Grinning at the sun.

This can be set in contrast to the complexity of the second stanza of XXXIV, the image of Mary at twilight.

> Her soft doveslippered eyes strayed in the dusk
> Creaming backward from the fallen day,
> And a haughty star broke yellow musk
> Where dead kings slept the long cold years away.

There are echoes of A *Marble Faun* in the images of any number of the individual poems, enough to give the careful reader a sense of continuity in Faulkner's entire poetic work, and the dominant mood of the whole book is pastoral.[12] The cycle of the seasons in a classical landscape merges with the figure of a plowman at sunset in X and evokes an image that haunts Faulkner's prose as well as his verse.

> Nymph and faun in this dusk might riot
> Beyond all oceaned Time's cold greenish bar
> To shrilling pipes, to cymbals' hissing
> Beneath a single icy star
>
> Where he, to his own compulsion
> —A terrific figure on an urn—
> Is caught between his two horizons,
> Forgetting that he cant return.

If there is continuity in Faulkner's verse there is, as in his prose, a restless experimentation, and an attempt to achieve, within the limitations which he demanded for verse, new variations on the oldest themes. The final effect is not one of "immature romanticism." It is rather one of strenuous effort to create a poetry which, had it been continued, might have been a sophisticated lyric strain in contemporary verse. The final poem of A Green Bough, XLIV, which had been previously published as "My Epitaph" and This Earth significantly closes Faulkner's career as poet on a note of subdued tranquillity and a return to roots in the earth he has chosen not only to celebrate, but as his home. A Green Bough shows a poet, not always successful, or equally skillful, who knows the value of words, rhythm, image, texture, and, above all, structure; and it shows us a writer who, contrary to popular myth, was a meticulous craftsman, aware of the tradition of letters and the best contemporary work. Faulkner never achieved all that he asked of himself in poetry, but he could at least have the sense of satisfaction he put into the words of the natural poet in the sketch "Out of Nazareth": "You see, I wrote this, and I liked it. Of course it ain't as good as I wisht it was. But you are welcome to it."[13]

The Poetry of William Faulkner

Notes

1. Of the thirty-one poems published during this period by Faulkner, six were to appear in *A Green Bough*. I include the unsigned poem "Nocturne," *Ole Miss*, 25 (1921), 214–15.
2. Introduction to the Modern Library edition of *Sanctuary* (New York: Random House, 1932).
3. Mr. Runyan also prints a checklist of Faulkner's poetry which adds nothing to the list compiled by Robert W. Daniel, *A Catalogue of the Writings of William Faulkner* (New Haven: Yale University Library, 1942).
4. Still, this has been done. Eda Lou Walton, reviewing *A Green Bough* for *New York Herald-Tribune Books*, April 30, 1933, p. 2, wrote: "If William Faulkner had not been interested in becoming an important novelist and short story writer, it seems most probable that he would hold rank as one of the better of the minor poets of this period." Similarly, *The Marble Faun* received a perceptive review which saw the poems of that book as promising real achievement: John McClure, "Literature and Less," the *New Orleans Times-Picayune*, Sunday magazine section, January 25, 1925, p. 6.
5. A. Wigfall Green, "William Faulkner at Home," *Sewanee Review*, 40, no. 3 (July–September 1932), 300. Reprinted in Frederick J. Hoffman and Olga W. Vickery, eds., *William Faulkner: Two Decades of Criticism* (East Lansing: Michigan State University Press, 1951), 40. Faulkner's study of the French symbolists is confirmed by Phil Stone in a letter to James B. Meriwether, February 19, 1957: "As to the French symbolist poets, Bill read a good many of them that I had, some in the original and most in translation, and I think they had some influence upon his own verse."
6. *The Double Dealer*, 7, no. 43 (April 1925), 129–31.
7. Answering a question about Eliot and Poe, Faulkner made his distinction between the aims of poetry and the aims of prose quite clear: "Well, with Eliot there is this difference—Poe dealt in prose, while the poet deals with something which is so pure and so esoteric that you cannot say he is English or Japanese—he deals in something that is universal. That's the distinction I make between the prose writer and the poet, the novelist and the poet—that the poet deals in something universal, while the novelist deals in his own traditions." *Faulkner at Nagano*, edited by Robert A. Jelliffe (Tokyo: Kenkyusha, 1956), 16.
8. *William Faulkner: Two Decades of Criticism*, 18.
9. In line thirteen, "his fierce embrace by riven boughs in shaped," "in" is obviously a misprint in the original text. This is corrected by R. N. Raimbault in his bilingual edition, *Le Rameau Vert* (Paris: Gallimard, 1955), 182.
10. An excellent discussion of the trend toward "mythological" subjects as against "occasional" subjects is W. H. Auden's foreword to W. S. Merwin's book of poems *A Mask for Janus* (New Haven: Yale University Press, 1952).
11. Frederick L. Gwynn, "Faulkner's Prufrock—and Other Observations," *The Journal of English and Germanic Philology*, 52, no. 1 (January 1953), 63–70. Mr. Gwynn's article actually deals with the influence of Eliot on the early novels but he finds that the first two poems of *A Green Bough* "owe their situation and tone and many of their phrases to Eliot's 'Portrait of a Lady,' while No. XXVII is almost a parody of 'Sweeney among the Nightingales.' "

12. Something remains to be said of the continuity between Faulkner's verse and his prose. The pastoral feeling of *The Hamlet* echoes many images in *The Marble Faun* and *A Green Bough*.

13. *New Orleans Sketches by William Faulkner*, edited by Ichiro Nishizaki (Tokyo: Hokuseido, 1955), 79.

15

Faulkner's Early
Literary Criticism
(1959)

With as much accuracy as humor William Faulkner once wrote: "All that is necessary for admission to the ranks of criticism is a typewriter."[1] In general Faulkner has tended to ignore the critics and has given no sign of having a high regard for their discipline. An example of his contempt for bad criticism is his letter to *Time* in 1950; there he broke his usual silence to attack the critics and reviewers of the new Hemingway novel, *Across the River and into the Trees*, comparing them to bad little boys in school, spitball throwers who "don't have anything to stand on while they throw the spitballs."[2] With the exception of some of the published interviews, and recently in seminars at Nagano and Charlottesville and Princeton, Faulkner has had little to say in public *about* literature, has joined no schools, developed no critical position, and he has stated few preferences or sympathies outside the demonstrable activity of the critic implicit in the work of the artist. Some of the published interviews do contain brief but significant critical remarks, and the number and variety of literary subjects he has called on with ease during interviews to answer specific questions indicate a wide-ranging interest and an appreciation-in-depth of the literary tradition, past and present. But observations in the context of an interview are not to be taken as formal criticism. The interviews deserve separate and careful study.

Recent scholarship has brought to light the fact that early in his career, indeed before he had begun writing his first novel, Faulkner wrote a number of critical pieces.[3] Some of these are most valuable to an understanding of the critical assumptions behind the artist's work. No previous study has dealt with Faulkner's published criticism and its relation to his work.[4] Faulkner is the author of twelve critical pieces, eight of which were published during the important formative years of

1921–1925. His earliest known critical production is a review of Conrad Aiken's *Turns and Movies and Other Tales in Verse.*[5] His most recent is "Sherwood Anderson: An Appreciation."[6] Five of his critical essays appeared in *The Mississippian*, the weekly student newspaper at the University of Mississippi. They are little known, not easily accessible, and of more than passing interest. Faulkner's contributions to the paper included poems, translations, narrative sketches, letters, and criticism. The criticism is of special interest since, like many a young writer, he was more sure of what he liked and wanted to do than his creative efforts at the time might indicate.

His review of Conrad Aiken's book of poems is doubly significant. It shows that, contrary to the usual picture of him at that time, Faulkner had a keen awareness of the contemporary literary situation. And the qualities he isolates and praises in Aiken's poems are closely related to the direction he was taking and was to follow in his own poetry. In general he was critical of the American poetic situation for its second-hand romanticism, for "sobbing over the middle west," and for the "impenetrable thickets of Browningesque obscurity." He contrasted the work of Aiken with these tendencies, and in praising Aiken he attacked what he viewed as specific abuses:

> Nothing is ever accidental with him, he has most happily escaped our national curse of filling each and every space, religious, physical, mental and moral, and beside him the British nightingales, Mr. Vachel Lindsay with his tin pan and iron spoon, Mr. Kreymborg with his lithographic water coloring, and Mr. Carl Sandburg with his sentimental Chicago propaganda are so many puppets fumbling in windy darkness.

It was more than Aiken's individuality that merited Faulkner's admiration. Three qualities were assumed by him to be at once praiseworthy and promising: the obvious control of the material by the poet, the degree of technical skill, and the "musical forms" of the verse. The emphasis on control and technique is significant. Faulkner favored artifice in verse, and by technical skill he meant the use of and variation on formal, traditional means. "Mr. Aiken has a plastic mind," he wrote; "he uses variation, inversion, change of rhythm and such metrical tricks with skillful effect, and his clear impersonality will never permit him to write poor verse."

The notions provide a background for the appreciation of Faulkner's own poetry and his later comments on verse. A few years later he wrote "Verse Old and Nascent: A Pilgrimage," in which he described his own appreciative progress from Swinburne to his contemporaries, especially praising Robinson, Frost, Aldington, Aiken, and Housman.[7] From there he had moved into the past: "From this point the road is obvious, Shakespeare I read, and Spenser, and the Elizabethans, and Shelley and Keats." It is interesting to note that Faulkner's description of the development of his taste parallels to some degree T. S. Eliot's later discussion of his own.[8] From his experience of appreciation Faulkner emerged with an idea of the use of poetry. Its purpose was the communication of "spiritual beauty"; its method in our time should be to "revert to formal rhymes and conventional forms again." His ideas on poetry, suggested as early as the Aiken review, seem to have remained basically unchanged. In the *Faulkner at Nagano* he is quoted as distinguishing between poetry and prose by asserting that poetry should deal with the "universal" while prose must deal with the particular.[9] Poetry is international, cosmopolitan; prose is of necessity regional. The review of *Turns and Movies* shows an already developed point of view and a considerable knowledge of the contemporary literary milieu. Most of the progress later to be described in "Verse Old and Nascent" was already behind him, and what remained was the refinement of his own poetic talents in *The Marble Faun* (1924) and *A Green Bough* (1933).

Only one of the *Mississippian* pieces is concerned with fiction, an essay-review treating three novels by Joseph Hergesheimer.[10] It is a curious review, containing at once a strong attack on Hergesheimer's work and yet, in part, a description of characteristics that would later be evident in the work of Faulkner the novelist. There is a kind groping and wrestling here. In an effort to articulate his discontent with Hergesheimer, Faulkner summoned up some images which have remained constant and recurring in his own work, as for example: "He has never written a novel—someone has yet to coin the word for each unit of his work—Linda Condon, in which he reached his apex, is not a novel. It is more like a lovely Byzantine frieze: a few unforgettable figures in silent arrested motion, forever beyond the reach of time and troubling the heart like music." Or, in another case, he described something in the technique which pleased him, a device which was to become a powerful weapon in his own arsenal: "The induction to The Bright Shawl is good—he talks of the shawl for a page or so before one is aware of the presence of the shawl as a material object, before the word itself is said; it is like being in a room full of people, one of whom one has not yet directly looked at, though conscious all the time of his presence." The qualities Faulkner disliked in Hergesheimer's novels, as he viewed them, were the absence of inner reality in the characters, the imitation of the method of Henry James, and, more subtle, a quality of nihilism he detected. "He is subjective enough to bear life with fair equanimity, but he is afraid of living, of man in his sorry clay braving chance and circumstance."

In addition to two appreciative essays on Sherwood Anderson, [11] there are three later book reviews by Faulkner in which he takes critical positions on the novel. The earliest of these is a review of *The Road Back* by Erich Maria Remarque. [12] His reaction to Remarque's book was mixed. He was troubled by the despair of defeat, the sentimentality, and the absence of the devices of art. "Granted that his intent is more than opportunism, it still remains to be seen if art can be made of authentic experience transferred to paper word for word, of a peculiar reaction to an actual condition, even though it be vicarious." We have again his early distinction between art and reality. The most significant observation in the review is again a question of practical technique arising from the problem of decorum in characterization. Faulkner was bothered because Remarque had given to his characters "speeches which they would have been incapable of making." Discussing this, he worked toward a distinction between what might be called *imposed* and *inevitable* heightening of a character's powers:

> It is a writer's privilege to put into the mouths of his characters better speech than they would have been capable of, but only for the purpose of permitting and helping the character to justify himself or what he believes himself to be, taking down his spiritual pants. But when the character must express the moral ideas applicable to a race, a situation, he is better kept in that untimed and unsexed background of the choruses of Greek senators.

It is a distinction which, perhaps, applies to the difference between the flights of Gavin Stevens and the complex anonymity of *A Fable*. His next book review, a review of the nonfictional *Test Pilot* by Jimmy Collins,[13] is again concerned with distinctions between the experience of art and the experience of life, between fiction and nonfiction. It is clear that in Faulkner's mind art is always highly ordered experience. "They [the sections of the book] are wide in range and of varying degrees of worth and interest, and one, an actual experience which reads like fiction, is excellent, concise, and ordered, and not only sustained but restrained." Excellence, concision, order, restraint are the qualities of art. But Faulkner's main interest in this review was the "folklore of speed" which he said was yet to be written. *Pylon* had been published the previous spring. That statement of what this new folklore would imply stands as a significant contrast and, perhaps, a corollary to the grandeur of his well-known Nobel Prize address. The review concludes:

> It would be a folklore not of the age of speed nor of the men who perform it, but of the speed itself, peopled not by anything human or even mortal but by the clever willful machines themselves carrying nothing that was born and will have to die or which can even suffer pain, moving without comprehensible purpose toward no discernible destination, producing a literature innocent of either love or hate and of course of pity or terror, and which would be the story of the final disappearance of life from the earth. I would watch them, the little puny mortals, vanishing against a vast and timeless void filled with the sound of incredible engines, within which furious meteors moving in no medium hurtled nowhere, neither pausing nor flagging, forever destroying themselves and one another.

Faulkner's only other known review of a novel, a review of Hemingway's *The Old Man and The Sea*, indicates an added dimension of his concept of character:[14]

> His best. Time may show it to be the best single piece of any of us, I mean his and my contemporaries. This time, he discovered God, a Creator. Until now, his men and women had made themselves, shaped themselves out of their own clay; their victories and defeats were at the hands of each other, just to prove to themselves or one another how tough they could be.

It can be seen that from his earliest critical piece on the novel Faulkner has been greatly concerned with the problem of character, where and from what the fictional character draws the breath of being, with the distinction between the worlds of art and reality, a distinction which he had maintained for poetry as well, and, too, with the importance of meaningfulness, of positive human values in art. The position on characterization is most significant in his own development as a novelist. From the beginning he realized that no fictional character should be a puppet, but must be animated from within. This is a consistent point of view. An addition to this, the next dimension, is apparent in the Hemingway review, the necessary sense of a Creator breathing life into the dust of an imaginary character. It may be that this slight addition to an original point of view parallels the gradual shift from the tragic vision of *The Sound and the Fury* to the comic reality of the great Snopes trilogy, begun in *The Hamlet*, extended in *The Town*, and to be concluded in *The Mansion*. There are three other critical pieces written by William Faulkner for *The Mississippian*, which are of considerable interest. All three are concerned with the drama.[15] The first of them was a short review of Edna St. Vincent Millay's *Aria da Capo: A Play in One Act*.[16] Faulkner praised the play for its simplicity of design, its condensation, artifice, and language; and he used the occasion for one more smack at the imagists and Carl Sandburg.

> A lusty tenuous simplicity; the gods have given Miss Millay a strong wrist; and though an idea alone does not make or mar a piece of writing, it is something; and this one of hers will live even though Miss Amy Lowell intricately festoons it with broken glass, or Mr. Carl Sandburg sets it in the stock yards, to be acted, of a Saturday afternoon, by the Beef Butchers' Union.

It is amusing, if slightly irrelevant, to note that Faulkner's syntactical independence was asserted so early. It may also be of interest that though his belief in formalized verse seems to have remained unchanged, he appears to have changed his mind about the importance of Carl Sandburg. He has more recently spoken in praise of him as one of the "indigenous American writers who were produced and nurtured by a culture which was completely American."[17]

More important are two essays devoted to Eugene O'Neill and to the contemporary theater in general.[18] They show an alert awareness of the contemporary theater, American and European, and they are riddled with references to important figures, indicating that the young

Faulkner was much less provincial than his critics have ordinarily assumed. He talks easily of Flaubert, Balzac, Conrad, Hauptmann, Moeller, Synge, Kreymborg, Marsden Hartley, Ezra Pound (whom he views with not much approval), Freud, and Robert Edmund Jones. His concern in the first essay is with the possibility of a national literature in any literary form. The best possibility that he sees is in the developing work of Eugene O'Neill. Faulkner was torn between two notions, one "that art is preeminently provincial: i.e., it comes directly from a certain age and a certain locality," and the other that somehow a national literature must manage to be universal as well. He saw Synge's work as exemplifying both these characteristics. He found O'Neill at that stage (*Anna Christie* had just been produced) an exception in the sense that he did not seem to *need* a particular region. This led him to consider what it was that could create a national literature in America. He concluded that the best hope was in the language:

A national literature cannot spring from folk lore—though heaven knows, such a forcing has been tried often enough—for America is too big and there are too many folk lores: Southern negroes, Spanish and French strains, the old west, for these always will remain colloquial; nor will it come through our slang, which also is likewise indigenous to restricted portions of the country. It can, however, come from the strength of imaginative idiom which is understandable by all who read English. Nowhere today, saving in parts of Ireland, is the English language spoken with the same earthy strength as it is in the United States; though we are, as a nation, still inarticulate.

Against this possibility, he described in the second article the many threats to the writer's integrity in this country. These included the Broadway market, the movies, expatriation, the literary life, and "dragons which they, themselves, have raised." The latter he illustrated by the story of an artist who submitted himself to psychoanalysis to the detriment of his art. For the material of a new and vital literature he offered two suggestions as examples—the Mississippi River and the growth of the railroads. Both of these he was to use, one way or another, in later work.

These early critical pieces in *The Mississippian* would be of interest if only for the picture they give us of the young Faulkner, back from the war, at the University of Mississippi, deeply interested in a variety of literary subjects, and struggling to find his own way. They show a young man whose literary awareness at any time would have to be called considerable, and they also give an indication of what he was reading in those days. But perhaps most important are those ideas which he has not outgrown or abandoned, but has continued to cultivate in his creative work: an emphasis in all literary forms on artifice to distinguish art from life, a concept of complete fidelity to character, a devotion to the American scene, a sense of the vitality of language, and, finally, a position that art, however truthful and tragic, must be a positive statement against anarchy and chaos. Few of his professional critics can show as much consistency.

Notes

1. "On Criticism," *The Double Dealer*, 7 (January–February 1925), 83.
2. *Time*, 56 (November 13, 1950), 6.
3. James B. Meriwether, *William Faulkner: A Check List* (Princeton: Princeton University Library, 1957); of particular value to this examination is the list of Faulkner's contributions to *The Mississippian*, pp. 22–23.
4. For a short, and inaccurate, piece dealing with some of Faulkner's creative contributions to *The Mississippian*, see Martha Mayes, "Faulkner Juvenilia," *New Campus Writing No. 2* (New York: Bantam, 1957), 135–44.
5. *The Mississippian*, February 16, 1921, 5.
6. *Atlantic*, 191 (June 1953), 27–29.
7. *The Double Dealer*, 7 (April 1925), 129–31.
8. T. S. Eliot, *The Use of Poetry and the Use of Criticism* (London: Faber, 1933), 32–36.
9. *Faulkner at Nagano*, ed. Robert A. Jelliffe (Kenkyusha; Tokyo: 1956), 16.
10. *The Mississippian*, December 15, 1922, 5.
11. In addition to the *Atlantic* piece, there is "Sherwood Anderson," *Dallas Morning News*, April 26, 1925, III: 7; reprinted in *Princeton University Library Chronicle*, 18 (Spring 1957), 89–94.
12. "Beyond the Talking," *New Republic*, 67 (May 20, 1931), 23–24.
13. "Folklore of the Air," *American Mercury*, 36 (November 1935), 370–72. See also William Faulkner, *Essays, Speeches, and Public Letters*, ed. James B. Meriwether (New York: Random House, 1965), 192.
14. *Shenandoah*, 3 (Autumn 1952), 55.
15. Faulkner displayed more than a little interest in the drama at this time. In addition to these critical pieces, he wrote at least two plays while a student at the University of Mississippi, including *Marionettes*, according to Carvel Collins in the introduction to *William Faulkner: New Orleans Sketches* (New Brunswick: Rutgers University Press, 1958). A copy of *Marionettes*, hand-lettered, bound, and illustrated by

Faulkner, was displayed in the Princeton University Library exhibit "The Literary Career of William Faulkner," May–August, 1957.

16. *The Mississippian*, January 13, 1922, 5.

17. *Faulkner at Nagano*, 140.

18. "American Drama: Eugene O'Neill," *The Mississippian*, February 3, 1922, 5; "American Drama Inhibitions," March 17, 1922, 5, and March 24, 1922, 5.

The Influence of
William Faulkner
(1964)

No contemporary writer can ignore the work of William Faulkner. If they are young American writers, the chances are that they will have read and studied books by Faulkner and about Faulkner in school; and it is likely that our next wave of writers, those now in schools and colleges, will have been even more extensively and systematically exposed to his art. What effect this latter development will have remains to be seen. It is possible that it may tend to generate the inevitable rebellion of bright students against what they are made to read and told to like. However, those who cherish the work of William Faulkner can be sure that the power and mastery of that great artist will overwhelm even the natural recalcitrance of the student and the well-meaning ineptitude of teachers.

It is difficult in many ways for a young writer to have to stand in the long shadow of a master. Dryden no doubt voiced the deep feeling of many other poets when he complained about having to follow after Shakespeare. Yet he went on working, and our young writers will go on writing novels and hoping to write better ones as long as our language lives. Whatever happens to the novel, even if, as pessimists in unison declare, it dwindles in its audience and importance to the tiny, insular world of poetry in our time, novels will go on being written, just as poems go on being written and dutifully, hopefully, sent off (with return postage and self-addressed envelope) to cross the chaotic desks of magazine editors who are at best jaded and at worst indifferent. (I have been editing the poetry for *The Transatlantic Review* since it was founded in 1959 and I confess to being a little of both.) There is no stifling of the creative impulse, though that impulse may, indeed, become less and less rational as it offers fewer rewards. It is *especially* difficult to be a "Southern" writer, that is, a writer born and raised in the

South, at home with its traditions and history, and to follow in time after William Faulkner. One of the most exciting discoveries about Faulkner for the young Southern writer is his use of the *material* of Southern life and history. The South is many places and peoples, all quite different, yet there is much that is common to it all. The Southern writer is very much aware that Faulkner did not invent his material. It was there to be mined and explored. The close student and the scholar of Southern literature become increasingly aware of how much of that basic material was *already* a part of the literary tradition of the South before Faulkner came on the scene. Some of this will begin to show up in forthcoming studies—the extent to which Faulkner deliberately worked within and with a tradition of whose conventions he was acutely knowledgeable. Professor Joseph Blotner of Virginia, who has had the privilege of examining Faulkner's library with some care, has remarked that the number of "old southern books" is surprising. It should not be so. If it were not for the public myth Faulkner so carefully cultivated in order to preserve his precious privacy, that of being an inspired "farmer" who just happened to write books, it would surprise no one.

The Southern writer is able to see Faulkner as realist. He is capable by birth and inheritance of divorcing subject and treatment and thus able to acknowledge the real genius involved in the choice of subject and the supreme mastery of technique, a dazzling virtuoso performance of more than thirty years of professional writing without ever going stale or ever repeating himself. The trouble for the Southern writer begins with the old, immutable fact that most of his editors and a large proportion of the book reviewers and critics with whom he must contend are *not* Southern and not versed in the Southern tradition, literary or actual. Of course, it isn't their fault. They can't really be blamed for being born elsewhere. But they can and should be blamed for failing to recognize that many of the themes and subjects he used do not belong to Faulkner, who never for one moment proposed that he was inventing them, but to a time and a place, already changing fast as the world changes, but still all of a piece and close enough in time for his history to be our history. In fact the works of William Faulkner are now a part of our Southern history. The sane solution for the young writer is, of course, not to avoid writing about something he knows just because Faulkner also may have written on a similar subject. But the enormous difficulty of convincing editors, publishers, and finally readers who are strangers to the South (except in the Press version, also composed and contrived by strangers and for strangers) that one's work is merely a bucket from the same deep well has forced many Southern writers of recent times into the strategy of innovation for its own sake or into exile from their proper subject. Most of the old Fugitives are fugitive indeed, expatriates living in the suburban North, far, far from their real soil or their nostalgic, agrarian dream.

These same expatriate Southerners have not helped the situation by insisting in public and private that William Faulkner might have been a better man and a better writer had he only moved north and surrounded himself with literary types, rather than living in Oxford and working alone. Many Northern critics have suggested this as well, and it was with some astonishment that I heard Faulkner's editor, the late Saxe Commins, express the same opinion. I have heard this from a number of distinguished writers, editors, and critics, some of them Southerners by birth. The most recent example in print I know of is in a piece by Allen Tate written for the *New Statesman* (28 September 1962), which Tate calls "a memoir, or perhaps it had better be called an obituary." There Tate takes the occasion of an obituary to bring up the old saw, though in literary terms, of William Faulkner wasting away in the benighted wilderness:

> I suppose my main source of annoyance with him was his affectation of not being a writer, but a farmer; this would have been pretentious even had he been a farmer. But being a "farmer," he did not "associate" with writers—with the consequence that he was usually surrounded by third-rate writers or just plain sycophants. I never heard that he was a friend of anybody who could conceivably have been his peer.

Friendship, "belonging," "togetherness" seem important to Tate here. One need not be so cynical or unkind as to ask whom Tate would name as Faulkner's peers. Still, this view is important because Faulkner, indeed *belonging* by choice to a time and a place and a literary tradition, did not need the additional stimulus of being deeply involved in "the literary life." It is just as well. The work might not have been written at all if he had allowed himself to be surrounded by literary friends and enemies and cliques, all chattering brightly over the edges of martini glasses about the latest news from Olympus, the latest quotations from what Frost always called "the literary stockmarket," and the latest gossip and odds on who will win what prizes year after next when the judges and committees change. The combined novels of all the Fugitives add up to less work than Faulkner's. Which in itself stands as an example of dedication and professionalism for any young writer and, as well, an estimate of the price that must be paid in the coinage of misunderstanding by one's own countrymen, by long neglect, and by the indifference of the reading public.

Faulkner made a definite and significant choice at a certain point early in his career. When his third, and most ambitious book at that stage, *Sartoris*, was rejected by everybody and finally accepted by Harcourt Brace with some humiliating provisos and stipulations, he suddenly realized that "the literary world" was a world well lost. He rejoiced in his new freedom and set about the writing of *The Sound and the Fury*, *Sanctuary*, and *As I Lay Dying* in rapid order. Of this decision he has written: "I seemed to shut a door between me and all publishers' addresses and book lists. I said to myself, Now I can write."

Most of the young writers I know have been *inspired* by William Faulkner. All have been influenced one way or another. There are clear and present dangers in the process of influence. There is something marvelously hypnotic about the style and method; though, contrary to the opinion of most critics, there never was *a* style, but many and all designed to fit a subject. Perhaps even more than with the single style of Hemingway, Faulkner's stylistic virtuosity has a way of so overpowering the young and highly receptive talent that the young writer can shake off this specific influence only with effort and difficulty. There are a few writers who have on occasion deliberately, and not without some success, cultivated this process rather than resisting it. I would cite Shelby Foote's *Jordan County*, William Styron's *Lie Down in Darkness*, and William Humphrey's *Home From the Hill*. Humphrey has stated in talks and interviews that he subscribes to the notion of Robert Louis Stevenson, that of a deliberate, conscious imitation in detail of the methods of a master whose work one admires. Styron has managed to outgrow the initial effect of this influence, improving through two other novels and gradually finding his own way and his own voice. It is significant, however, that Styron's most successful novel to date, *Set This House on Fire*, is only briefly and partially set in the South. Calder Willingham has been called a satirist of the Faulkner style. This may indeed be so, but it is difficult to establish and, if so, pointless except as a typical example of a young Southern writer living with and wrestling with the problem.

In my first novel, *The Finished Man*, I tried something else, a fancy trick for which I got my knuckles rapped and probably deserved to. Only once in the book did I attempt to use something reminiscent of Faulkner's style, a vague echo, for a particular purpose. One character was telling another of the most crucial event in his life. I tried, in a somewhat different vocabulary, to imitate some of the sweeps and pauses of the Faulknerian rhythm, hoping to suggest to the ideal, alert reader that my character was not really telling the truth, that he had already over the years made something "literary" out of the event. (My character was decently educated and would very likely have read some Faulkner, though I never explicitly said so.) It was intended to be a kind of allusion, not for the purpose of satire or parody, but as a part of the preparation for revelations to come. It did not work. One reviewer after another quoted this particular passage, a very brief one in a longish book, as typical of the book and as an example of how much I had been "influenced" by Faulkner. I had and have been much influenced. But not in that particular passage. And not in that particular way.

The influence of technique, of course, has not been confined to Southern writers. A great many American writers dealing with other regions and sometimes radically different subjects, show the signs of a careful study of Faulkner's narrative techniques. Wright Morris, for example, is clearly indebted to Faulkner in a number of his novels; this in spite of the fact that in his critical writings he has not been altogether fair to his model, accusing Faulkner of being the victim of a vague nostalgia and further arguing that the only really soundly created characters in Faulkner's work are his Negro characters. The latter, Morris insists, is the result of the fact that the Negro is inherently superior to the Southern white and not a result of Faulkner's deliberate characterization in the context of a given story. In other words, Morris sees this as *unintentional*. These points deserve some scrutiny, if only because Wright Morris is a very "literary" writer, much involved, *engaged* in the literary scene, and therefore these opinions are apt to be as much shared as they are original. There are, in fact, three myths of current literary criticism at work behind Morris's statements: the myth of Faulkner as the "unintentional," spontaneous writer, a misunderstanding, deriving from that rather incredible and far-reaching assumption, about "the message" of his work, and coming from both these misconceptions, a conclusion that characterization in Faulkner's books was overcome by a propensity toward symbolic statement. The first of these myths, what might facetiously be called "the unintentional fallacy," is partly attributable to the mystery Faulkner himself deliberately cultivated in order to protect his privacy. But now, with many of his manuscripts and papers available for study at Virginia and Texas, this has been shown to be sheer nonsense. If anything Faulkner was a finicky, compulsive reviser of his work. Another factor which gives the lie to the unintentional theory, and one that has not been seriously considered in its relationship to his whole body of work, is Faulkner's considerable experience and success as a screenwriter. A chapter in James B. Meriwether's fact-filled *The Literary Career of William Faulkner*, with careful reference to other little known studies of Faulkner's Hollywood work, indicates that he worked on films over a considerable period of his career. He has an impressive list of credits, and when one realizes that until quite recently credits were not given as a matter of course or right, it is probable that he worked on a good many more. It is also likely that we shall never have the whole story. The point is relevant to this extent: screenwriting, though it may not be art in itself, is terribly exacting work. All effects are and must be calculated. As one who has done a stint in Hollywood, I am amazed at the variety and success of William Faulkner's work there. Most "serious" writers cannot stand the strain. Judging by his interviews, I believe he was able to do the job well because he never took it seriously, always realizing that a multiple form, involving so many disparate hands, could never be controlled by the writer. He was careful never to become deeply involved in the filming of any of his own books, thus allowing himself a proper distance. If the screenplay is highly calculated in all its effects and if Faulkner was a good screenwriter, it follows inevitably that in his serious work he was at least capable of control. It is high time that we give an artist the basic credit he deserves. He knew what he was doing.

Brief mention should be made, even at the expense of digression, of the fact that we need someone to study with care and dedication the extent of the influence of the film on Faulkner's writing. Visiting at the University of Virginia recently, John Dos Passos admitted the film, even certain precise films, as a major influence in his own documentary and chronicle method. It is possible that Faulkner, who was a good deal more involved with the industry of making movies, was also influenced. I see this influence in two ways. First, a kind of anticinematic method of narration in the novels, as if to dare adaptation. He has created the kind of books that break the heart of the hack adaptor. They are not easily converted to the medium. They must be translated like poems in another language. Which may be the reason why the successful adaptations of his novels have been so few and far between. Ironically, he showed the way, *how* it can be done, by his own freewheeling film adaptation of Hemingway's *To Have and Have Not*. At first glance it shares little more than the title. Yet the whole milieu of this film is the milieu, the world of Hemingway. Bogart is the perfect Hemingway hero. (Perhaps there is even a bit of literary criticism subtly at work there. As if Faulkner were saying: "This is what it *really* adds up to.") In any case *To Have and Have Not* is a far better film than any of the more "accurate" adaptations of Hemingway's work, except, perhaps, the first version of *A Farewell to Arms*. The second way in which I believe the film form influenced Faulkner is more positive. This would take some doing to *prove*, a patient Ph.D. dissertation. I think it can be shown that the methods of transition—cuts, dissolves, and fades—are at work in his prose fiction, as well as cameralike angles—pans, high shots, close shots, long shots, montage effects, and finally even the curious continual present time of the framed celluloid world. Of all our major novelists William Faulkner has been the most successful as a screenwriter, a fact that is not without honor and one which certainly cannot be safely ignored by the critics.

Back to the fallacies of Wright Morris (and others). The problem of "message" and character. Morris's notion is old and new. *The Art of Faulkner's Novels,* by Peter Swiggart (University of Texas Press, 1962), is entirely based on this idea. Swiggart states it explicitly at the outset. "Faulkner's narrative achievements may be explained in terms of his ability to express abstract themes by means of stylized characters without detracting from the dramatic force, and the apparent realism, of his narrative situations. Arbitrary stylization is compensated for in his work by the creation of characters who have explicit symbolic functions, yet live in the reader's imagination as if they were real people." Reduced of its excess of jargon and critical terminology, what this adds up to is that Faulkner *fools* the reader. He was more interested in saying something than in character, that his people are really two-dimensional. If this is so, it is a serious charge; for it means Faulkner failed in his primary intention. Talking to a writing class at the University of Virginia, Faulkner, who was always interested in young writers (recall that his Nobel Prize speech was in part addressed to "the young men and women already dedicated to the same anguish and travail"), said this about message: "A message is one of his [the writer's] tools, just like the rhetoric, just like the punctuation. . . . You write a story to tell about people, man in his constant struggle with his own heart, with the hearts of others, or with his environment." Another time he told the students: "I'm not expressing my own ideas in the stories I tell. I'm telling about people, and these people express ideas which sometimes are mine, sometimes not." He went on to say that in his fiction he was neither satirizing his own country, nor trying to correct it, though he might do both publicly as a private citizen. He was writing about people. Too many critics and some writers (who ought to know better) have tended to blame Faulkner for the opinions, prejudices, and defects in his characters. In one sense this is a tribute to his mastery, but it has created problems. James Baldwin, with both error and ignorance, has assumed Faulkner to be a racist and denounced him for it. Norman Mailer in his incredible example of exhibitionism, *Advertisements for Myself*, reveals the same bias and ignorance. Both these writers have clearly been influenced technically. There are many recent books which show the signs of technical influence. Edmund Keeley's *The Libation* takes its intricate time scheme, along with certain other details, directly from Faulkner. The very new book *The One Hundred Dollar Misunderstanding* is a student exercise in the Faulkner technique of alternative viewpoints.

There is another kind of influence which, paradoxically, while seeming negative is more positive. It is perhaps best illustrated by the beautiful statement of another kind of fiction presented in Glenway

Wescott's *Images of Truth*. Wescott, along with others, is for a return to the fabric and pace of narration, the avoidance of technical fiddling and foolery for their own sake, and, as far as possible, the divorce of the novel from the deliberate cultivation of the effects and devices of modern poetry. Faulkner began as a poet, was much influenced by the directions of modern poetry in his prose; and it is at once a tribute and a criticism that no two of his novels employ the same narrative method. He blazed trails, broke ground, opened up new country for the American novelist. But it does not follow that the novelists now writing should do the same thing or try to duplicate his pioneering. His achievement is a fact. That may be what the subtle and gifted Mr. Wescott meant when he told students at the University of Virginia (in reply to a direct question about Faulkner) that the works of Faulkner were for him like the Blue Ridge Mountains in the distance, beautiful to look at, but he did not intend to climb them.

From his earliest critical writings while still a student at the University of Mississippi William Faulkner showed a great desire to be a part of the creation of a worthy *American* tradition of writing. He saw himself as a pioneer, not the first, for he honored Twain, Dreiser, and above all Sherwood Anderson, but among them. He left behind a large, varied body of work and the record of a long professional career. He preserved much of his past. He opened new vistas for writers to follow. It is hard to guess what his influence will be in the future. It is as certain as the changing weather that his reputation will go up and down. And it looks as if it will be a long time before a great many myths and misconceptions about the man and his work are dispelled. There are good people trying to get at the truth, for example the dedicated scholar Meriwether, now at Chapel Hill and, as well, Carvel Collins of M.I.T. But the articles based on other articles and the books based on other books, most of them just plain bad, proliferate like Error. No doubt they will always be with us like the poor.

For myself, and for many of the young writers I know, Faulkner stands as a master, an *example* from whom we can always learn. There is no sense of competition. Art is not a horserace. Nor is there any particular need for technical thievery. We will borrow when we need to, just as he did, but we will strive not to be copycats, but instead to find our own voices. Just as he did. Most of all he is a model for behavior as novelist. He kept going, kept writing in spite of indifference and hostility, praise and blame for the wrong reasons. And through it all he preserved his sanity, his humor, his courage, and his integrity. When Homer began the *Odyssey* with Telemachus, the untried son, he was giving us the point of view from which to regard the fabulous adventures to follow. Besides the story of the hero's homeward journey, Homer tells the story of the education of a young man (one of Faulkner's favorite subjects), not so that Telemachus could make the same journey, but so that he could profit by the example and one day become a man himself. We have in the long and full career of Faulkner a heroic example against which to measure our woes and joys. If there is any meaning in human history or the life of a great man, then some of us, with luck and with perseverance, will be better writers than we deserve to be because he has gone before. All of us are given a literature in our language that is better than it deserves to be because of his selfless dedication to the craft and art of fiction.

17

Afterword
to *The Road to Glory*
(1981)

We know the basic facts of life behind the creation of this filmscript. From Joseph Blotner's biography, as well as from other scholarly and critical studies, we know now how William Faulkner went out to Hollywood to work on this project. Went to work out of commonplace need and with an uncommon urgency. The need was, of course, for money. Survival money. His books had not sold (and would not sell much for a long long time). His stories weren't finding happy homes. There were not any other easy possibilities, and this was a full generation before serious American writers could find for themselves places in the universities and sell a portion of their precious time for money. Time was more precious than ever for him at just that time. Never mind the details of his personal, private life. They were complex and aggravating enough. But the true urgency was that he was desperately trying to complete a draft of *Absalom, Absalom!* And, in fact, he managed to finish the complete draft while he was out there working on the property which would become *The Road to Glory.*

All that we need to know, to think about here and now, is that this very great writer under very great pressure, at a time when his life was troubled, when his drinking was a serious problem—enough so that it could easily have cost him the chance even to hold down the assignment on the picture—when time to complete his work-in-progress had to be bought and paid for, earned the hard way by hard labor, parceling out his time and energy and creativity, like a gambler nursing cards and chips over a long night's game for the highest stakes, while holding in reserve within himself the secret, invaluable, still unrecognized treasury of his word-hoard, that this great writer, one of our precious few masters in this century, managed to get the movie job done, also, and to do it well. For even at this stage, a while before the final shooting

266

script, which would come along all in due time, it is a first-class professional job of screenwriting done, as it had to be, in brief, intense collaboration with a whole group of first-class professionals, ruthlessly demanding, utterly unsentimental movie people. More about them, more about all that a bit later.

Here at the outset we need to acknowledge that there were real difficulties which had to be overcome and were, and we need to draw at least some of the inferences which are simply there. For instance, we are obligated to recognize his courage. The risks were then, as now and always, very great. These risks did not, of course, include all of the corruptions of success you can read about in boring and conventional Hollywood novels. His very modest salary, a boon to him but a bargain for his bosses, was not likely to corrupt anybody. What could have happened, what has happened to many talented and evidently stouthearted, strong-willed writers and artists in that brutal milieu, was that he would have been drained of energy, shattered of the confidence needed to take the wild artistic gamble and surmise from which every rare artistic achievement, and also the cemetery of countless artistic failures, derives. To save his real life, which was always a work-in-progress, he had to risk losing it. We can safely infer that William Faulkner was at the time brave enough and tough enough and possessed of faith enough, if not in himself then in his gifts, to do what he had to, whatever he had to at whatever risk. Which means, among many other things, that he was almost perfectly attuned to the spirit of the French combat veterans in this story. One can say, and we will, that in a literary sense he was exactly the right man for this story; but we should also understand that in an inward and spiritual sense he was singularly appropriate to the task. For he understood, at the deepest and most ineffable levels of himself, the inner lives of these characters. And all this comes through quite clearly in the screenplay.

Almost without exception, screenplays, like the finished films they sometimes become, are committee work, characterized by all the familiar confusion, interchange, friction, clash, and compromise that any attempt to create anything by a group consensus inevitably arouses. In the making of screenplays and movies the inherent problems are intensified because of the differences in rank and authority and practical experience among the members of the group. Almost without exception the writer is awarded an unenviably low place in the hierarchy. And yet, paradoxically, it is an essential position, absolutely necessary and important at least until a satisfactory, usable, workable screenplay exists and has been accepted as such by everybody else concerned. This group, the number and variety of people concerned with any given script, ranging from important peripheral types like bankers and lawyers and accountants and agents and casting directors through the entire production company in all its component parts, all the cast and the huge, skilled crew to the people at the other end who must promote and distribute the finished film, is very large and various. The script must serve all of them and most of them quite differently. It becomes a crucial document in a variety of ways. And it is the writer's responsibility.

Two things need to be said and understood about all this, as it relates to the film. First, we have to understand that there is no way simple and truthful to attribute authorship, in a conventional literary sense, to a screenplay. Everyone concerned contributes one way or another and to a greater or lesser extent. The writer, in essence, becomes for a time the voice of the committee and, indeed, the larger group which the committee comes to represent. In the sense of a poem or a short story or even a novel there is no screenplay author at all. (Of course, we should remember that the finished product, the printed book, the actual object itself by means of which we can come to know and experience the words and work of the creator, has engaged the professional services and attentions of a great many people and can, in that strict sense, almost as much as any movie, be said to be the work of a group, an institution, rather than any individual. Writers, after all, write manuscripts. Publishing companies publish and seek to sell books.) Nevertheless, credit for screenplays is in fact earned and given; and this attribution is controlled by a variety of rules. So that no matter how many people in how many ways may or may not have contributed toward the creation of the screenplay for *The Road to Glory,* the official credits are to Joel Sayre and William Faulkner for both the story and the screenplay.

In any collaboration of this kind it is, finally, impossible to distinguish who contributed what since ideas, notions, whims must be blended and fused together into a unity which is largely inextricable, into the sources of the bits and pieces which make up its parts. In other words, another paradox, if not an outright contradiction: it doesn't matter, except for the quality of the final film, how many contributions have been made by how many different people, the screenplay is created by the author or authors who are credited with it. Thus the rules of the Guild (the Screenwriters Guild in those days, today the Writers Guild of America, West or East) reflect that reality. And so it follows that we can, honestly and accurately, discuss all aspects of this screenplay as the work of William Faulkner, with the understanding that he shared the authorship equally with Joel Sayre.

What I am trying to suggest is that it would be pointless, and probably wholly inaccurate, to attempt on the basis of external and internal evidence to isolate precisely the separate contributions of either writer to the finished whole or to separate those contributions from the suggestions and even the specific demands (made much more often in discussion than in writing) of the producer and the director, and so forth. Even documents would not, do not, prove much. The crucial single document, at any stage of the development of a picture from idea to film, is the officially accepted version of the screenplay at that stage. Attempts, by those who were actually involved, to disentangle the complex process into its component, individual parts later on are not of much value or authenticity either. Even when (rarely!) recollection is honest and clear, it is neither easy nor accurate to isolate one item or another as originating exclusively from a specific source. All that we have to go on is the composite and finished object, the screenplay. Thus the convenience of credit, of attributed and accepted authorship, turns out to be the only fact of the matter worth worrying about.

With all due respect to Faulkner's collaborator and partner on this film, it is Faulkner's involvement and authorship that matter to us now. Simply for convenience in this afterword, and with full acknowledgement of Joel Sayre's full share in its creation, I intend arbitrarily to talk about this screenplay as Faulkner's. It should be noted, though, that the seamless collaboration evident in this screenplay indicates another truth about Faulkner—an ability to work well and closely and honorably with another writer, when he had to. This is certainly not a unique ability, but a great many gifted writers have found that they simply could not collaborate effectively.

The collaborative process of *The Road to Glory* must have been more than usually complicated and demanding. Working for Darryl F. Zanuck was, evidently, an unusually stressful experience; and the evidence is that he fiddled with and fine-tuned several versions of this screenplay between the first surviving version, this version, by Faulkner and Sayre, and the final shooting script. But this film was top-heavy with talent, quite aside from Zanuck. Zanuck's assistant producer was the screenwriter Nunnally Johnson, who, we can be sure, made himself responsibly influential. And the director, evidently from the beginning, was Howard Hawks, who would, significantly, continue to use Faulkner on film projects for years to come. Plenty of talent and ego there. It is safe to assume that Faulkner and Sayre had to work with at least three bosses; two of them legitimately knew more about screenwriting and filmmaking than both of the collaborators taken together. And all three must, unquestionably, have been very powerful and often contradictory presences during the process of creating the script.

A writer who went to Hollywood in the 1950s to write a script for Stanley Kubrick has told me that he had occasion and opportunity to ask William Faulkner's advice. "Don't take the work too seriously," Faulkner is said to have told him. "But you take these people very, very seriously." As one who has gone down that long row to hoe myself, I cannot imagine better advice. Or more difficult advice. It is hard not to take the work seriously. That is, all of the artist's impulses, taken together with his acquired professionalism and his earned sense of honor—an essential and ritual sense of honor which demands complete, unstinting integrity and commitment must be engaged in every exercise of his craft, be it ever so humble and insignificant; demanding not that it be "good" or "important," but that whatever it is, it should represent his best, all that he has to give to that subject and occasion at that moment; demanding all this at the very grave risk that any conscious lapse from duty, that any withholding, slacking off, or saving of self and gifts for some more serious purpose and occasion may result, most likely *will* result in the permanent loss of a certain kind of purity, something like artistic virginity; and that loss bearing with it the even more grave prospect that the Muse will no longer visit the house defiled not by commerce or greed or strange passions but by indifference— combine to make him wish to create the best possible screenplay, once

Afterword to The Road to Glory

he is engaged in and, for one reason and another, committed to complete the chore.

But that way, the natural way for the artist to work, leads to crippling frustration and, thus, to poor and shoddy work. It overlooks the essence of the creative process in moviemaking—that it is corporate, that it is political, also, in the sense that the final product is a choice arrived at through constant negotiation and compromise. I remember hearing, many times concerning any number of projects, the old cliché of the business, "If everybody involved got fifty percent of his ideas into the final version, it would be the greatest picture ever made." This was almost always followed by a shrug and a faint smile. "What the hell," they'd say, smiling and shrugging, "it's only a *movie*." To which should be added yet another old saw, tossed around like a frisbee in the industry and largely ignored outside of it, to wit, "Nobody ever *tried* to make a bad picture."

All this was obviously understood by William Faulkner. (Remember that he was speaking to a fellow workman and professional. His comments addressed to others, to outsiders, in interviews and such, tended to reach for humor and to satisfy the preconceptions of outsiders, to tell them more or less what they wanted to hear, and would hear in any case, about the subject. Knowing that they would not understand anything else and no doubt believing that they had no right to try to understand the artist's choices, his risks and wounds, no right to presume to stand in his shoes.) All this was understood by him and is implied by him in his reply to the younger writer. It is also suggested, if you pause to think about it—and the remark was, like many of his apparently offhand comments, made to make the hearer pause and, perhaps, think about it—that to do a good work, to do the work well, which, after all, is the proper aim of every artist and craftsman and is also a matter of simple, commonplace pride and honesty, the desire to earn fairly the money one is being paid for the job, one must be loose, light on his feet, quick, adept, flexible, supple. The work can break your heart if you let it, and that will carry over into all your other work. *Don't take the work too seriously.* If you do, it won't be any good. If you do, you won't be any good. If you do, it will be harmful to you.

As for the people. His advice is well taken also. All of the clichés and stereotypes have roots in the truth. They, the movers and shakers, the wheelers and dealers of the motion-picture crap game which they call, partly out of a deep and deeply frustrated desire for respectability, The Industry, are, just as depicted in so many of the plays and novels, and even movies, about Them, rude and crude, gross and sly and greedy and ignorant and ruthless, cruel and funny, and dedicated to . . . *something*. Hard to say precisely what that something is. Yes, they want to make good pictures that make good money and, as a spinoff, offer them a little prestige and repute. Yes, they enjoy dealing and, yes, too, the power to treat with and often to mistreat artists and craftsmen, their envied betters, the power to humble others by constant giving and withholding. (Oh, in a very literal sense, everyone who works in The Industry is reamed on a real or metaphorical casting couch. There are endless stories, many of them true enough, of how They have savaged artists, how they have used them up and discarded them without qualm or even second thought.) So part of Faulkner's advice was, predictably, to stay awake and alert, to watch out. Don't take Them lightly. They can tear you to pieces.

But there is more to it than that. I believe that he understood Them more deeply than that. Understood that these arrogant and insensitive, sly and shifty, slippery and shrewd, wildly piratical codgers, aesthetic gangsters, probably moral cripples, babbling their Immigrant English as they sought to con everyone around them, restrained only and finally, and only slightly, by the Law, They were nevertheless deeply dedicated to a number of things, at least to all of the things, the implausible, manifold combinations of energies, talents, and things which are necessary to transform an idea, a whim, a notion into ninety minutes, or more, of finished film to be shown in theaters to people who could be persuaded to pay good money to come inside and see it.

And most of all, beyond even the excitements and challenges of producing this particular product (which most of Them had to conceive of as similar to and a more complex version of the designing and producing and promoting and selling of the garments, in that other Industry out of which so many of Them came and which, therefore, served as the foundation of and the model for that first generation of American filmmakers), They loved the pure and simple crapshoot and roulette whirl of it, loved the game in and of itself, the points of it, winning and losing, loved the gamble most of all. Is it any wonder that so many prominent people in the movie industry, then and now, have been literal gamblers as well, throwing away ransoms and fortunes at the tables of Las Vegas, Reno, Tahoe, Monaco? They love the action. More, finally, than the results. This is something They share with artists. Of course, that was the very heart of the Depression, when Faulkner was working on *The Road to Glory* and learning how to tell a hawk from a handsaw in Hollywood, and, as the late Sam Goldwyn once remarked, "We have passed a lot of water under the bridge since then." But Faulkner's advice was offered twenty years later, as the next generation came to power in Hollywood, the second generation.

The second generation, and now the third already, is disguised behind college educations, good tailoring, all the outward and visible benefits of expensive upbringing, health, and welfare. They are slicker, smoother, maybe as clever and far less flamboyantly colorful than their real and metaphorical parents. These barbarians wear togas and look good in them. But the game is the same and the risks are the same. And, as Faulkner suggested, the best thing to do when dealing with Them, moving among Them, is to take Them very seriously. On the strength of my own admiration for the mind and sensibility of William Faulkner, and out of my experience of his work, I can only conclude that he meant, too, that, weighing all, beyond all risks and rewards, these people deserve to be taken seriously, that They can be of both interest and value to the artist who can go beyond the garment-truth of stereotypes and clichés and open himself to what is wonderfully different. Faulkner was always fascinated by passionate and obsessed characters, characters who want something, love something. He could see this obsession and desire in the people who make the movies.

He seems to have known and understood enough, more than enough, to have written a really first-rate Hollywood novel. And it would be fun if there were one, one we could put alongside Fitzgerald's and O'Hara's and Nathanael West's. He took the people seriously enough. But I think it is clear that he didn't love Them enough, or the work either, to want to do it. He came and went. He endured and finally prevailed. Instead of a work about Hollywood, we have examples of his work for Hollywood. Which, in a real sense, offers its own commentary.

His advice to a young writer has its parallel in the tenth chapter of Matthew. "Behold, I send you as sheep in the midst of wolves: be ye therefore wise as serpents and innocent as doves."

Faulkner was faced with another problem, a special kind of problem, in writing the script. There are still (probably always will be) unanswered questions about the nature and details of this adaptation. But it seems that the property which Zanuck had acquired, and now wished to develop into a script and an original film, was not a story idea, not a book or a play to be adapted, but rather an existing French movie, *Les Croix de Bois* (1932), itself said to be based upon the story line of a French novel. It appears that Zanuck was chiefly interested in using some of the extensive and expensive combat scenes from the French film, incorporating them as stock footage in his own film. So it became the assignment of the American screenwriters to come up with a story line and structure (in which task it is said that Howard Hawks contributed some anecdotes and reminiscences) which would make the most efficient and effective use of the footage from the French film. Early on in the script we see scene headings—"(STOCK C. de B.)"—which indicate that stock footage is to be used. Fairly often, however, that heading is simply dropped, and it remains uncertain as to how much, if any, of the French combat footage was actually used in the American film.

Here a brief digression on the state of this particular script is called for. The opening sequence, and several other places, have the detail of camera angle and transition written in and thus have the look of a *final shooting script*, broken down into its smallest component parts. Soon, however, we get *master scenes*, units of a page and more sometimes, with or without any indicated transition. Brief specific shots—see, for instance, scenes 37, 38, and 39—are indicated only to make story points or character reactions. Later (see, for example, scene 204) there are fairly long master scenes not broken down into individual shots. And in some places (see 215, 216, and following) there are scenes which are not scenes at all, really, but rather are synoptic sequences. There is nothing unusual about this. Several stages of development are represented in this script. In some places it could, conceivably, be shot as is. In other places there is a good deal of work, by several hands, left to be done before it is ready.

The idea of a script at this stage of development requires, among other things, that it should look like a final script, that it can and should be read more or less like a final shooting script. All these camera angles and directions, as well as the means of transition from one scene or shot to the next, even though these details may well have been suggested by the producers and the director, are really expendable. The cinematographer and the editor will, later, have a lot to say about those things. Meantime, though, the details give a sense of the *style* that the picture will probably have. And they give a not wholly inaccurate impression that the filmscript is almost finished. It can be read and budgeted, roughly, by those whose business it is to estimate schedules and costs. Can be read by investors, agents, actors, technicians, and so forth.

The writers have here established a basic story line, a general structure (this, of course, can change in shooting and in editing); and they have created the central characters. At this stage, dialogue (what they call "the words," as in "The leading man could not learn the words") is apt to be, as it is, fairly full, making plot and character points, where necessary, as overtly and as clearly as possible. Later, in the acting, shooting, and editing much of this may well be changed. Words can be added where points are not made or are not clear. Words can be cut where, thanks to acting, direction, and context, they are redundant. At this point the script remains primarily the work of the writers and is as close to being a *literary* document as a movie, in its metamorphosis of many shapes, can be. It is at this stage that the contributions of the screenwriting are most evident and important.

There are some wonderful cinematic moments and devices here which, whether or not they were able to survive to appear in the film itself, set a style and tone for it. The arrival of Pierre Delaage (scenes 8–20) by means of a hearse to join the Fifth Company of the Second Battalion of the Thirty-ninth Regiment is an excellent example. It immediately catches attention and establishes Pierre as a lively and sympathetic character. It is, moreover, exactly appropriate to both the form and the content of what follows, establishing that this war is almost more myth than fact, even for those most actively engaged in it. It makes the point, among others, visually and dramatically, that the differences between the living and the dead, thus between living and dying, are at once less clearly defined and more a matter of accident than anyone might wish to allow. This is good movie-writing.

And there are other things, the Old Man's bugle, for instance, and the Captain's set speech to all new recruits, among many other similar devices throughout, which depend upon repetition to work their rhetorical, cinematic effects. (Those familiar with other Faulkner scripts—*The Big Sleep, To Have and Have Not,* and *Air Force,* for instance—will recall how he liked to use echoed and repeated phrases and actions to establish an intimacy with the characters and the experience.) These also serve to emphasize the cyclical nature of the action, a particularly important point in *The Road to Glory,* where the war is seen as an unending cycle. And there are any number of well-executed cinematic and dramatic sequences here. The sequence dealing with the mining beneath the dugout, beginning with scene 59, through the sudden silence and then the noise of digging again in 64 and 65, is powerful and effective. The bombing of the village (scenes 87–100) leading into the sequence of Pierre and Monique together in the cellar (101–20, with intercuts) is almost textbook screenwriting. And there is a whole series of strong dramatic scenes, fully realized. In short, the script seems to me to be at the very least a solid, workmanlike job, well constructed and full of interesting details. Faulkner was worth what they paid him.

Yet, having said that, it remains to be said that the real job of the writer is not, in fact, a matter of cinematic devices and gimmicks (whether they are good or not) or even, finally, of dramatic writing. What the writer must do is create characters and situations in which those characters can be tested and developed. And out of all this, deriving from his story line, emerges an attitude toward the material. There may or may not be a "message" in a movie. That depends. But there will almost always be a *statement* of one kind or another, even if that statement is primarily manifest as an attitude. Here is where, I believe, William Faulkner really gave them their money's worth and where we, who are mainly interested in how his screenplay fits into his life's work and relates to it, should focus our most serious attention.

The *New York Times* review (August 6, 1936), by Frank S. Nugent, of the released picture gives us a good place to start. It is a mixed review, really, praising the skill of the picturemakers while criticizing the implications of the story, the apparent statement it seemed to be making. Nugent allows that the treatment of war in this movie, "objective, but romanticized," is unacceptable after the experience of Erich Maria Remarque's *All Quiet on the Western Front,* Humphrey Cobb's *Paths of*

Afterword to The Road to Glory

Glory (which would much later be made into an exceptional film from a screenplay by Calder Willingham), and Irwin Shaw's play *Bury the Dead*. Nugent criticized Faulkner and Sayre for writing their screenplay "with the impersonality of a veteran newspaper man's account of a fire" and was disturbed by what he inferred, from "the swift chronicling of these disassociated events," to be the principal theme of the story, namely "the glory of service, of regimental tradition, selfless discipline and sacrifice." He went on to say that the audience had a "right to expect something more, a word or two, perhaps, on the significance and ultimate value of their sacrifice." Exactly, then, what Faulkner did not, would not, do. Nugent found it technically exciting and gripping, but, as it were, ideologically upsetting. This entirely honest, if naive, reaction gives us a good deal to consider.

First, it seems to me typical of Faulkner that he should create something against the grain of the current literary fashions in treating the subject. This demands that the writer be fully familiar with the literary conventions and clichés he would either use or discard. In everything he did, poetry, prose, fiction, essays, even the screenplays, Faulkner showed on the one hand a considerable, indeed an unusual familiarity with the precise literary fashions of the times and, on the other hand, a clear determination to distinguish his own work from those fashions by seeking to approach subjects (and forms) freshly, in new and different ways. Poetry, as it has been practiced in America in this century, did not give him the freedom or the room to do much. I am convinced that, even in the limited terms of verse writing, Faulkner was a better poet than has been allowed, but that the poets did not then and do not now understand what he was trying to do with their forms. The novel gave him the most opportunity, so that he was able to explore that form for all his working lifetime without ever repeating himself. Film, as a form of narrative, did not offer him as much latitude as prose fiction; but at least he could apply some of the same energies, albeit in the cruder, simpler forms of the screenplay.

In everything Faulkner created (as I see it), Faulkner showed great familiarity with the habits and fashions of a given form, or a given subject and its usual treatment, together with a strong impulse to distinguish his work by shattering as many of the habits and habitual reactions as he could. The reason behind this artistic impulse seems to have been the simple realization that habitual thinking and feeling, no matter how moral or uplifting, are the enemies of truth. He wanted, like Mark Twain, only differently, always *differently*, to tell the truth, mainly. *The Road to Glory* tells the truth, as best it could be told in this form, about the experience of war.

It is a strange thing that in this century of wars, wars in which millions and millions have been involved, our intellectuals and critics (and, alas, so many of our artists) seem to have learned so little, to know so little about war. Faulkner knew something about it all without being there except in his unflagging imagination. He wore a uniform, he served a time; and if he never did go overseas and into combat, he didn't have to. He learned enough and knew enough to understand war as well as any others who have written about it. And he wrote very well about war—in the stories of World War I, like "Turnabout" and "Ad Astra." In the novels—*Soldier's Pay, Sartoris, The Unvanquished, A Fable,* and so forth—he showed, it seems to me, a deeper comprehension of the texture of the experience of war, and its aftereffects, than did Hemingway in *A Farewell to Arms* or *For Whom the Bell Tolls.* (*Across the River and into the Trees* comes closer to Faulkner.)

As late as the recent war in Vietnam, people who ought to know better were discussing the rights and wrongs of warfare, acting as if one side or the other in a war was strengthened or weakened by moral or ethical considerations. Acting as if ideology has ever had anything to do with survival. Believing that there are "good" wars and "bad" ones. Every soldier who has experienced combat knows that ideology, the Cause (whatever it may be), morality, and ethics are not so much expendable as utterly inessential. At best as ludicrously out-of-date as the Old Man's battered bugle. Scenes 170 and 171, in which Morache and Regnier examine the packs and equipment of the new replacements and order them to get rid of everything that is not essential, make this point. "We see that their equipment is in sharp contrast to that of the veterans." This is a story about veterans. Not about the "meaning" of sacrifice. Not even a statement against war. Which would be completely irrelevant. War speaks out against itself. And, in truth, war is the only life these people know and experience, while we know and experience them, until they die. War is shown to be unending. The cycle goes on and on, attack and retreat, without any hope of a conclusion. There may be intervals of peace and quiet, of love and festivity, but the war is always there.

In that sense, *The Road to Glory* is as much prophetic truth as it is accurate history. Mid-1930s—Hitler already in power and arming, Mussolini seeking empire in Africa, Japan at war in China, Stalin preparing for war and meantime purging and slaughtering his own people, merciless. *The Road to Glory* becomes, in retrospect, an allegory for our times. Without ideology, Cause, honest historical memory, or any real hope for the future, for any future, what was left for these people? Duty and honor among comrades remained. That is all that is left for the veteran soldier, his loyalty not to a nation or an idea, but to his fellows. Duty, honor, courage, and, on occasion, compassion remain. And love, if and when it can be found, though both Delaage and Morache are willing to give up love out of a deeper sense of honor. There are no true heroes, though Morache is shown to be exemplary throughout, the finished veteran. There is only one real villain. The man who trades in evil, for whom war is commerce, is the orderly Bouffiou. He is shown to be a coward and a conniver who can profit from the misery of others. The scene (177) where he burns the Old Man's orders, for a price, mixes disobedience with commerce and is, in fact, presented as the most wicked single act in this story. Much as Jason's burning of the circus tickets in *The Sound and the Fury* is the most wicked act in that tragic story.

What I am suggesting is that, within the limits of the conventions of the war story, this screenplay is remarkable for its integrity and its authenticity. It is a pared down, tough story. It is about as ruthlessly unsentimental as it could possibly be and still qualify for release and distribution as a major motion picture. Soon enough, after revisions and polish, with the aid of Howard Hawks's direction and with the benefit of a superb cast (Warner Baxter as the Captain, Lionel Barrymore as the Old Man, his father, and Fredric March as the Lieutenant), it was made into an outstanding motion picture, one of our finest, then or now, on the subject of men at war, and one which has clearly influenced many later films. The whole process began with the story and this script. There are faults and flaws in the script. There always are. And there was still time to correct many of these in revision. But the story line, the tone and truth of it, was absolutely essential to the success of the movie. Faulkner earned his money, finished *Absalom, Absalom!*, and headed home. With still many years to go before he would receive any recognition for the work he had done, was doing, and would continue to do.

He was, in a way, like a figure in his own story. It was, like most good stories, just that personal in implication, though well disguised. Something of him was the Old Man with his bugle and his dreams of old glories. Something of him was as weary, as battered, and as dutiful as the Captain. Something was still young, at that time, as lively and sardonic, as fond of whiskey and love and the quixotic gesture as the Lieutenant. And something in him deeply understood Bouffiou; for here he was, making commerce of his art, selling his time in an effort to earn more free time for himself, trying to survive at all costs.

If nothing else, this screenplay proves he had the ability to survive and to persevere, by hard labor, on his own. It proves, among other things, that he could do a job on order and for hire, when he had to. It proves here to be a good job, one worthy of the gifts of the man who was writing *Absalom, Absalom!* at the same time. If nothing else, the quality of this work should change the picture of Faulkner as someone who was "carried" by and through the kindness of Howard Hawks. That may have been the case later (who knows?). But here he did the job right and made Hawks look good. A good script makes everyone involved look good. It is always a gamble, but when Hawks hired Faulkner later on, he was betting on a winner. And I would guess he knew it.

18

"Fix My Hair, Jack": The Dark
Side of Faulkner's Jokes
(1984)

My title comes from the final chapter, chapter 31, of *Sanctuary*, the penultimate sequence of scenes just before the final closing down of that story in the set piece of Temple Drake and her father at the Luxembourg Gardens in gray Paris. It is the next to last scene of the next to last sequence in what amounts to an entire sequence of endings set in a row, an ending as final and thorough, wrapped neatly and tied with a bowknot, as anything you can think of offhand. (It is as thorough and as satisfactory an ending as any of the Oz books and shares with them at least the elegant paradox of seeming to invite a sequel to challenge its finality.) My title is the last words in this world, and in this book, of Popeye, as he stands on the scaffold with a rope around his neck waiting to die in payment of and for not any of the divers crimes committed in this story or anything else he may have done or left undone, but for the murder of a policeman in Alabama, a crime of which, to our sure and certain knowledge, he is perfectly innocent.

Here is how Popeye dies. In William Faulkner's words:

> They came for him at six. The minister went with him, his hand under Popeye's elbow, and he stood beneath the scaffold praying, while they adjusted the rope, dragging it over Popeye's sleek, oiled head, breaking his hair loose. His hands were tied, so he began to jerk his head, flipping his hair back each time it fell forward again, while the minister prayed, the others motionless at their posts with bowed heads.
>
> Popeye began to jerk his head forward in little jerks. "Psssst!" he said, the sound cutting sharp into the drone of the minister's voice; "psssst!" The sheriff looked at him; he quit jerking his head and stood rigid as though he had an egg balanced on his head. "Fix my hair, Jack," he said.
>
> "Sure," the sheriff said. "I'll fix it for you"; springing the trap.[1]

Well, then. A little gallows humor. An ending for Popeye, a moment which is grotesque, grotesquely funny, and completely satisfactory in terms of the demands of the narrative and the conventional expectations of the imaginary reader. Popeye surely has to die after all he has done since he first appeared to Horace Benbow, reflected in the clear spring at the root of a beech tree, a man introduced as possessing, in Benbow's way of seeing, "that vicious depthless quality of stamped tin."[2] Popeye is involved from that point on in many kinds of unpleasant and indecent activities, the most formidable, objectionable, and memorable of which (and memorable in the larger sense to people who have never even read the book) is the corncob rape of the archetypal coed—Temple Drake. It was that crime which was to cost Popeye most dearly, which rendered him most liable to the appropriate punishment of hanging by the neck until dead for a crime he did not commit.

Writing about it, making it up and seeing it through its various drafts and versions into print, was something for which the author would have to suffer also. As witness, this brief incident from Blotner's biography. The time is the fall of 1938, seven years and a number of books after the publication of *Sanctuary*:

> It was not all business for Faulkner. Haas pitched horseshoes with him, and Commins took him to see Columbia play Army. At one crucial point in Columbia's last minute game-winning drive, Faulkner leaned over and predicted the next play. When the Columbia quarterback called it, Commins congratulated him.
>
> "From now on you'll always be known as the grandstand quarterback," he said.
>
> "No," Faulkner replied. "I'll always be known as the corncob man."[3]

The truth is that the execution of Popeye, together with the sequence leading up to it, is an extraordinary and virtuoso performance which, continuing up to that gritty, bitter, brutal last moment, ending with the sheriff's brisk one-liner, becomes one of the great fictional hanging scenes in our national literature. It will stand tall and well beside such moments as the execution of Billy Budd, Truman Capote's hanging of Perry and Dick in *In Cold Blood*, and Norman Mailer's celebrated disposal of Gary Gillmore in *The Executioner's Song*. If I digress a moment . . . I find Faulkner's the best achieved and most interesting of the lot. Billy Budd dies completely in character (as I reckon, all tragic characters have to), as good and as innocent and as simple-minded as he has always been, first to last. Capote and Mailer, each differently, spend a whole book making a kind of case for their criminal protagonists. While not denying their crimes, they work very hard, in text and in subtext, to establish reader engagement and sympathy, long before they bring their people to the edge of the grave. At that edge they then pull out all the conventional rhetorical stops, hoping to move you and me to some kind of pity and terror, and, indeed, succeeding to a considerable extent. Faulkner had a much bigger problem to deal with, and his success is really remarkable. This is a sequence I give to writing students to see how something marvelous, an almost complete turnabout, can be deftly and economically achieved in just a few pages. I justify this brief excursion away from the general topic with the claim that, as elsewhere in many places in the work of William Faulkner, humor of various kinds and forms, several kinds of jokes, then, threaded into the rich texture of complex and often contradictory moods, is an essential part of the whole (and successful) rhetorical effect. Here, as elsewhere, it wouldn't work without the benefit of various kinds of laughter, some of them examples of dark laughter to be sure. We are never far in Faulkner's works from what James Cox has called (in this conference on Faulkner's humor), "the incredible laughter that is at the heart of his world." In any case, throughout *Sanctuary* Faulkner, in a fairly unusual gesture for him, made Popeye a strictly consistent, almost fixed character. We get different angles on him which give some sense of change and development, but he, himself, seems to be consistently malevolent and altogether unsympathetic. He is known to us by his actions; but, present even in absence in this story's structure, he is also depicted by the effects, accidental as well as planned, of his actions on others and by the juxtaposition of his acts and many others which are related to him only in the reader's world. That is, on top of everything else, all he has been up to, Popeye also picks up bits and pieces of the sins of others like nettles and beggar's-lice as we follow the ways Faulkner has chosen for him to walk in through this story. Finally, in exactly the opposite gesture to those of Capote and Mailer, the narrator, from and through several points of view, heaps negative coals upon Popeye's head from first to last or, anyway, almost the last. The steady consistency of this latter strategy works to create a kind of backlash in the reader, not of open sympathy or understanding or any such, but at least a feeling that Popeye, perhaps alone among the crew of characters in *Sanctuary*, is not getting the fully dimensional exploration which the others seem to receive. Then in chapter 31 Faulkner turns things around—not by violating his original presentation of Popeye, but by *adding* two elements: first, a background, horrendous enough and of mixed values, partly composed of terrible suffering and deprivation, partly composed of first acts of wickedness, a background known only to God and the narrator and now, of course, the reader, just as Popeye is caught, tried and convicted for the crime he did not commit. Throughout this last sequence Popeye remains consistent, as tough and arrogant and essentially uncomprehending as ever. But the clever and amazing difference is gained by surrounding him with strangers—District Attorney, Turnkey, his appointed lawyer and his Memphis lawyer, the sheriff, a minister—all of whom find him intriguing and mysterious, all of whom become, to one degree and another, sympathetic. This time, just before he dies, we see him as we have not before, and he suddenly gains some stature, grows right before our eyes. So that finally, even when he goes out to the tune of a hard-nosed joke, there is a certain odd nobility about his death. In a Shakespearean sense it is Popeye's most becoming moment of life. And yet he is still the same man who, on the first page, broke up Horace Benbow's enjoyment of his own reflection in a clear spring.

The dark side of Faulkner's jokes, his jests so often played at the expense of our best expectation that we gradually begin to expect them as much or more than anything else, comes from the fact that they are almost always present, even in the most serious works (again in a Shakespearean manner), never more than a paper-thin partition away from the most tragic or poignant or pathetic or simply horrifying scenes and events. If at any moment (sometimes by no more than the purest and simplest and most thoughtless of gestures, like going the wrong way around the town square) the known world can collapse into a bellowing chaos—a chaos composed of murder and mayhem, rape and mutilation, crimes and punishments, a dance of the seven deadly sins and the spectacle of the violation of the deepest taboos of our tribe—just so at any moment, again and again, moments as closely associated as, say, in

---

Macbeth the bloody murder of Duncan the King with the drunken Porter's soliloquy, at any of these moments the world, like that clear spring Popeye spat in and shattered, can fall apart helplessly into one kind of laughter or another. The major novels of William Faulkner, whether they *end* as comedy or tragedy, share with *King Lear*, for example, the inextricably mixed patterns of comedy and sorrow. Clearly it was his aim to make us *care* (something which separates him from most writers then and even more writers now), and clearly he figured out very early on that laughter is essential to the deepest kind of caring. The Elizabethans had a proverb that may have some validity—"The maid who laughs is half taken." I'm inclined to believe the proverb applies accurately to the necessary seduction of the imaginary reader.

Since I used one of the final scenes of the final version of *Sanctuary* as my basic example, I'd like to add to it by citing the *beginning* of the original version of the same novel, taken from *Sanctuary: The Original Text*, edited by Noel Polk. The first paragraph or two work much the same way (with some important differences) as the earlier example, from a context of crime and horror to a one-line joke and, in another of Faulkner's habitual gestures, from the contrast of complex style with the simple, from grandiose high style and the vernacular and idiomatic:

> Each time he passed the jail he would look up at the barred window, usually to see a small, pale, patient, tragic blob lying in one of the grimy interstices, or perhaps a blue wisp of tobacco smoke coming raggedly away long the spring sunshine. At first there had been a negro murderer there, who had killed his wife; slashed her throat with a razor so that, her whole head tossing further and further backward from the bloody regurgitation of her bubbling throat, she ran out the cabin door and for six or seven steps up the quiet moonlit lane. He would lean in the window in the evening and sing. After supper a few negroes gathered along the fence below—natty, shoddy suits and sweat-stained overalls shoulder to shoulder—and in chorus with the murderer, they sang spirituals while white people slowed and stopped in the leafed darkness that was almost summer, to listen to those who were sure to die and him who was already dead singing about heaven and being tired; or perhaps in the interval between songs a rich, sourceless voice coming out of the high darkness where the ragged shadow of the heaven-tree which snooded the street

lamp at the corner fretted and mourned: "Fo days mo! Den dey ghy stroy de bes ba'ytone singer in nawth Mississippi!"[4]

Speaking of style, though this may seem and, indeed, may well be yet another diversion from the true course, the hard straight ploughed furrow, on my part, I would like to mention a daring and endearing comic device often used by William Faulkner to snatch at more meaning from one event or another and in so doing, among other things, to move us more than usually, to make us care. This device is the seemingly inappropriate use of the high style often to describe the most ordinary things or to deal with events which seem to call for the most direct and transparent prose. Since the high style which Faulkner invented was hypnotically his very own, replete with its own special rhythms and its own rich and repetitive vocabulary, this making fun with that style constitutes almost making fun of it; that is, it constitutes a brave kind of self-parody, one result of which is to make the narrator more sympathetic and the style more acceptable, able to be used grandly precisely because it has also been used humbly and humorously. There are, inevitably, other important effects of the contrast, and (sometimes) confusion of styles. For instance, even in parody humble things gain a certain grandeur by being caught and exposed in the net of the grand style. Likewise pompous and important things, captured in the vernacular, are awarded some measure of vital simplicity. Always the two extremes of style inform the spirit of each other. There are so many wonderful examples that you could put together an anthology of them, one of those "Exotic Flowers from Faulkner's Garden," nineteenth-century kind of books. Even so I would like to mention briefly, a couple or three examples as illustrative of this humorous tendency.

Who can forget the description of a memorable fart which opens book 3, "The Long Summer," of *The Hamlet?* "Sitting in the halted buckboard, Ratliff watched the old fat white horse emerge from Varner's lot and come down the lane beside the picket fence, surrounded and preceded by the rich sonorous organ-tones of its entrails."[5] Could Rabelais have done it any better?

How about this, from *Pylon,* for a man's sudden awareness that, immediately following one amazing sexual experience, in the front cockpit of a flying airplane, he is already triumphantly tumescent again? "It was some blind instinct out of the long swoon while he waited for his backbone's fluid marrow to congeal again that he remembered to roll the aeroplane toward the wing to which the parachute case was attached because the next that he remembered was the belt catching him across the legs as, looking out he saw the parachute floating between him and the ground, and looking down he saw the bereaved, the upthrust, the stalk; the annealed rapacious heartshaped crimson bud."[6] That is the same remarkable organ he had earlier described as "between himself and her wild and frenzied body, the perennially undefeated, the victorious."[7]

For the vernacular style, which is changed and refined by its close proximity to the high style, just as the latter is leavened by association with the former, take the impact of inflation upon Mink Snopes, fresh out of spending thirty-eight years in Parchman and here in the midst of trying to keep trace of the thirteen dollars he carried with him as a free man into a strangely altered world. This from *The Mansion:*

> He had given the man at the store one of the dollar bills and the man had given him back change for bread, eleven cents, lunch meat eleven cents, which was twenty-two cents, then the man had taken up the half-dollar for the sodas, which was seventy-two cents, which should have left twenty-eight cents; counting what remained slowly over coin by coin again, then counting the coins he had already set aside to be sure they were right. And still it was only eighteen cents instead of twenty-eight. A dime was gone somewhere. And the lunch meat was just eleven cents, he remembered that because there had been a kind of argument about it. So it was the bread, it would have to be the bread. *It went up another dime right while I was standing there* he thought. *And if bread could jump up ten cents right while I was looking at it, maybe I cant buy a pistol even for the whole thirteen dollars. So I got to stop somewhere and find a job.*[8]

If Mink's reasoning is comic, it is right. And it is no more comic than many of Gavin Stevens's tormented and tortuous musings which are more often likely to be wrong.

Now I would like to shift tone and stance slightly, moving away from the strictly literary to something closely related, but still something else, something which has to do with Faulkner's lifetime and ours. These times are, to begin with, much more different from each other than we might care to acknowledge. Just as his life proved to be (I do believe) quite different from what he could possibly have imagined—

even he, who was at times painfully, exquisitely prescient, to the sheer edge of prophecy. Keep in mind his sensitivity to the tides and trends of things in this terrible century whose own apt symbol may well be a mountain of human skulls in modern Cambodia, the warehouses of shoes and glasses and false teeth at Auschwitz, or the frozen heads in the freezer of Idi Amin, heads he liked to talk to in the late and lonely hours of the night. Don't forget for a moment the century he saw arrive and lived in; from which Oxford, though quiet and stable, was, clearly, no kind of refuge. Do not forget, either, that it was, *is* precisely his generation which saw more radical changes in the shape and form of things than any other in memory. Ours has merely seen the exploitation of changes which arrived for his generation. A time of arrivals—of the automobile and the airplane, of electricity and modern plumbing, of the radio and motion picture and the television, of the vast and intricate communications network or environment which, however distorted and destabilizing, allows selected events any place to have some impact on any other. An event in Sri Lanka can, for a time at least, impinge upon the peace and quiet of Oxford. For the first time, in his generation, for better and worse, it became possible for anyone in Oxford, Mississippi (or Truckmire, Georgia, or Kissimmee, Florida, my old home town), to know as much and as easily as anywhere else. It has been a hundred years since people in New York have had the actual ability to know any more than people in Oxford, though they are not among the first to admit this. There are many implications of all this. A single and obvious one is that by turning to consider the world as it was to be found here on his own postage stamp of territory, William Faulkner did so at a time when he was depriving himself of very little and sparing himself of even less except, perhaps, the noise of strangers.

One other bit of background. We have heard, eloquently and provocatively, if briefly, how he was a small man and how that smallness of stature served to shape his vision and a Napoleonic ambition. All of which may well be the case. Who knows? What is undeniable, undebatable, really, is that he was a very small man in a large world of larger men—and women—who was frail and vulnerable, even delicate in flesh as well as spirit, who suffered considerably because of that frailty; but who schooled and taught himself a toughness in a stoic sense, who lived, literally, with his outer and inner wounds without flagging in his work or complaining very much. Had he been larger, stronger, more confidently at ease with himself, his vision (if any other than a private one) might have been uniformly lighter; but I think we can safely agree that a lighter, more moderate vision of reality would have been grotesquely inappropriate to his times and ours and would have betokened not health, but a sort of lobotomized lunacy. It is my best judgment that his styles and forms, and equally his minted currency of dark comedy as the ne'er-do-well cousin of stark tragedy, are more aptly suited to this century than the styles and forms of any other writer of his generation.

In any case, in a practical *literary* way, Faulkner imagined that he lived in a world which was sequential, chronological, and mostly progressive. He was fully aware that he was living in a changed and different social world from that of Charles Dickens or of his own great-grandfather. But he did not know, at least at the beginning, that it was also a radically different *literary* situation; that neither writers nor readers nor publishers were the same or doing the same things; that all this had been changed also. Faulkner's failure to perceive or to understand that his literary generation was radically different from the previous generation or two (and the evidence of and for this misunderstanding is overwhelming in the published letters and the biographical studies) is not surprising. It is, indeed, an altogether typical misapprehension fully shared by the finest literary artists, the masters of his own generation and of ours. As far as I can tell, only a few true crazies were undecided. And these, in their turn, allowed themselves to be deluded by the fundamentally absurd notion that because things were now radically different, there was, therefore, *no* possible connection between now and then. I should add that Faulkner's folly (if that is what it is) appears to be widely embraced by my own generation of writers who, by and large, imagine that they are living in roughly the same literary world which Faulkner knew. Ours is, in fact, so different from that of the earlier generation, his generation, the generation of the masters, that a good case can be made for the idea that what we are doing is not at all the same thing, is almost a different art form. Of course, even if there were no difference between his time and ours, we would still be forever divided from the literary scene and situation faced by William Faulkner by the immutable fact that he who was there is now here. It is he (among others, but perhaps chiefly among them) who has changed things for better and worse for us and for the rest of the world—especially the lately celebrated small band of Latin American authors. If Faulkner was a literary conservative, in the sense that he believed he was living more or less in the same literary world as, say, Hawthorne and James and Conrad, if he was, as a result, a preserver of literary tradition, he was also, at one and the same time, our most adventurous and successful literary pioneer. There is hardly any place where an American writer can go or would want to go today that William Faulkner hasn't been first. At the same time, as an artist, he didn't stay long in any one place, which means, in fact, that all the literary settling, surveying, exploration, and exploitation remains to be done. To put it another way, if William Faulkner came along now, he would be inhibited, if not prevented, from doing the same kind of literary pioneering he was able to accomplish then. Places which he had not discovered then would surely be labeled terra incognita now. What I mean to say is that our debt to him is much greater than most of us can or will know.

Nevertheless in the thick of his own literary times, William Faulkner gives every sign and clue of being baffled, befuddled, and often almost desperate, trying to survive and perform as an artist. The letters and the biographies tell a sad professional story. Until after he was awarded the Nobel Prize, there hardly seems to be a day, even part of a day, in which he was free from real practical worries. Not a day of genuine stability or temporary security in which he could count on time to do his work. There were not any fellowships or grants (most of them did not exist then) to help him, to tide him over. Educational institutions paid him next to no attention or mind. He had a very hard row to hoe. All of us should keep that in mind. All of the time until the Nobel Prize he was in fact on very thin ice, earning a shamefully meager living by his work and by writing for the movies. And even after the Nobel Prize, he found himself as a man with a better than average income (at last), but having forfeited twenty-five lean years to what might well be called subsistence writing, he had no capital assets to speak of or draw on except Rowan Oak and the farm, both of which proved, at times, to be very expensive assets. When he came to buy a fine house in Charlottesville, he was forced to borrow the down payment from a wealthy dilettante because there was no other way he could make the down payment. Nobel Prize or not, his publisher wasn't in the moneylending business. Not in his case. They put their money where they expected a return in kind. Thus, writers like Irwin Shaw and Philip Roth routinely received advances ten times those of William Faulkner. A so-called serious writer—I am not speaking now of "popular" writers, but of those deemed to be prestigious literary figures—a writer like John Irving has received in advance for one book, even allowing for inflation, more than the entire lifetime earnings from all sources of William Faulkner. You are to understand that Faulkner's famous agent was not much help at all (though Harold Ober was very helpful and generous to F. Scott Fitzgerald). You need to understand that his publishers gave him contracts which were, in my opinion, less than generous. And they held him strictly to them, their basic premise being that he should, like any other of their authors, earn just what he sold, nothing more and nothing less. Which sounds fine and dandy until and if you choose to consider the inestimable value which his publishers, and chiefly Random House, gained by having him on their list. A good agent or a good lawyer probably could have come up with fairly exact numbers to prove his actual worth to them. And none of that would consider the enormous actual value his work has gained posthumously.

As for honors. Well, they came along all in due time. Some of them, anyway. But they came late, too late to catch up with, if not make up for the times when he was ignored or greatly underrated. It is clear that he was painfully conscious of his status in the literary world, of exactly where he stood. He didn't need Malcolm Cowley to tell him, though he had to put up with Cowley's telling him that, among other things, if he wanted to see the Viking *Portable Faulkner* come to be. Try to understand it—Kurt Vonnegut and John Updike have (separately and equally) both received far more critical attention and support than Faulkner did in his lifetime. James Dickey has many times the number of honorary degrees. Barry Hannah has already received at least as much favorable critical attention as Faulkner did up until the Nobel Prize. Believe me, it does not make a writer happy or fulfilled to work hard and honestly and as well as he is able to and then receive, in a relative sense, next to nothing, minimal response and reward for his efforts. Believe me, he was not kidding or playing with rhetoric when he described his work in the Nobel Prize address as "a life's work in the agony and sweat of the human spirit, not for glory and least of all for profit."[9] That is not a modest statement of good intentions. It's a harsh description of reality.

Never forget that at the high tide of his career and creativity, Faulkner lived in a world where J. D. Salinger was widely regarded as clearly his artistic superior.

I mention these little practical matters, often considered too boring or sordid for serious critical consideration, because he had to live with them constantly. Because they had something to do with the way he wrote. He was free, *liberated*, to be an explorer of the form, precisely because it didn't matter much to anybody, beginning with his pub-lisher, what he did. He might as well do what the spirit moved him to do. From this situation, endured, and ultimately prevailed over, came something of his pride, his gravity (which replaced a wild levity of youth), his rare (oh very rare) impeccable integrity as an artist. From it also came a certain professional bitterness. Some fellow writers who were acquainted with him, one way and another, have described him as "bitter." And there is, in his words and deeds, dealing with other writ-ers of all kinds, ample evidence of a kind of bitterness so strong that it might have crippled a lesser artist, a lesser man. We can thank God that he was strong enough to have it both ways and that his urge to make art, to leave his name and works on the wall, *Faulkner-was-here*, overcame everything else, both reason and passionate disappointment. It is a dark and comic thing, comic at the last because there was a be-lated happy ending (an ending of just the kind he was so contemptuous of, almost an old-fashioned Hollywood ending), that he persisted, that he lived and wrote the books.

If his professional life was a very hard one (and it was and, for the most part, a good deal more so than that of anyone he knew or knew of), his personal life was hard and disappointing also, full of bitter times and frustrations. The death of his firstborn, Alabama, a death at least partly his own responsibility, was devastating. The death of his brother, Dean, was heartbreaking and terrible too. His health was bad and so were his habits. He felt bad a lot of the time. His marriage was often very difficult, more like a bed of nails than a bed of roses. His love affairs were complicated, difficult also, and usually ended badly . . . for him, at least. None of the women in his life, at least those mentioned in the biography, hasn't, one way or another, profited greatly from her association with him. It is harder to imagine what happy rewards there were for him, beyond the most fleeting, in these matters. Even in these affairs, he seems to have allowed comedy to triumph in the end. It appears in the letters and the biographies that he broke off with each of them, exercising the same formulaic farewell— "Between grief and nothing, I'll take grief." Betting, without any great risk, that his lovers were encountering those words for the first time. Is that a dark joke or not? I think so.

When he was young and had more energy and was still defended by innocence and ignorance, he had a wonderful sense of irrepressible levity. Here he is in a very early interview (1931): "I was born male and single at an early age in Mississippi. I am still alive but not single. I was born of a Negro slave and an alligator, both named Gladys Rock. I had two brothers, one Dr. Walter E. Traprock and the other Eagle Rock, an airplane."[10] All in good fun. It is a dark irony, if not a dark joke, that Faulkner, who so cheerfully had fun and games with the press as a young man, came by the end of his life to view the press as the enemy of privacy and the American dream, as a deeply destablizing force. But he could still joke about it in those days.

Similarly, back in the early days, he had high spirits and creative energy to burn. There are, for example, the surviving letters (there were probably more) of Faulkner to Sherwood Anderson about the mythical Jackson family the two of them invented. Here I quote from Joseph Blotner's one-volume biography:

> Faulkner wrote Anderson a three-page typed letter about Al Jackson and the sheep he raised in the swamp to make their fleece more luxuriant, only to find that in time they began to change until they resembled beavers and then alligators. The same thing happened to Al's son Claude, from herding the creatures in the swamp.[11]

I have seen some of these letters and they are really very funny, more amusing than simple description can make them.

There are many kinds and forms of humor in Faulkner's work, early and late. And there is always a strong thread of dark, sometimes bitter joking found throughout his career. No one has called him a comedian in real life, but the odd thing in the biography is that they all seem to remember funny things he said or did, almost always straight-faced and deadpan. I have heard my share of these stories outside of the biography. A good many of his jokes took planning and preparation. Some of them are very private, so much so that we may not ever know about them, beyond guessing. He became a guarded and secret man. But all the stories from his life serve to confirm the portrait of a great man whose vision was so open and inclusive that if he always felt the tears of things, he likewise could hear, as some hear voices, the sourceless laughter which is at least half the music of this world.

Notes

1. *Sanctuary* (New York: Random House, Vintage Books), 307–8.
2. Ibid., 4.
3. Joseph Blotner, *Faulkner: A Biography* (New York: Random House, 1984), 400.
4. *Sanctuary: The Original Text,* ed. Noel Polk (New York: Random House, 1981), 3.
5. *The Hamlet* (New York: Random House, Vintage Books, 1956), 157.
6. *Pylon* (New York: Random House, 1962), 195–96.
7. Ibid., 195.
8. *The Mansion* (New York: Random House, Vintage Books, 1965), 263.
9. *The Faulkner Reader: Selections from the Works of William Faulkner* (New York: Modern Library, 1971), 3.
10. *Lion in the Garden: Interviews with William Faulkner, 1926–1962,* ed. James B. Meriwether and Michael Millgate (Lincoln: University of Nebraska Press, 1980), 9.
11. Blotner, 134.

19

"When I Showed Him the Check, He Asked If It Was Legal":

What William Faulkner Got and Gave Us from Pop Culture

(1990)

The relationship of the American writer to popular culture has been and remains tenuous and difficult to describe, constantly changing. The role and station (status, if you will) of the American writer has changed radically in my own professional lifetime. And it has changed much since the prime time of William Faulkner's career. Truth is, it was changing all along, during his lifetime, too, though this is not something he would need to have noticed until late in life and late in his career. And evidently he did not notice it much. There are good reasons for that apparent inattention. For one thing he was much too busy trying to get his own work done, completed and published, and trying (somehow, day by day, month by month, year by year) to survive in order to be able to do his own work.

Faulkner never had enough money, not until the very end of his life, to rest easy about money, that he was always wheeling and dealing, on a very polite and very small scale, just to make ends (briefly) meet.[1] And even at the end, when there was, at last, public honor and a modest measure of financial security, he could not easily come up with the necessary front money on his own to make a down payment on Red Acres near Charlottesville. This was at the peak of his reputation and his earning power. He could raise the money, but would go broke unless he could borrow it expeditiously.

You don't have to know much about money to know that even a sudden influx of money near the end of a lifetime career cannot make up for years and years of break-even subsistence. Money does not work that way. Your own poverty claims you.

May I say, by way of a parenthesis, that the way money works, and is generally understood, is part of our American popular culture now, perhaps the most important part, in that it is the *bonding element*, the universal glue that is shared by all the various and sundry activities which can be considered popular culture.

What Faulkner was desperately trying to raise in the summer of 1962, through his longtime publisher and through the collector Linton Massey, was $50,000 for the down payment on Red Acres. Considerable money now and even more then. Here is some of what he said in a letter of June 29, 1962, to Linton Massey: "I want to make an offer for Red Acres. I can make the offer as is. But if it is accepted, I will be broke. I will have to guarantee to write a book or books. I can earn about $10,000 or more a year from lectures etc. I will do this, write books or lecture [notice, at his age and state, he doesn't promise to do both], to own Red Acres, but I don't want to have to guarantee to."[2] He offered his manuscripts as security if need be.

As an example of changes in the scene, may I be so bold as to mention some figures from 1988? Recall that Faulkner in 1962 guessed he could make about $10,000 for a year's worth of lecturing. In 1988 the asking fee for a single lecture by Margaret Atwood was $7,500; Toni Morrison, $10,000; Ann Beattie, $12,500; Tom Wolfe, $16,000. And those figures are peanuts compared to the fees asked for and received by the likes of Henry Kissinger and Timothy Leary and G. Gordon Liddy. Since Faulkner's day the public lecture has become an odd little part, a cranny of popular culture. And, of course, there has been the great inflation, everywhere, even in the world of literature. But as I understand it, inflation has multiplied prices by about eleven times since 1900, not since 1962.

We should also notice that William Faulkner believed he could raise $50,000 in 1962 by signing on to do a book or *books* plural.

Compare that with the situation of novelist James Jones only two years later in 1964. Two publishers, Dell and Pocket Books, made offers to win him away from Scribner's. Here I quote from my own biography of James Jones: "Each was a complex, stepped contract with various escalator clauses, offering bonuses and increases according to the size of sales. Essentially, Dell offered an advance of $350,000 for the first book and $150,000 each on the second and third plus all the complexity of 'steps.' His royalty was to be 17 percent in hardcover and 10 percent in paperback. Pocket Books came up with something similar—$300,000 for the first book, $200,000 for the second, and $150,000 for the third."[3]

One thing, among others, which this discrepancy means is that Faulkner had been so busy writing he was somewhat out of touch with the contemporary literary scene. He said as much to the students at the University of Virginia, admitting that "there was a gap of about twenty-five years during which I had almost no acquaintance whatever with contemporary literature."[4] However, Faulkner also told University of Virginia undergraduates: "I think the artist is influenced by all in his environment. He's maybe more sensitive to it because he has got to get the materials, the lumber that he's going to build his edifice."[5]

That image of lumber puts me in mind of how in 1599 James and Richard Burbage took down the lumber of the old playhouse, the Theatre in Shoreditch, and put it up on a Bankside as the brand new and improved Globe. Somewhere in a back closet of your consciousness, keep Shakespeare in mind—a writer who had tried his hand first at high art and culture, but who was deeply involved in pure popular culture for most of his working life. So often our greatest literary artists, submerged in the present, get and guess wrong, either or both, their past and future. Certainly Faulkner, like most of the rest of his generation, really, honestly believed (at least for a long time) that he lived in roughly the same literary world which had recently been inhabited by the likes of Henry James and Conrad, even by Twain, Melville, and Dickens; believed that there was a kind of continuum, that the new generation was, essentially, up to the same thing the earlier ones had been, faced with similar problems and challenges. And, just so, my generation of American writers has awkwardly assumed that we still somehow belong to the same literary world as William Faulkner and the masters of his generation. The evidence is overwhelming that we do *not* live or belong in the same world. If we could be more objective than we are able to be, I am convinced that we would see clearly that not only is the world we live and work in radically different from Faulkner's but also that what we are doing, the *writing* we are doing, is by definition and design, something else, something quite different from what he and his generation were up to.

Be that as it may, Faulkner's generation was the last one in America which could plausibly, sanely accept the illusion that the so-called serious novel had any prospect of general popularity. It is a matter more of irony than anything else that Faulkner and Joyce and Hemingway (and many others) began as writers wishing and hoping to earn some form of conventional popular success; that such a goal seemed entirely possible and plausible. And that in the end the masters, of that generation of masters, had as much to do as anybody else in removing the so-called serious novel from the realm of popular culture.

Other factors were at work, not the least being the kinds and forms of literacy the nineteenth century had (briefly) known. But nevertheless when, one by one, the masters saw that their art form was likely to endure, if at all, only as a kind of high art rather than part of popular culture, they embraced the inevitable and thus bear a full share of the responsibility of and for the decline in simple popularity of their kind of modern novel. I say their kind of novel because what we now call the genre or public novel—novels of suspense, of fantasy, of romance, even the cult of celebrity—is now enjoying an enormous, blooming, though small-scale success. There are some greatly gifted writers, playing other artistic games by other rules, who are doing very well indeed in our time, who are closely involved, to the extent that anything in print still can be, in popular culture. Very few critics and scholars, with the notable exception of our own inimitable Leslie Fiedler, have demonstrated the courage and the chutzpah necessary to deal seriously with these works. But it seems at least likely that the last half of the American literary century may be said to belong more to (for example) Elmore Leonard and John D. MacDonald, Harlan Ellison and Arthur C. Clarke, Stephen King and Alexandra Ripley than, say, to Pynchon or Coover, or Gass or Gaddis, or even Roth.

Which does not mean that the *finest* of the modern masters are in much danger of losing place and/or face, but that some of the lesser lights of high art may very well find themselves in a similar situation to some of the earlier (and now lesser) Elizabethans—people like Barnabe Barnes and Sir John Davies and Michael Drayton, Fulke Greville and George Tuberville. Sidney and Spenser and Chapman were justly regarded as great writers in and of their age, but by now have to give way and precedence to the likes of Marlowe and Jonson and Shakespeare. Which tells us only that there are both upward and downward mobility in the arts as well as real life.

Faulkner's generation began by imagining that somehow they could be, at one and the same time, serious artists and popular novelists. They could—if they were both good and lucky like Faulkner, or Scott

Fitzgerald, earn some kind of living with *literary* popular art—short stories and screenplays. Sooner or later, they were entitled to hope, their novels would catch on.

Among the many snarls of irony in the celebrated and much-discussed, and often-misunderstood, introduction to *Sanctuary*, one of the threads of irony in that introduction, is that it constitutes a farewell to the hope (not the idea or ideal but the *hope*) of the novel as popular art. In the heart, the dead center of the Great Depression, in (of all places!) America, William Faulkner begins with an apology for even entertaining the vague idea that he might possibly earn some money from writing this book, any book. And he ends with a parodic commercial: "So I tore the galleys down and rewrote the book. It had been already set up once, so I had to pay for the privilege of rewriting it, trying to make out of it something which would not shame *The Sound and the Fury* and *As I Lay Dying* too much and I made a fair job and I hope you will buy it and tell your friends I hope they will buy it too."[6] That the complex introduction was and still is widely misunderstood and that *Sanctuary* was a success, but that Faulkner was not able, at the time at least, to enjoy the full fruits of that success, compound the ironies associated with this book, this time in Faulkner's life. It is surely debatable, but it seems to me that after *Sanctuary* Faulkner never really or seriously imagined being a conventionally *popular* novelist again. He would enjoy various kinds of success. But I think his introduction to *Sanctuary* can be taken as a personal valediction, a farewell to the novel as an artifact of popular culture.

Can we return to Shakespeare for a moment? It is relevant (at least to myself) because I can and do consider William Faulkner to be an artist of the kind of magnitude, depth, and breadth of William Shakespeare. Allowing for many obvious things in which they are widely different, there are some less obvious things which they have in common. For instance, at the outset of their extremely productive professional careers both of these artists believed that they were working in popular art forms. With some differences—the Elizabethan stage was a fairly new medium; the novel, though not by any means fully explored or exploited, was aging fast. The plays of Shakespeare, though early and often praised, did not acquire the patina of intellectual respectability in his lifetime. Faulkner lived to see the novel, at least his kind of novel, become for better and for worse a form of highbrow art, the texts of novels actually studied, investigated, and explicated, in the groves of academe.

In March of 1958, in an informal session at the house of Professor Willard Thorp of Princeton University, the following exchange took place and was remembered and reported.

> STUDENT: Mr. Faulkner, how do you feel about having your books studied in classrooms and people writing Ph.D. dissertations about you and your work?
>
> FAULKNER (lighting pipe, Puff Puff): Well (puff, puff), I expected it.

Which may indeed be true. William Shakespeare had a confident and ingrained sense of his past, a vision of it, but Shakespeare had no real sense of the future at all—if he had, even a hint of it, the short term future (Revolution, regicide, end of the theater as he knew and imagined it, Reformation) or even longer term, it would probably have stunned him into perfect silence.

Faulkner, though he knew and could imagine the past as well as any artist and seems to have understood everything about the past except his own place in it, Faulkner had an amazing prescience, a prophet's dreamlike flashing awareness of what future time was most likely to bring. There are many examples of this characteristic—and it is something we are going to come back to—but here and now I just want to remind you of one superb example of his prophetic powers. In 1935, in a book review of *Test Pilot* by Jimmy Collins, Faulkner turned to the idea of a folklore of speed, a folklore of the future which (as you can see) certainly encompasses the apocalyptic environment we have since come to live in, a world at home with such concepts as Mutual Assured Destruction: "It would be a folklore not of the age of speed nor of the men who perform it, but of the speed itself, peopled not by anything human or even mortal but by the clever willful machines themselves carrying nothing that was born or will have to die or which can even suffer pain, moving without comprehensible purpose toward no discernible destination, producing a literature innocent of either love or hate and of course of pity or terror, and which would be the story of the final disappearance of life from the earth. I would watch them, the little puny mortals, vanishing against a vast and timeless void filled with the sound of incredible engines, within which furious meteors moving in no medium hurtled nowhere, neither pausing nor flagging, forever destroying themselves and one another."[7]

That flash was more in the line of genre fiction in 1935. If you listened carefully you heard even a hint of futuristic *literary* criticism—a prophecy that out of the *folklore* of the future, that is the popular culture, would come a nonjudgmental, flat-affected, spare, and unengaging literature (what, for lack of better terms we now call minimalism and metafiction)—"a literature innocent of love or hate and of course of pity or terror."

Something else contained there, in that visionary passage, is an awareness of how popular culture constantly changes as the whole culture is also changed. No generation of Americans witnessed more obvious and radical changes in the whole texture and fabric of our society and culture than William Faulkner's own generation. It is in his lifetime that automobile and airplane, electricity, telephone and radio and motion picture and television changed and evolved, rapidly, from newly invented oddities (the "passing fancies" Rogers and Hart identified in "Our Love Is Here to Stay"), changed from odd and interesting inventions to universal, entirely mundane and somehow, finally, necessary commonplaces.

And bear in mind, also, the fantastic changes wrought by World War II—the end of the grinding Great Depression, the end not only of international isolation, but also of national isolation and immobility. With the new mobility came the possibility of more uniformity than this society or culture had ever known or even known that it wanted. Simultaneously with these huge changes came such sometimes contradictory forces as what the late René Dubos used to call regionalism by choice and, at the same time, the new Federalism, redefining the national constitution and greatly limiting, severely diminishing, both the independence and the power of local and state governments, of whole regions of the nation.

All of these changes surface somewhere in the works of William Faulkner.

Prior to World War II, then, American popular culture tended to be much more regional, localized, thus (his term was correct) more a matter of *folklore* and custom and tradition than anything else. Locally there were the events and adventures in the pulpit, in the courthouse, on the political stump, events and adventures at once defined and maintained by local gossip and memory. All these things shape Faulkner's language and his subjects. The world came calling in other ways, in the revivals, carnivals, fairs, football games, all of which Faulkner wrote about.

Yes, there were the funny papers and Faulkner surely seems to have read them, alluded to them, used them. Yes, there was the radio—though here Faulkner's use of the familiar elements of radio shows seems to me minimal for the era. There were the national magazines that he depended on as a potential marketplace for his short stories—for example the *Saturday Evening Post, Collier's* and *Liberty* (we should keep in mind that the first full-fledged example of the now dominant form of illustrated journalism, *Life*, came on the scene, and tentatively enough, on November 23, 1936). Ross's *New Yorker* and the old *Vanity Fair* existed, not yet making any serious claims on more than their own sophisticated local consciousness. And I don't recall many incidents involving the wild improbability of one of Faulkner's authentic Mississippi characters being aware of or any way interested in such things. There is the celebrated and significant exception—the picture of Candace Compson, brought by the spinster county librarian of Jefferson, in 1943, to the attention of Jason Compson: " a picture, a photograph in color clipped obviously from a slick magazine—a picture filled with luxury and money and sunlight—a Riviera backdrop of mountains and palms and cypresses and the sea, an open powerful expensive chromium-trimmed sports car, the woman's face hatless between a rich scarf and a seal coat, ageless and beautiful, cold and serene and damned; beside her a handsome lean man of middleage in the ribbons and tabs of a German staff general."[8] It is absolutely appropriate that the only person in Jefferson in 1943 who would have ever seen and noticed and clipped and folded the photo in the slick magazine would be the librarian. Try to imagine the difference, what kinds of attention in all forms a beautiful and well-born Mississippi woman in the company of an enemy general would attract in 1988.

The New York Times and the old *Herald-Tribune* were at the top of the national newspaper heap; but even in the limited world of literature, they had far less power than they now have come to possess. And, anyway, any news they brought to the South, the Midwest, the West, arrived days late. Local papers, still mostly independently owned, if not noticeably independent, were pretty much all that mattered. Newspapers and reporters figure in a variety of Faulkner's works, in a folkloric kind of down-home *Front Page* fashion. That is, they were a useful stereotype in popular culture, one which could be at once exploited and revised, as in *Pylon.*

In his last years, the years of his fame and, as well (as he saw it), of his service—traveling the world for the nation, speaking out in many ways on many issues, he became increasingly aware of the inherent and implicit, as well as the overt and explicit, dangers of what we now call the media. We have some idea of what his bitter and ironic thoughts were concerning television from the answer he gave in November 1958 to J. Robert Oppenheimer's question, "I wonder what you think of television as a medium for the artist."[9] To avoid serious offense, I won't repeat Faulkner's answer here out of a complex context; but even with all it contextual ironies, it does not suggest an enthusiastic appreciation of the artistic possibilities of television.

We know more of Faulkner's reaction to the growing power and pervasive influence of journalism in the two published essays out of the five or six he once planned to be a book, tentatively titled "The American Dream: What Happened to It." And especially from the one more personal essay, "On Privacy," recounting some part of his own unhappy experience with contemporary journalism and his awareness of the deeper dangers of its ruthless impact upon liberty and equality and, as he put it, " hope for the individual man."[10]

Speaking of the American dream (and note that it has nothing to do with the dream of upward mobility advanced by both political parties in 1988 as a desirable purpose and goal in life), he wrote in 1955: "It is gone now. We dozed, slept, and it abandoned us. And in that vacuum now there sound no longer the strong loud voices not merely unafraid but not even aware that fear existed, speaking in mutual unification of our one mutual hope and will. Because now what we hear is a cacaphony of terror and conciliation and compromise babbling only the mouthsounds; the loud and empty words which we have emasculated of all meaning whatever—freedom, democracy, patriotism—with which, awakened at last, we try in desperation to hide from ourselves that loss."[11]

Faulkner was dead and gone before the aspect of popular culture now called the cult of celebrity had fully come into focus. There was not yet a *People* magazine or "Lifestyles of the Rich and Famous," or, for that matter, personal posters and T-shirts; no bumper stickers except for political campaigns; no vanity license plates except by pure accident. Yet he sensed very strongly the direction things were taking: "Perhaps it is impossible now for any American to believe," he wrote, "that anyone not hiding from the police could actually not want, as a free gift, his name and photograph in any printed organ, no matter how base or modest or circumscribed, in circulation."[12]

What he, as an artist, died without having to know and to deal with was the present situation wherein it can be seriously argued that the reputation and success or failure of contemporary American artists, of popular art or, as Saul Bellow names it, private art, of literature as well as rocking and rolling, depend not much at all upon the inherent quality of the work or indeed upon any perception of quality by others, but purely and simply upon the publicity one way or another engendered or aroused by the artist. Thus a Truman Capote, a Norman Mailer, a James Dickey, a Joyce Carol Oates, in their ceaseless struggle to gain and hold public attention (that is, to get publicity), though they are opposites to William Faulkner in almost every way conceivable except that all are, in Capote's case were, workers with the word, wordsmiths, different as they may be and have been, they could argue that if he had the bad fortune to live in their world and their time he would have to make his intricate persona even more a matter of public record and curiosity than he did, would have to spend more time cultivating his image and somewhat, maybe a good deal less, cultivating his art and craft.

Come on down to the next generation, our very youngest writers here and now, and you'll have to agree that if a meeting between William Faulkner and, say, Jay McInerney or Tama Janowitz were miraculously possible it would not be a meeting of like human beings, but a classic close encounter of the Third Kind. Among the very young and new writers only one that I know of so far, Madison Smartt Bell, though he speaks with the tongues of our own fin de siècle, has a fully realized sense of the American literary tradition, including the masterwork of William Faulkner.

It needs to be pointed out that even our discussion of the matter of popular culture is rich with ironies. If the novel—or at least a certain kind of novel—is at home in academic enclaves, so also (as we here bear witness) is popular culture. You can now get a Ph.D. in popular culture in many places, which really ought to be the death knell of much popular culture, but may not be. It takes one to know one, so it shouldn't surprise you that the journalists have been having a field day lately writing about the study of popular culture. For the deadly serious side there is the *Washington Post's* Jonathan Yardley whose "Pop Culture: The Academic Undiscipline" (June 13, 1988) is a one-thousand-word feature rage against "This trend toward trivialization and lazy professors and lazy students, permitting the standards of academic life to be undermined by people whose interests lie not in genuine scholarship but in careerism and self-indulgence." More fun—and maybe more typical—are pieces like this one from the July 26, 1988, *New York Times*, "Academics Analyse TV / As If Soaps Were Opera." But the place of popular culture in the scheme of things is also a matter of millions of dollars. A little over a week earlier (*New York Times*, July 25, 1988) S. I. Newhouse, Jr., head of many newspapers, head of Random House, and, in the magazine world, head of Condé Nast Publications, announced that it is now time to "reposition *Vogue* for the 90's." He gave a *Times* reporter some serious predictions for the coming decade: "He characterized coming cultural changes as 'profound' and said they included 'increasing informality' and a blurring of the rigid guidelines of what is high art and kitsch, all of which, he said, would be manifest in fashion."

Emblematic of the elaborate interchange of high art and kitsch is the much-publicized career of writer Bobbie Ann Mason, who was first of all a Ph.D. with a dissertation on Nabokov, next the author of a book in the popular culture field, *The Girl Sleuth: A Feminist Guide* (1975), and more recently a novelist of the New South, rich with brand names and flaky characters and as essentially cute as anything Disney ever dreamed up.

The one area of American popular culture which, in the end, engaged a great deal of Faulkner's time and attention and energy was of course the movies. The thing itself, the movies and going to them, doesn't play a large part in his fiction. His people don't have the time or spend a whole lot of it going to the picture show. But, in the absence of support from academe, the possibility of which arrived for the American writer just as Faulkner's life was coming to a close, and must have been yet another culture shock, he earned a lot of his living writing for the movies. Bruce Kawin has done some wonderful work on the subject in *Faulkner and Film* (Ungar, 1977) and I strongly recommend it to you. He is especially fine in indicating subtle interconnections—how the nature of film clearly influenced William Faulkner's novels which, in turn, have been an important influence on a lot of filmmakers, especially among the Europeans. And, in addition, Kawin has contributed some good, solid scholarship, information which is greatly helpful to all of us.

There isn't a lot I can add to what has already been done by him and others. Except, maybe, to call to your attention a couple of things. One is that, in a relative sense, according to the times when he was working, William Faulkner worked on a lot of screen projects—more than most "outsiders" (writers whose primary form was not screenwriting) and more than many full-time screenwriters. Then and now there are whole successful screenwriting careers based on a lot less work. There may have been a lot about film, as art and craft, he did not know, but there simply could not have been a whole lot about *screenwriting* in America that he didn't know except how to get rich at it. Screenwriting, especially in the days of the big studios, but always, really, is a very important activity but only a very small part of filmmaking. They can't get very far without a writer, true; and it is also true that no film is likely to be a whole lot better than its treatment and its shooting script. But it is, most of the time, deeply frustrating and unsatisfying work. Faulkner figured that out pretty early. Writing screenplays teaches any writer of fiction some new things to do with narrative and language. These are the positive lessons. The negative ones are things you don't ever want to have to do again in your own work. I can see signs of both the negative and the positive reactions in William Faulkner's work after he began to write screenplays for money.

But there is something else. Except in a very few cases—*Intruder in the Dust* is one prime example of the exception to the rule—Faulkner's work is almost impossible to adapt faithfully to the screen in its own terms. Story line seems so wedded to the way of telling that translation is virtually impossible. I believe that he didn't want them hacking away at his work; but I think there is something else. Jelly Roll Morton somewhere described the elaborate and intricate harmonies he and his friends used in Gospel quartets at wakes in New Orleans. The primary motivation for the difficult harmony, he said, was to make it impossible for anybody else to jump in and join the singing. Unlike a lot of writers, Faulkner from the beginning showed a willingness to adapt his own work for film. Not much came of it; but his thinking was sound. I like to think, anyway, that he made books that he alone was capable of adapting, in spirit if not in precise detail, for the screen. That is where the money, the desperately needed money, was and would be—in selling the "property" and then in writing the screenplay for it.

I think in some of the books there are marvelous moments where we get more than a hint as to what he might have done with his own material in a screenplay adaptation. Meantime, though, he took the hackwork and did it as well or better than could be expected.

There is another seldom admitted fact about working for the movies. Because it is a specialized and group enterprise, you can only learn your own part of it really well, well enough. The problem for many writers (Fitzgerald, surely, for one) was trying to learn everybody else's craft also. Faulkner knew better than that. But he also learned what everybody in the business learns sooner or later—that this astonishing new art form arrived on the scene almost fully formed. That, *essentially*, Griffith and Eisenstein did everything that could be done with film right at the outset. As Hitchcock put it more than once, the only real difference between the early films and later films is the introduction of sound. And the only difference there is that you can now hear what you had to imagine hearing. Film keeps changing all the time, but it is like a deck of cards dealt out in different hands, different arrangements. Old-timers will tell you that there is probably a clear precedent for everything that can ever be done with film by 1919 or a little later.

Here, then, is the restless artist William Faulkner. No two of his novels are alike in ways and means. They may have the same voice or voices and the same complex of characters, but every single one of them has a completely different way of telling a story. Maybe if Faulkner could have exercised the power of Irving Thalberg or Sam Goldwyn or even Harry Cohn he might have made some great films. There are enormous odds against it, however, as the odds are against all filmmakers.

Perhaps if one or another of the great buccaneer producers of the age had been able to recognize the genius of William Faulkner . . . who knows? But never mind. What we do know, and all that we need to know is this—that he was the man who wrote the books. And that they live.

Notes

1. My title comes from an incident reported in Joseph Blotner, *Faulkner: A Biography,* 2 vols. (New York: Random House, 1974), 1:768.
2. *Selected Letters of William Faulkner,* ed. Joseph Blotner (New York: Random House, 1977), 461.
3. George Garrett, *James Jones* (San Diego: Harcourt Brace Jovanovich, 1984), 142.
4. *Faulkner in the University: Class Conferences at the University of Virginia, 1957–1958,* ed. Frederick L. Gwynn and Joseph L. Blotner (Charlottesville: University of Virginia Press, 1959), 243.
5. Ibid., 57–58.
6. *Sanctuary: The Corrected Text* (New York: Random House, Vintage Books, 1987), 339.
7. William Faulkner, *Essays, Speeches, and Public Letters,* ed. James B. Meriwether (New York: Random House, 1965), 192.
8. *The Portable Faulkner: Revised and Expanded Edition,* ed. Malcolm Cowley (New York: Viking, Penguin, 1987), 712–13.
9. *Faulkner: A Biography,* 2:1705.
10. *Essays, Speeches, and Public Letters,* 63.
11. Ibid., 65–66.
12. Ibid., 68.

Inch by Inch

One of the things writers do all the time nowdays, when they ought to be reading or writing, is give talks. Here is one I confess I enjoyed giving—my acceptance, in Chicago in 1989, of the T. S. Eliot Award given by the Ingersoll Foundation.

I. Two Epigraphs

A text, or an epigraph, for what I am going to say. Some lines from John Ciardi's poem about the Birdman of Alcatraz who was, among other things, a trickster of sorts. These words from Ciardi's poem, "Snickering in Solitary":

> In every life sentence
> some days are better than
> others; even, sometimes,
> better than being free.

And one other, the basic aesthetic and ethical principle I have tried to live by and act on all my life as a writer and now find firmly stated in these lines by W. H. Auden from his poem "The Cave of Making," which is an elegy for another good poet—Louis MacNeice:

> Even a limerick
> ought to be something a man of
> honor, awaiting death from cancer or a firing squad,
> could read without contempt.

II. Ancient Pistol Thanks You Kindly

In the fall of 1940, a dark and dangerous year for our civilization, General Sir Archibald Wavell, commanding an ill-equipped, ragtag-and-bobtail force, an army of Anzacs and Indians, South Africans and Scotsmen with, at its core and center, a few impeccably cool battalions of the Brigade of Guards, a force which could still be called, then, without irony or apology, Imperial, attacked a much larger force of what was very likely the best *equipped* army in the world (now that the superbly equipped French, together with their extravagant claims to superior civilization and culture, had collapsed like a shack in a hurricane). Wavell attacked and drove Mussolini's army out of Egypt and halfway across Libya, taking more prisoners in the process than the total number of all his own forces. Even allowing that it was an Italian army, it was a stunning victory, a bright brief moment amid the dark times on either side, before and after.

At the moment of Wavell's triumph, Winston Churchill, prime minister, sent a simple message: "Matthew 7:7." In immediate response to which Wavell signaled to him, with the same cheerful irreverence: "James 1:17."

That is. Churchill to Wavell: "Ask and it shall be given to you; seek and ye shall find; knock and it shall be opened unto you."

Wavell's reply had been, then: "Every good and every perfect gift is from above, and cometh down from the Father of lights, with whom there is no variableness, neither shadow of turning."

I stand here grateful for your good gift and astonished that it has come to me.

And although a shifty and sneaky shadow of myself (who may even be real) keeps whispering in my ear the eleventh verse of the last chapter of the Book of Job—"Then came there unto him all his brethren, and all his sisters, and all that had been of his acquaintance before, and did eat bread with him in his house: and they bemoaned him and comforted him over all the evil the Lord had brought upon him; every man also gave him a piece of money and an earring of gold"—that other part of me which I had rather call the real, the true self, is, at this moment, reminded of the first words of Queen Elizabeth upon being told that her sister Mary was dead and gone and that she, Elizabeth, last of the Tudors, was now Queen of England, Ireland, France, Defender of the Faith, etc. She turned to the Psalms and said "This is the Lord's doing and marvelous in our sight."

You can see that my mood is blatantly celebratory. I am grateful to all of you who are here, grateful to the Ingersoll Foundation and especially grateful to the judges, even as I am admiring and envious of their courage and independence. By which I mean to say, more or less seriously, that had their responsibility fallen on my shoulders, I doubt very much that I would have chosen me for this award. It is not a matter of being deserving or undeserving. None of us, not even among the high and mighty, can ever be called fully deserving. Some, I suppose, are utterly undeserving. But, I must confess that I think, and hope I have not lost all good sense of the power of humility by saying now that I do not feel I am one among them, either. Truth is, as Joyce Cary more eloquently put it in his preface to *The Horse's Mouth*, speaking to the point of whether Gulley Jimson was a "good" or a "bad" artist, neither justice nor injustice has any true place in the arts. In that preface to the Carfax Edition of his great novel Cary had this point to make about Gulley and all artists: "He is himself a creator, and has lived in creation all his life, and so he understands and continually reminds himself that in a world of everlasting creation there is no justice. The original artist who *counts* on understanding and reward is a fool." The arts, all of them, high and low, crafty and profound, have always to do with creation, The Creation. And secular justice, that concept carried over from the stone world of Caesars with fat lips and broken noses, has nothing to do with the energy and ineffable motion and direction of Creation. Though we are one and all almost endlessly fascinated by the doomed attempt to apply the rules of secular justice, or injustice, to the arts, so much so, indeed, that it sometimes may seem we think and talk of very little else, we know in our hearts (as we have to; for we live always in Creation) that except for the fool, whose heart is softened by every sort of sentimental denial, and the knave whose heart is as hard as a mailed fist, none of us can believe that there is any appropriate application of the ideals or practice of secular justice, of punishments and rewards, to the arts. The Elizabethan image of Fortune's wheel—O long before Vanna White appeared to impersonate the blithe spirit of pure greed!—is a more accurate model. The wheel goes round and we

---

rise and fall, win and lose. As old Job, already dutifully mentioned, neatly put it, "The Lord giveth, the Lord taketh away. Blessed be the name of the Lord."

Put it another way. I am as happy as a kite dancing on a string in an April breeze to receive this award and this attention, but I hope and pray I am not so foolish (dotage will follow soon enough) as to imagine that I earned it. Or that I belong in the company, the visionary company, if you will, of those six other writers, who have been honored here before me. If I may revert for a moment to that snickering Birdman of Alcatraz, I may be allowed to parody some genuinely heroic words:

Old men forget; yet all shall be forgot
But he'll remember with advantages
What feats he did that day. Then shall our names
Familiar in his mouth as household words,
Borges and Ionesco, Naipaul and Percy, Anthony Powell and
Octavio Paz—
Be in our flowing cups freshly remembered. . . .

I toast and salute them one and all, feeling, however, a little less like King Harry and a lot more like Ancient Pistol. Nevertheless he, too, was there with his part in the play to play.

My reasons for a respect, close to awe, for the Foundation and the judges are more simple. There is a strong element of discovery here, and discovery seldom, if ever, is characteristic of honors of any kind awarded in the arts. It is a bold gesture, bordering on the outrageous, not to select someone already established as officially honorable. Have you ever noticed how the high-ranking officers of the Eastern Bloc nations, as well as many a fierce-looking leader in Latin America and the Third World, and now, too, I am sorry to report, many of the military leaders of our own nation, are draped, top-heavy with row after row of ribbons representing more medals and decorations than a body could wear at a time. We know very well that these things do not necessarily represent heroism or betoken valor. We know very well that heroism and valor undeniably exist, with and without these tokens. But it is our habit safely to continue to honor those who have already been established as worthy of honor. No harm done, and it is a hard habit to

---

break, especially in *this* peculiar age where we find ourselves, an age where publicity and notoriety have equal billing with whatsoever things are good and true and beautiful and of good report.

In a world full of much-decorated and high-ranking officers (albeit officers of the literary establishment) you have elected to honor an enlisted man from the trenches. And I thank you kindly for it. And I accept it, in some part, at least, for all of the others, my brothers and sisters, fellow hard laborers in the vineyard whose work is often not only not as well known as it ought to be, but also not noticeably inferior in quality and value to the work of many of their more celebrated contemporaries. There is more democracy in the arts than anyone, and least of all the most honored and celebrated artists, chooses to admit. Even the absence of a strong sense of community feeling does not prevent our accomplishments and our failures from being communal, a communal enterprise. We are, as John Berryman wrote in *Homage to Mistress Bradstreet,* "on each other's hands who care." When I go back to the trenches to join the others I shall carry with me more than my own private good feelings and more than the lighthearted joy which comes from the lifting of the spirits, flagging a little if not yet cast in weary lead, of a sixty-year-old man who had long ago thrown away idle hopes the way veteran soldiers always used to discard their gas masks on the battlefield (keeping the container because it was waterproof). It will also be my bounden duty to share with my fellows something of your warmth and good will and recognition.

III. What Saves a Man

Here I should quickly move to a close, on a note of celebration and gratitude, a *Nunc Dimittis,* as sincere if somewhat more modest than Simeon's in the second chapter of Luke. But I would be remiss not to say a general word or two about the state of the art (as I view it) at this time.

Plurality and diversity may be desirable social qualities, or admirable buzzwords anyway, highly valued by the society at large. But in the American literary arts, where there is true diversity and plenty of plurality, the factions are fighting each other to the death. Fortunately for one and all, the battles are almost exclusively on what Kierkegaard called the *aesthetic* level of reality. Writers very seldom rise to the next, the ethical level. Because their hearts are turned toward the buried treasure of aesthetics, they are all too often ethically—that is, socially and politically, as primitive and as alike as peas in a pod. We need not look to our writers for much political and social wisdom or even the excitement and challenge of serious individual eccentricity. As for truth, which is, after all, inward and spiritual, we have to be honestly aware (as so many of our writers are not) that we all live together in the same social world, sharing not merely experiences, but judgments and follies, as well. As a nation, as a society, our outward and visible problems are not beyond solving. But our inward and spiritual weaknesses, our true faults and flaws then, are more intractable. For instance, we have become accustomed to, indeed inured to atrocity. Nothing, not the continuing Passover and the continual slaughter of the innocents can raise our eyebrows in shock and surprise. The pain of strangers is meaningless to us. Yet at the same time we are desperately, sentimentally afraid. As I wrote once, long ago, in a poem:

> We have lived too long with fear. We take
> fear for granted like a drunken uncle,
> like a cousin not quite all there
> who's always there.

We are compassionate in the abstract and without much human charity. We are sentimental and self-pitying in the particular. And we are not even ashamed of it, because we have lost our capacity for shame. We luxuriate in a bubble bath of private guilts and lack the essential common and communal sense of shame without which there can be no community of secular justice. Even the most brutal Caesars were capable of some shame. Without shame there can be no conscience. Without conscience there can be no true compassion, only the illusory comforts of wealth, of youth and beauty, of good health while it lasts. No wonder that the words "and there is no health in us" were struck from the General Confession in *The Book of Common Prayer*. They are too painful and exact to utter even in prayer.

There is one more small thing that should be said about the state of the literary arts in the two post-World War II generations in America;

namely that, like the larger society itself, having freed themselves from the inhibitions of ethics and religion, many of our best-known artists have been busy seeking to manage and control not merely the present—or, like commonplace contemporary totalitarian leaders, revising the past to suit their present purposes—but also, with what earlier generations would surely and immediately have identified as hubris, they have sought to manipulate and control the unborn future, making it a colony, a captured possession and an extension of the present. That is, they are trying to create and to write their own history before it happens. That they are bound to fail goes without saying; though precisely how they will come to fail is an interesting, mildly suspenseful mystery. Equally interesting is the nature of the cockeyed innocence which allows them to imagine that they can possibly succeed.

All aesthetic claims aside, the artist is not charged with any priestly duties. We must work out our own salvation and do so separately and diligently. But the artist can, if he will, spare us somewhat from the heavy yoke of our abstraction from Creation. And the artist can also, like others in the active vocations (which is to say that the practice of the arts is not essentially contemplative), offer us the example of continuing performance, of risking by doing. As an important character in Saint-Exupéry's *Wind, Sand and Stars* says: "What saves a man is to take a step. Then another step. It is always the same step, but you have to take it." Not a great claim, but a huge demand, if you think about it.

I have tried, as one must do in an elegy for an admired artist, to put much of this into images and poetry, in a poem in memory of John Ciardi, an old friend I wish (for all kinds of reasons) could be here with us tonight. Here it is:

Dear John

Even as, inch by living inch,
I contrive to chip and cut and carve
myself into various and sundry parts—

first, of course, the fingers
and toes, then ears and nose,
these offered, as it were, in words

---

of *The Book of Common Prayer,* to be
"a reasonable, holy and living sacrifice."
Eyes before sex, arms before legs,

next the thin peeled skin and last
the bloody mess of muscles and meat,
fat and the lonely internal organs.

Must we be universal donors, John?

Too much to wish for.
Better (and you knew it and said so,
to well, so many times)

to spend our skin and bones, to pay
out blood and breath upon
the wholly unimportant poem:

something reasonably simple and simply
(while memory endures) unforgettable;
you and I one time, late on my front porch

in York Harbor, Maine, drinking
stone fences—your special favorite,
apple jack and apple cider, all

the fumes and essences of Eden;
two old guys, feeling no pain,
beneath the brightly reeling stars

while nearby, shiny and smooth
as a blacksnake, the river is rising up
to high tide, inch by living inch.

Index

317
